Joyful Toddlers & Preschoolers

Joyful Toddlers & Preschoolers

Create a Life That You and Your Child Both Love

FAITH COLLINS

HOHM PRESS
Chino Valley, Arizona

Cover Design: Becky Fulker, Kubera Book Design, Prescott, Arizona

Interior Design and Layout: Becky Fulker, Kubera Book Design, Prescott, Arizona

Library of Congress Cataloging-in-Publication Data

Names: Collins, Faith, 1975- author.
Title: Joyful toddlers & preschoolers : create a life that you and your child both love / Faith Collins.
Other titles: Joyful toddlers and preschoolers
Description: Chino Valley, Ariz. : Hohm Press, [2017] | Includes bibliographical references and index.
Identifiers: LCCN 2017011943 | ISBN 9781942493280 (trade pbk. : alk. paper)
Subjects: LCSH: Child rearing. | Preschool children.
Classification: LCC HQ774.5 .C65 2017 | DDC 649/.123--dc23
LC record available at https://lccn.loc.gov/2017011943

HOHM PRESS
P.O. Box 4410
Chino Valley, AZ 86323
800-381-2700
http://www.hohmpress.com

This book was printed in the U.S.A. on recycled, acid-free paper using soy ink.

To all the children who've taught me how to listen,
and especially my own daughter, Sophie

CONTENTS

FOREWORD

It was such a rich experience working with Faith every day at Rainbow Bridge—a LifeWays program for twelve children, ages one to five, that we offered in her home for several years. While I handled the business aspects and brought the Waldorf Kindergarten activities for the older children, I considered myself her apprentice when it came to working with the younger ones. Her joy was contagious, and observing her was a constant source of learning and inspiration. Faith *gets* and *loves* children this age—she appreciates toddler humor and laughs at preschoolers' jokes; like an orchestra conductor, she leads nonintellectual yet coherent and inspired conversations with them during lunch; and she provides both the connection and the high expectations they need to foster healthy relationships and develop self-control in this unique stage of life.

How did Faith come to the insights she shares in this book? Over the years, I have watched her countless times start with experimenting and searching for what works, then look for *why* something works, and then re-formulate it to be most useful for others. As she explains, finding herself in a classroom with ten one-year-olds who were crying much of the time propelled her to rapidly explore what worked and what didn't, and to immediately start applying the principles she was learning in her LifeWays Early Childhood Training, based on the work of Rudolf Steiner, founder of Waldorf education. She describes how, in addition to working with rhythm and simplifying the day, she explored ways to strengthen the children's desire to cooperate and create a life that was satisfying for all of them—what she calls "Cultivating a Habit of *Yes*."

After working together at Rainbow Bridge, Faith moved with her husband to England, where the practical experience she had had was supported and deepened by her master's degree work in early childhood at Roehampton University. She discovered that what she had been creating with the children, and working to help parents create at home—a life that both they and their children loved—was what was called, in academia, *a mutually responsive orientation* and that studies backed up how she was approaching it. Her research dissertation, on "Pitching in: Toddlers helping with household tasks," also supported the value of using life as the curriculum with young children, another of the LifeWays principles she had been using in her work.

Upon returning to America, Faith was able to apply all these things in her own family after her daughter Sophie was born in 2014. She also continued to share her insights with hundreds of parents and childcare providers through online classes and parent–child classes in her home and at a school. Throughout this time, she was always honing her message based on feedback from parents and professionals as they transformed their lives with young children, and this book is the result.

Joyful Toddlers & Preschoolers is filled with practical suggestions backed by mainstream research as well as by the LifeWays/Waldorf understanding of child development. It can bring immediate results for anyone who is willing to try any of the ways Faith recommends of pairing high expectations with high levels of warmth to support children in learning the skill of becoming responsive. I see the book as a companion volume to *You Are Your Child's First Teacher*, going more deeply into the behavioral and relational aspects of being with young children. Referring to my own parenting journey described in *First Teacher*, I have often told parents, "I made every mistake in the book—that's why I wrote the book!" I certainly wish I had had *Joyful Toddlers & Preschoolers* as a young mother raising Faith and her brother and sister . . . Lucky you!

—Rahima Baldwin Dancy, early childhood and parenting educator
May 2017, Boulder, Colorado

PART I

Transforming "No" Into "Yes"

The Link Between Connection and Cooperation

CHAPTER 1

Parent–Toddler Relationships at Their Best

This chapter starts by looking at research on parenting styles (particularly Baumrind's work on *authoritative* parenting), and then goes on to explore the secret to healthy parent–toddler relationships: healthy relationships are **mutually responsive**, meaning that both people respond quickly and positively to each other, even—and especially—when they cannot do what the other person wants. We discuss what that means and what it looks like in real life.

With the mutually responsive relationship in mind, we look at **The Two Great Parenting Tasks** of the toddlers years: 1) To support our children as they practice controlling their impulses and learn to be responsive to us; and 2) To shift our parenting to be responsive to children's deeper needs, rather than reacting to their whims. We look at how to start doing this, and introduce three universal human needs: the need to feel *connected* to others, the need for *competence* or mastery, and the need to know that we are *contributing* to something greater than ourselves.

Life with young children can be frustrating, joyful, infuriating, tender, rage-inducing, boring, inspiring, and interminable, all in a single day. Each way we turn, we are greeted with conflicting instructions: we're told about the importance of staying connected to our children on the one hand, and we're told about the importance of establishing and maintaining boundaries on the other. However, we aren't given many tools to do both at the same time. In fact, these two directives often seem to be at odds with one another: at any given moment, do we choose to be connected, or do we choose to set that boundary? And how exactly do we go about setting boundaries with toddlers, if we don't want to use punishments or time-outs? Most relationship-based, positive-parenting books seem to be aimed at children over age four, and involve a lot of explaining, reasoning, and discussion. If explaining and convincing don't work, then what's left?

We all want to give our children what they need to be happy and successful in life. In addition, we want to enjoy our own lives, not feel like we're putting our own needs and desires on hold. We want to increase the times that we enjoy our children's company and minimize times of conflict, without "giving in" to our children's every whim. This book is a guide for how to do all of these things.

The first Part of this book looks at why explaining and convincing don't tend to get buy-in from children under five, and what we can do instead to get that *yes* in a way that strengthens our relationship, rather than undermining it or getting stuck in power struggles. When we know what makes parent–toddler (and nanny–toddler, teacher–toddler, or grandparent–toddler) relationships strong and healthy, we can develop a new set of tools and set our own internal compasses so we're able to help children be their best selves more and more often, today and every day, not only some day when they're more mature.

The second Part explores what to do when we can't get "buy-in" from our children, how to address constant meltdowns and tantrums, and how to deal with our breakdowns and anger.

In the third Part, we investigate ways to teach our children how to be polite, patient, and enjoyable.

The fourth Part looks at how to create more time for ourselves and our own interests while still getting all of the must-do items done, by doing housework while our children are awake and present, helping or playing happily nearby. Sound impossible? It's not. It's eminently doable and we will go over what it takes to be successful and provide your children with exactly what they need while you're at it. Even very young children long to live a life that is not just filled with activity, but feels fulfilling, where they know they are making a difference in the world. We'll address how to weave your own passions into your day in ways that are child-friendly. It truly is possible to create a life that you love, that includes and is welcoming to children.

WHAT DO TODDLERS NEED?

With babies, the route to a secure bond between parent and infant is relatively intuitive for many people, and the phrase "you can't spoil a baby" has been backed up by decades of research. The research has shown that a secure bond is formed when the baby lets his or her needs be known, and the adult responds as quickly, lovingly, and effectively as possible. When we are able to do this as consistently as we can, then babies learn to trust us deeply, and a secure attachment is formed that sets a foundation for life. (For a thorough book of research in this area, check out *Becoming Attached: Our First Relationships and How They Shape Our Capacity to Love,* by Robert Karen.) But, what happens when those sweet babies become demanding toddlers? How does the nature of the parent–child bond shift, and how does it stay the same? What actions continue to support that bond, and which ones no longer serve it?

Life with a toddler shows us quickly that responsiveness needs to change in some way. Wants and needs are no longer the same. If we continue to do what we did when they were babies, and try to do everything they want as quickly and effectively as we can, we don't necessarily end up with secure, loving, well-adjusted children. Instead, we are more likely to wind up with children who are either little dictators, imperiously telling us what to do and how to do it,[1] or with children who are fearful or anxious, relying on us to make everything safe and comfortable for them.[2]

Some people think that having little dictators is simply "how the toddler years are," and that our best option is to grit our teeth and wait for them to grow up a little bit. However, this is a fallacy: research shows that the patterns we establish with our toddlers are more likely to carry on than not.[3] In addition, there's no need to grit our teeth: positive, enjoyable relationships are absolutely possible during the toddler years. That's not to say that every moment will be enjoyable; children tend to bring up whatever our issues are, and being our best selves with our children is something we must constantly strive for. Even with these challenges, however, without having to be the perfect parent, and without our children having to be anything other than who they are, we can have healthy, enjoyable relationships with them.

What is it that's missing in our general knowledge of toddlers? I have spent a lot of time thinking about that, as an early childhood educator, parenting coach, and as a parent myself. When I went back to university after a decade of working with families, to get a master's degree in Early Childhood Studies, I decided to look into the research on this subject. I went in with the question: What makes parent–toddler relationships strong?

My first forays into the tomes of research left me surprisingly empty-handed. Just as with the popular parenting books, there is a plethora of research on parent–infant bonding (referred to as "Attachment"), and research on every aspect of childhood behavior and development over the age of four. The toddler years, though, seemed to have been given short shrift. (*I did eventually unearth quite a bit, and I'll share it shortly.*) I broadened my search, and the first thing that jumped out was the landmark research by Diana Baumrind on the long-term effects of different parenting styles. Her studies were not toddler-focused, but if we want to start with the end-goal in mind, then this is a good place to start.

THE EFFECTS OF PARENTING STYLES ON CHILDREN

In 1966, researcher Diana Baumrind started by examining dozens of studies on parenting, looking for trends across them.[4] She searched for effects of different types of parental control: punishments, threats, begging, etc. Based on these results, she identified three styles of parenting, which she and other researchers went on to study extensively.

Each of the three parenting styles was rated based on "demandingness" (also described as control, guidance, or expectations) and "responsiveness" (also described as supportiveness, understanding, or warmth). The first style she called *permissive* parenting, which has high warmth, and low demandingness. Permissive parents love and support their children, and generally let them do as they wish. They encourage their children to develop opinions of their own, and strive to engage in a democratic method of parenting. On the other end of the spectrum is *authoritarian* parenting, in which parents have high demandingness but low warmth. Authoritarian parents have high "maturity demands." They expect proper behavior and punish infractions, usually regardless of the reason a child has misbehaved. In the middle of the range is *authoritative* parenting. While *authoritarian* and *authoritative* sound unfortunately similar, there is a vital difference: *authoritative* parents hold high expectations, while also giving their children lots of emotional support. Authoritative parenting is high on both warmth/supportiveness/responsiveness *and* guidance/expectations/demandingness. These parents expect children to do well, and they provide the support for them to do so. They care about what their children think and feel, and why children do the things they do, but at the end of the day, they are the ones who are in charge. Later research identified a fourth style, *uninvolved* or *neglectful,* which is low on both warmth and expectations.[5] Here's a table that depicts these categories:

RESPONSIVENESS	low DEMANDINGNESS	high DEMANDINGNESS
high	**PERMISSIVE** (high warmth, low expectations)	**AUTHORITATIVE** (high warmth, high expectations)
low	**UNINVOLVED/ NEGLECTFUL** (low warmth, low expectations)	**AUTHORITARIAN** (low warmth, high expectations)

The reason that these categories of parenting styles are important is that researchers discovered that parenting style has a large influence on how children develop. In looking at the results, there is a clear winner: children with *authoritative* parents do better than children of any other parenting type. These children do better academically, socially, and emotionally than children of uninvolved, permissive, or authoritarian parents. Permissive parents tend to have children who are bossy, immature, and less able to cope when things don't go their way, as I described in the beginning of the book. Authoritarian parents tend to have children who are either defiant, overly compliant and self-limiting, or sneaky (following rules in front of their parents, but breaking them when they can get away with it). Authoritative parents, with high responsiveness *and* high demandingness, are much more likely to have happy, curious, well-adjusted children who follow rules and expectations, even when nobody is watching.[6]

Baumrind's work on the effects of parenting style is important, because we all want children who are happy and well-adjusted! Many parenting books have been written based on this research; two good ones are *Parenting Without Power Struggles: Raising Joyful, Resilient Kids While Staying Cool, Calm and Connected* by Susan Stiffelman, and *No-Drama Discipline: The Whole-Brain Way to Calm the Chaos and Nurture Your Child's Developing Mind* by Daniel Siegel and Tina Payne Bryson. One of the key elements that Baumrind and these other writers focus on is that parents who are high in responsiveness and high in demandingness tend to get buy-in from their children, so that children accept their guidance and are more likely to do what they are asked. Baumrind emphasized that one of the ways authoritative parents tend to do this is through explaining and convincing: they explain *why* they are imposing a certain rule, listen to any objections, and engage in active, back-and-forth discussion with the goal of coming to a mutually-agreed-upon conclusion. Following her lead, that's also what most of the relationship-based discipline books recommend. Unfortunately, when parents of toddlers try to use the techniques suggested in these books, they can be left feeling frustrated. What nobody seems to mention is that of the studies Baumrind originally examined, the ones that found a statistical effect between discussion and compliance were largely focused on adolescents!

While explaining and convincing may work well to get buy-in from older children, explaining why you want a child to do something is not likely to get you far with a toddler. This approach relies on skills like reflection, perspective-taking, and cause-and-effect—abilities not developed yet in the toddler's growing brain. These skills are all aspects of "executive functioning," which is run by the neo-frontal cortex and only develops gradually over the first twenty years of life.[7] In the toddler and preschool years, that area is just starting to develop.

When the "explain and convince" tactic is unsuccessfully applied with children who are too young, it pushes well-meaning parents away from authoritative parenting, since many of these parents don't want to make their children do things if they are unable to convince them. This makes them high in warmth and low in demandingness, inadvertently slipping into permissive parenting. In contrast, authoritative parents get buy-in from their children when they can, but still insist on "right action" when they can't. Baumrind explains,

> *The parent who exerts authoritative control...does indeed exert vigorous efforts to shape the child's behavior in his early years. To the extent that her policy is effective, the child may argue and test the limits, but he is fundamentally satisfied with his relationship to his parents and does not revolt.*[8]

THE MUTUALLY RESPONSIVE RELATIONSHIP

If discussion-based discipline doesn't work well with toddlers, then how do we get buy-in and cooperation from them? How do we go about being *authoritative* with young children? What does being high on warmth and having high expectations look like in the parent–toddler relationship? To delve into these issues, I turned to the research once again. This time, I looked for data on toddler-specific interactions: what makes them go smoothly or poorly, be enjoyable or challenging, successful or unsuccessful?

When I dug into the research I found many studies that focused on these questions, but most of them were not well known at all. Not only did researchers approach the topic from dozens of different angles, but almost every researcher called it something different. They didn't use nice, user-friendly words, either. In talking about what's happening when things are going well, one researcher described it as "contingent responsivity," while another called it "dyadic synchrony"; a third dubbed it "reciprocal responsiveness"; a fourth, fifth and sixth labeled it "social contingency," "interactional harmony" and "affect attunement," respectively.[9] Small wonder that these ideas have never made it out of academic circles. Unlike parent–infant research on Attachment, in the field of parent–toddler relationships there has been no John Bowlby (the "Father of Attachment Theory"), Mary Ainsworth (who did decades of research to back up Bowlby's ideas), or Dr. William Sears (who developed the philosophy of "Attachment Parenting") to unify and popularize the message.

While none of those academic terms seemed particularly approachable, I noticed that one idea kept turning up, even though different researchers described it differently: the interactions that went smoothly between parents and toddlers, and the relationships that were strong and healthy, were all steeped in *reciprocity*. Not reciprocity as in constant negotiations, "I'll-give-you-this-if-you-give-me-that," but reciprocity as in parent and child each caring and being responsive to the other. In academic-speak, interactions were "bi-directionally coordinated," meaning that each party accepted the influence of the other.

As I noted before, in a parent–*infant* relationship, it's the baby's job to communicate his or her needs to the adult, and it's the adult's job to meet those needs as quickly and fully as possible. In a healthy adult-*toddler* relationship, no longer is the child giving all the cues and the adult doing all the responding. At the same time, neither is it a "children should be seen and not heard" model. One of my favorite researchers, Grazyna Kochanska, coined a phrase describing this type of interaction that I liked so much I've adopted it for use in this book: she said that things go most smoothly when adult and child are *mutually responsive*.[10] It's possible for adults and children to be mutually responsive (or not) in a given interaction, and the more interactions we have this way, the closer the relationship gets to being mutually responsive overall. Our goal in parenting our toddlers, then, is to develop mutually responsive relationships with these emerging and powerful individuals. In order to create a life that you and your child both love, this is the necessary foundation.

While we adults can generally control our own behaviors and choose how responsive to be in a given situation, the other side of the equation can feel more challenging: how do we get our toddlers or preschoolers to be responsive to *us*? How can we get buy-in from toddlers when we ask them to do something (or refrain from doing something)? This may seem nearly impossible if we've fallen into a pattern of behavior where our children are making frequent unreasonable demands, throwing regular tantrums, or ignoring us completely. We parents have been practicing being responsive to our children for months and years, but our children have had much less practice in being responsive to us. How do we change that balance, and help children become responsive?

The short answer is that being responsive is a skill, and we can teach children how to do it. The long answer is contained in the chapters of this book: we do it by having high expectations (the "demandingness" of Baumrind's *authoritative* parent), and then helping our children to follow through. We don't make our help punitive; on the contrary, we make it as fun and enjoyable as we can (the warmth of the *authoritative* parent). Ideas on how to do this gracefully and enjoyably to come.

THE ELEMENTS OF RESPONSIVENESS

In being responsive to babies, we simply do what they need and want. With anyone else, however, it isn't always feasible or even desirable to do what they want. Luckily, **being responsive doesn't require us to do whatever the other person wants**. What it *does* require is two things: that we respond quickly, and that we respond positively. Both of these are possible to do, even if we can't—or won't—do what the other person wants. Likewise, our children can also respond quickly and positively to us, even when they can't do what we have asked of them. Relationships are healthiest when both parties are responsive.

> *Being* ***responsive*** *requires two things: responding quickly and responding positively. This is especially important when we can't—or won't—do what the other person has asked.*

Perhaps it's not obvious what I mean when I say to "respond quickly and positively when we can't (or won't) do what the other person wants." Let's look at some examples. I'll use toddlers and adults, since that's what this book is about, but the principles hold true for two adults, or two children, as well.

Example 1: *An adult can't (or won't) do what a child asks.*
Nikko, aged twenty-three months, yells, "Milk!" in an imperious tone. Perhaps there *is* milk in the fridge, but mom feels resentful at Nikko's demanding tone. She can still respond quickly and positively, not by giving him milk while holding in her annoyance, but by telling him how to ask in a way that makes her want to say yes: "You can say, 'Milk, please.'" More often than not, children will respond by saying exactly what we've said, in the exact same tone.

But perhaps there is no milk to be had. In that case, mom could still respond quickly and positively: "Are you thirsty? There's no milk left, but I wonder if we could find something else for you to drink. Let's look together." She takes him by the hand and they walk over to the fridge. She's telling him no, but in a way that *feels* like yes. As we'll explore in the next chapter, both touch and getting children into motion are good ways to help them feel connected, so going to look together is more likely to have a positive response than simply telling a toddler what's available.

In both of those cases, the mother is being responsive to the child, without doing exactly what he asks.

Example 2: *A child can't (or won't) do what an adult asks.*
Dad asks three-year-old Emma to get her jacket on, but the task feels overwhelming to her. How could she still respond quickly and positively? One possibility would be to ask for help, preferably in a way that makes Dad want to say, "Sure!" Another possibility would be to bring her jacket over to him. Both of those are responding positively and quickly, even though she's not doing exactly what she was asked to do.

However, suppose that Emma simply doesn't *want* to get her jacket on. If she were verbal enough, she might still respond quickly and positively by asking, "Can I carry my jacket instead?" If she's not verbal enough, then she might show her desire by tucking her jacket under her arm, or grabbing a sweatshirt instead of her jacket. Alternatively, she might need dad's active help to respond quickly and positively: "You don't want to wear your jacket, huh? Would you like to carry it instead? Why don't you ask: 'Carry it, please?'"

That type of parental support, either helping a child *want* to say yes to us, or helping a child come up with a response that's still positive, even when she doesn't want to do what's been asked, is a vital piece in helping a child learn how to become responsive to us. In fact, it leads us to:

The First Great Parenting Task of the Toddler Years

While some children seem to pick up through osmosis how to be responsive, most children need our help and support. Shifting from their sense of being the center of the universe (as all babies are) to being half of a pair is monumental. To want one thing but choose to do another because of someone else's desires takes real self-control. To figure out how to respond positively when you can't or won't do what's been asked takes both skill and practice. Self-discipline is a skill that is just beginning to emerge during the toddler years, and parenting decisions can have a significant impact on whether it develops strongly or poorly. This brings us to the First Great Parenting Task of the Toddler Years:

> *In the toddler years, it is vital that we support our children in learning to control their impulses and practice being responsive to us.*

This book is all about how to do that task: you will discover practical ways to help toddlers and preschoolers say yes to you, even as they go through their own process of individuation or are overwhelmed by big emotions. You can set them up for success, cheer them on, help them recover when they fail, and encourage them to try again.

Establishing a mutually responsive relationship is powerfully important because being responsive to each other is not just what makes parent–toddler relationships strong: it's what makes any relationship strong. By helping toddlers learn to be responsive to us while being responsive in return, we are setting the groundwork for them to have healthy relationships for the rest of their lives. Indeed, we would be doing them a disservice to do otherwise. It is also vital for creating a life that we and our children both love; if one party is responsive but the other is not, this leads to an inherently unbalanced relationship where enjoyment is precarious and often fleeting.

With this view of creating a healthy, balanced relationship, there no longer has to be a struggle between connection and boundaries. We don't have to put connection aside to get children to do what we've asked; in fact, we will often do things we know they love when asking them to do something for us, to make saying yes as natural and enjoyable as possible—to help get their buy-in. We don't get buy-in through logic when they are at this age, since that part of their brain isn't developed yet; we get it through positive emotion. We are helping them *learn* to say *yes* to us. And, even when a child can't say yes, many people find that they have more patience when they can see a child as a person who's just learning the skill of being responsive, rather than as someone who's being defiant. Rather than punishing that child, we can help him come up with a positive response. When he is despondent because he can't have what he wants, we can help him develop the skill of recovering from disappointment. Our responses can foster connection without losing the "high demandingness" of the authoritative parent. We are working on developing a mutually responsive relationship.

The Second Great Parenting Task of the Toddler Years

There are two sides to a mutually responsive relationship. One side is asking—and helping—children to be responsive to us. The other side is our own responsiveness to children. We already looked at how being responsive isn't the same as doing what someone wants. Yet the waters are still murky when it comes to being responsive to a toddler or preschooler. When do we do what they want, and when do we "hold firm"? How do we know what to do in a given situation?

The way we can feel secure in our responses is to develop an internal compass to assess our responses—an internal compass that is tuned to the young child's needs, rather than to his desires. This attunement allows us to accomplish the Second Great Parenting Task of the Toddler Years:

> *In the toddler years, it is vital that we adjust our parenting to be responsive to children's needs rather than reacting to their whims.*

What does this adjustment look like? How do we distinguish between needs and whims, and what needs should we focus on? The idea that people have needs beyond those of food and shelter has been explored throughout history, and different classifications for our non-physical needs abound. Which needs will *you* focus on in your parenting? You can (and should) give that some real thought. What *do* young children really need? What do they *long for* on a deep level? This book focuses on three needs necessary to achieve a profound sense of belonging and usefulness: the first is the need for *connection* with others; the second is the need for *competence* or mastery; and the third is the need to know that one is *contributing* to something greater than oneself, making a difference.

Connection, competence and contributing are universal needs, and not age-dependent. The one-year-old reaches out to others, works on mastering skills, and tries to help others, as the three-year-old and five-year-old do, too. So do we. When we focus on being responsive to these important needs in young children, we achieve a broader perspective and a way to judge, in the moment, how to respond. This focus offers us a way to say yes to the need, even when we can't say yes to a specific desire. Additionally, this book offers practical suggestions for setting up a life in which there's room for a child to pursue and experience each of these areas, minimizing discipline issues and deepening your relationship.

Of course, there will still be times when we can't figure out how to connect, areas in which we're not comfortable letting a child practice competence, or situations when we don't have time to let a child try to contribute. We will discuss later what to do in those moments, too. Even in those moments, things can still shift if awareness of these three needs allows us to approach children's frustrations with compassion. Let's take a moment to look at each in turn.

The Importance of Connection

At all ages and all stages of development, human beings feel more satisfied and fulfilled when they are in authentic, meaningful relationships with one another. Extensive research exists on the effects of the quality of relationships on people's lives—from the lasting effects of babies' first relationships, to how social connections later in life prolong both life expectancy[11] and health[12] in the elderly. We are at our best when we are able to love and be loved, to enjoy one another and to be appreciated for who we are.

We can be responsive to children's need for connection by recognizing their efforts to connect with us (it may look different than you think), and by facilitating their efforts to connect with others. In later chapters, we'll look at ways that toddlers delight in connecting, and how to weave these activities throughout the day, without having to set aside "special time" to connect. Connecting works even better when we focus on weaving these activities into normally tricky times of the day—especially during transitions of all types, and tasks of bodily care, such as dressing and undressing, brushing hair and teeth, and diapering. When we integrate connecting into the necessary parts of the day, our days can become much more smooth and enjoyable. In fostering our children's sense of connection, we are fostering our own sense of connection at the same time. Taking the time to learn how children feel connected enriches both our lives.

The Need for Competence

The effort to challenge ourselves to learn and grow starts in infancy (see Robert White's research in the 1950s and 60s on babies' "competence motivation"[13]), and it continues throughout life. No matter where we are in our developmental journey, we strive for a place of balance in which we are neither overwhelmed nor bored, but are challenged just the right amount, confident in our abilities to handle what comes toward us. The need for competence encompasses both of these points: feeling confident in our abilities, and learning new skills.

We can be responsive to toddlers' need for competence by allowing them to watch us as we do practical tasks, by doing tasks slowly so they can join in, and by giving them space to practice through independent play. We'll also discuss a specific type of competence called *self-regulation* that's necessary for children to be responsive to us, and for them to form deep friendships. Such self-regulation is also essential for the development of executive functioning in the brain.

The Desire to Contribute

People feel both energized and grounded when they know they are making the world a better place, when they are helping others, and when they are contributing to something greater than themselves. A large body of research shows that people are healthier, happier and more fulfilled when they are able to contribute to the well-being of others: it reduces chances of dropping out of high-school,[14] contributes to job satisfaction,[15] can be an effective treatment for depression,[16] reduces symptoms of post-traumatic stress disorder,[17] and increases longevity.[18] Evidence is strong that these effects are causal rather than correlational.[19]

Unfortunately, our culture rarely recognizes the very young child's desire to contribute. Young children are expected to learn, play and have fun. They are rarely expected to be helpful. Adults are expected to help children, not the other way around! Part III will look more closely at the types of real-life interactions that can meet the young child's desire to contribute, and how to engage in them successfully—in ways that are enjoyable for everyone. This aspect of a fulfilling life is almost entirely absent from the mainstream messages about children, and small changes in this area can make big differences in your relationship with your child.

EVEN TODDLERS CAN LIVE A LIFE THAT'S FULFILLING

The idea that even young children could live a fulfilling life in the present—right now—is much different from the message we get about children from our everyday world, which encourages us to think mainly of what they need for their *future* development. To support future development, we work to provide enrichment activities for them. We think about ways to stimulate them. We do our best to spend "quality time" with them. We teach them and help them and try to manage their behavior, and we wait for them to reach the next milestone, and the one after that, and the one after that. It can sometimes be exciting (remember those first steps?), but it can also feel stressful and boring at the same time, especially if your child doesn't meet a milestone or has a delay.

On the other hand, when we consider the universal needs of *connection*, *competence* and *contributing* that even very young children have, this knowledge can change everything. When these needs are met, children can live a life that's not just filled with activity, but that's actually fulfilling—not sometime in the future, but right now. With this new awareness of children's needs, we can be responsive to them in new ways. Suddenly, many of their previously-frustrating actions will make new sense to us, and thus our responses can shift. Take courage! If you are living a life where you're constantly butting heads with your child, know that it really is possible to make changes that will boost your child's contentment and strengthen your relationship, all while making your own life more enjoyable.

What would these changes look like? When you recognize your child's longings to feel connected to you and to others, you can weave moments of connection into the necessary activities of the day, and respond to refusals as requests for connection. When you recognize your child's longing for competence and to learn new skills, you can perform actions in an expansive way that allows your child to participate, and you can back off to give her room to explore her world through independent play. And, when you recognize your child's longing to contribute, you can allow and encourage him to help in real, meaningful tasks that make your household run on a daily basis. When we consciously create a life that has space for children to do those things, then suddenly we and our children can be on the same team, pulling in the same direction, and our days can go more smoothly. When we do butt heads, as will inevitably happen sometimes, we will still strive to respond quickly and positively. When we can be responsive to these deep-seated, universal needs, then children will be better able to weather the storms of not having every whim granted. With these three needs met, life may not be easy, but it still feels good.

As children grow more responsive, we can also call on them to be their best selves more often: helpful, flexible, able to roll with the punches and recover quickly when things don't go their way all the time. In short, they will be able to be responsive to us when we ask it of them. Establishing a mutually responsive relationship takes work, but lays the groundwork for a close and productive relationship with your child for the rest of your lives together. Let's begin!

KEY POINTS

The Big Ideas in *Parent–Toddler Relationships at Their Best*

Authoritative parents have high responsiveness and high demandingness.

Healthy parent–toddler relationships are *mutually responsive:* where both parties respond quickly and positively to one another, even—and especially—when they can't do what the other person wants.

The Two Great Parenting Tasks of the Toddler Years:

1. In the toddler years, it is vital that we support our children in learning to control their impulses and practice being responsive to us.
2. In the toddler years, it is vital that we adjust our parenting to be responsive to children's needs, rather than reacting to their whims.

We focus on the universal needs of *Connection, Competence,* and *Contributing* to set an internal compass to guide our responses to children. Childhood is not just a time of preparation for adulthood, but is as valid as any other time, and children long to live a life that's fulfilling, just like we do.

ENDNOTES, CHAPTER 1

[1] Luoh, M. C., & Herzog, A. R. (2002). Individual consequences of volunteer and paid work in old age: Health and mortality. *Health and Social Behavior, 43,* 490–509.

[2] Brown, W. M., Consedine, N. S., & Magai, C. (2005). Altruism relates to health in an ethnically diverse sample of older adults. *Journal of Gerontology: PSYCHOLOGICAL SCIENCES, 60B (3),* 143-152.

[3] White, R. W. (1959). Motivation reconsidered: the concept of competence. *Psychological Review, 66*(5), 297.

[4] Moore, C.W., & Allan, J.P. (1996). The effects of volunteering on the young volunteer. *Journal of Primary Prevention, 17*(2), 231-258.

[5] Smith, T. W. (2007). *Job satisfaction in the United States* (University of Chicago National Opinion Research Center). Retrieved from http://wwwnews.uchicago.edu/releases/07/pdf/070417.jobs.pdf

[6] Musick, M. A., & Wilson, J. (2002). Volunteering and depression: The role of psychological and social resources in different age groups. *Social Science and Medicine, 56,* 259-269.

[7] Heirholzer, R. W. (2004). Improvements in PTSD patients who care for their grandchildren. *American Journal of Psychiatry, 161,* 176.

[8] Luoh, M. C., & Herzog, A. R. (2002).

[9] Post, S. G. (2005). Altruism, happiness, and health: It is good to be good. *International Journal of Behavioral Medicine, 12(2),* 66-77.

[10] Kochanska, G. (1997). Mutually responsive orientation between mothers and their young children: Implications for early socialization. *Child Development*, 68(1), 94-112.

[11] Luoh, M. C., & Herzog, A. R. (2002). Individual consequences of volunteer and paid work in old age: Health and mortality. *Health and Social Behavior*, *43*, 490–509.

[12] Brown, W. M., Consedine, N. S., & Magai, C. (2005). Altruism relates to health in an ethnically diverse sample of older adults. Journal of Gerontology: *PSYCHOLOGICAL SCIENCES, 60B* (3), 143-152.

[13] White, R. W. (1959). Motivation reconsidered: the concept of competence. *Psychological Review, 66*(5), 297.

[14] Moore, C.W., & Allan, J.P. (1996). The effects of volunteering on the young volunteer. *Journal of Primary Prevention*, *17*(2), 231-258.

[15] Smith, T. W. (2007). *Job satisfaction in the United States* (University of Chicago National Opinion Research Center). Retrieved from http://wwwnews.uchicago.edu/releases/07/pdf/070417.jobs.pdf

[16] Musick, M. A., & Wilson, J. (2002). Volunteering and depression: The role of psychological and social resources in different age groups. *Social Science and Medicine*, *56*, 259-269.

[17] Heirholzer, R. W. (2004). Improvements in PTSD patients who care for their grandchildren. *American Journal of Psychiatry*, *161*, 176.

[18] Luoh, M. C., & Herzog, A. R. (2002).

[19] Post, S. G. (2005). Altruism, happiness, and health: It is good to be good. *International Journal of Behavioral Medicine*, *12(2)*, 66-77.

CHAPTER 2

Being Responsive to Children: Don't Forget to S*M*I*L*E!

This chapter dives more deeply into the practical aspects of what it takes to create a mutually responsive relationship with young children. It starts with the radical idea that most of the times children say *no*, what they're really saying is "*I don't feel as connected to you right now as I wish I did.*" We'll look at how we can be responsive to this request by exploring different ways young children feel connected, and how we can use those to help them do what we've asked in the first place. In this way, we are helping them learn to become responsive to us.

Fascinating research, pioneered by Carol Dweck, examines how our mindsets affect our actions.[1] A "mindset" is a set of assumptions about *why*: for example, why we succeed or fail ("because I didn't try hard enough" vs. "because I'm dumb" vs. "because people are out to get me"); or why someone hasn't phoned back ("I must have annoyed him" vs. "he must be busy"); or why our children misbehave (more on that in a minute). As Brooks and Goldstein propose in their book *Raising a Self-Disciplined Child: Help Your Child Become More Responsible, Confident and Resilient,* "Although it may seem obvious that a person's mindset affects the person's behavior, many people don't reflect upon their mindset, or if they do, many accept it as truth, rather than as assumptions that can and should be challenged."[2]

Let's start this chapter by reflecting on our mindsets about why toddlers and preschoolers say no to us. This is vitally important, because our interpretations of why children are doing the things they do has an enormous impact on how much we enjoy or don't enjoy being with them. This, in turn, shapes how we respond to them. Our interpretation of the reasons behind children's actions shape not only our own feelings and actions, but theirs, too: children look to us to give meaning to the events in their lives, so it's easy for our assumptions about them to become self-fulfilling prophecies as they live up (or down) to our expectations.

When I ask the question, "Why do toddlers and preschooler say no to us?" in talks and workshops, the answers I get tend to run along these lines:

- They're differentiating themselves from us.
- They're testing boundaries.
- They're expressing their individuality.

As sensible as these answers sound, I'd like to suggest an alternative perspective (or mindset) that has the ability to change your day-to-day interactions with your child in an enormously powerful way. This new mindset starts with the idea that, while the answers given in the list above are indeed important developmental undertakings during the toddler years, they are actually *not* the reasons that children say no to us the vast majority of the time. In fact, I propose that most of the time when children say no to us, what they are really saying is, *"I don't feel as connected to you right now as I wish I did."* If we are able to hear *this* when they say no, our responses can more easily change so we'll be less likely to get into power struggles. Our days can go more smoothly and be more enjoyable.

Let's look at the following interaction with the new mindset that many *no*'s are really requests for connection, rather than requests for independence. We set the stage with Ashley (age two years eight months) and her mom:

"Ashley, it's time for us to put our jackets on!"

"No!"

"What?!" Mom puts her hands to her cheeks with a shocked expression on her face. Ashley looks at her mom with a devilish glint in her eye, and her mother responds by stretching her hands out and wiggling her fingers, leaning forward and saying, "I'm gonna get you! I'm gonna get you!"

Ashley shrieks happily and runs away. They play chase for a moment, and then Mom picks her up and slings her over her shoulder. As she walks to the coats, she turns from side to side, saying, "Where's Ashley? Where did she go? I know she was here a minute ago!" Giggles emanate from behind her back. Mom puts her down and says, with exaggerated surprise, "Hey, how did you get here?!" More giggles.

Mom takes Ashley's jacket down from its hook and Ashley hides her hands. Mom ignores this action and instead sticks her own hand up the cuff of the sleeve, wiggling it around and saying, "Cheep-cheep! Cheep-cheep!" She looks at Ashley in mock amazement. "What's that? Is there something in your jacket sleeve?" She wiggles her hand again. Ashley looks intrigued, and when Mom opens the coat, Ashley puts her arm in the sleeve, reaching down toward the hand. As one hand nearly touches the other, Mom pulls her own hand out and lets it flutter away, whistling a little birdy tune. "A bird in your sleeve!" She and Ashley share a happy smile.

"Do it again!" Ashley exclaims, holding out the other sleeve. They go through the exact same routine with the other sleeve, and then Mom starts the zipper and holds the bottom so Ashley can pull it up the rest of the way. They slip their shoes on and go to the door, where Mom pauses.

"Are you ready?" she asks, making eye contact. Ashley nods eagerly, clearly aware of what's about to happen. Mom opens the door and they break into a rendition of *I've Been Working On the Railroad* together, and march out the door, knees high.

Does this type of scene feel familiar? Or does it seem like that mysterious "toddler magic" that some people have, but is totally out of reach for you? In fact, what is it that makes it "toddler magic," and why does it work? Perhaps, rather than seeming like "toddler magic," this interaction between Ashley and Mom seems more like rewarding bad behavior, or raising a child for whom saying no becomes too much fun. We'll discuss how to avoid that last pitfall later in the chapter, but for now let's look at *why* Ashley is happy to go along with her mother's response.

When Mom turns getting ready to go into a game, Ashley's resistance melts away. Not because Ashley no longer cares about differentiating herself from her mother. Not because she no longer needs firm boundaries. Nor is her mother somehow tricking her, or distracting her into forgetting her own needs. Although Ashley started out with a negative response, she ends up happy to go along with what her mom has asked because her mom has responded positively to her request for connection, which Ashley had voiced by saying no. Once mom has been responsive to Ashley, Ashley is able to be responsive to her mother in return. (*Fun and games are not the only way to connect with children; we'll go over examples of many different ways below.)*

Not quite convinced? Let's think about an alternate scenario, where Ashley's mother is tired, or in a hurry, or just doesn't have the energy for chasing-games and imaginary birds and song-singing. This time, when Ashley says *no*, Mom gets serious. She looks Ashley in the eye and says in a stern tone, "Ashley, it's time to go. Come get your coat on, right now." Mom picks up the coat and holds it out. If Ashley were really asking for boundaries, don't you think that this firm stance would make her feel reassured? But it doesn't reassure her. Instead, her response is likely to range somewhere between grudging acceptance and a full-on meltdown complete with Mom stuffing her daughter's arms into the coat and carrying her to the car because she won't get her shoes on.

When we meet a child's no with firmness or impatience, the intense negative reaction we can get often takes us by surprise. A complete meltdown because we asked her to put her jacket on? By translating no into *"I don't feel as connected to you right now as I wish I did,"* a lot of pieces can click into place. If the child is truly asking for connection, that response starts to make more sense. Consider how you might feel if something similar happened to you:

Imagine that you're feeling distant from your spouse or partner. Perhaps he or she has been extra busy lately, spending more and more time on the computer. Finally, one evening, you take a deep breath and say, "Honey, I've been feeling really disconnected lately. Will you put your work down for a moment and just give me a hug?" Instead of stopping and hugging you, however, your spouse looks up with a sigh and bit of an eye-roll and says, "I really just don't have time for this right now. Why are you always doing this? Can't you see I'm busy?"

Ouch. When we screw up our courage to ask for connection and we're rebuffed, it's not fun. We might even feel like having a bit of a meltdown ourselves. Imagine how much better it would be if, instead, your partner looked up at you and said, "Thanks for reminding me to take a little break. I love you so much," and then he or she got up from the computer and gave you a juicy, heart-felt hug. Your partner might still need to keep working on the computer after that, but perhaps you wouldn't mind so much, once your sense of connection had been restored. The same thing is true for children. We don't need to connect deeply with them in every moment; rather, we need to give them a few moments of real connection when they let us know that they need it.

Getting back to little Ashley and her mom, if we translate Ashley's *no* into "I don't feel as connected to you right now as I wish I did," then her mother's response is just right. She's not distracting her child, and she's not tricking her in any way. She's responding to Ashley's request for connection, and when Ashley feels reconnected she doesn't just grudgingly go along with what her mom has asked her to do; she does it joyfully. Many parents confuse connection with permissiveness, but they are not the same at all. Ashley's mom didn't give up on getting ready to go, she just made it easier for Ashley to say yes by making the actions more connecting. She is exhibiting high demandingness and high warmth at the same time, the hallmarks of authoritative parenting.

It seems counter-intuitive that when we ask children to do something and they refuse, it's really because they want to feel closer to us. And, in reality, we don't actually know what young children are feeling or thinking at any given time. However, whether it's "actually" true or not, thinking in this way can change our actions and change our lives for the better.

Certainly it would be so much nicer and easier if our young children would calmly state, "When you ask me to get my coat on, I feel resistance because I'm enjoying my play. Your energy feels rushed and you're not even really paying attention to me. Could you please take a moment to reconnect first? Then I'd be happy to get my coat on." Unfortunately, they can't say such a thing. Even most adults couldn't be that clear, and young children are at a double-disadvantage over even average adults.

The first disadvantage is that children don't have the adult consciousness, experience, or vocabulary to say something like the sentence above. They simply know that when we are hurried or distracted they feel resistance, and when we are fun and connecting they're eager for more.

The second disadvantage stems from *when* they are most likely to feel disconnected: when we're tired, when we're running late, when the baby's fussy and needs to be changed, or when we're over-committed or overwhelmed. In short, children tend to say *no* at the very times when saying no is the *least* likely to get a laugh and a fun game out of us. Perhaps we even know that things would go better if we could turn the *no* into a game, but, like the partner in the adult example, we think, "I don't have time for this." A game doesn't feel worthwhile if we're tired or in a hurry. Consequently, we don't have the patience, and we don't take the time, and when the meltdown ensues we sigh and grit our teeth, and carry our child to the car. (*It's only a phase, right? Just get through it…*) Realizing that a game is really honoring a request for connection makes it feel more worthwhile.

SIGNS OF CONNECTION: "LET'S DO IT AGAIN!"

If a *no* is often really a request for connection, then the next practical question is, "What can I do to connect with my child?" Practically speaking, what types of interactions feel connecting for young children?

While the enjoyment of connecting with another person happens at every age, the actions that foster connection change over the months and years, and depend on a person's character, experiences, interests, etc. Regardless of all those factors, you can tell that connection is happening when a person's reaction is: "Yes! Let's do it again!"

Adults might feel connected by having deep conversations about past experiences that have helped shape who they've become. A pair of teenage boys might feel connected by doing adrenaline-inducing activities together. As an eight-year-old girl, I can remember spending hours upon hours with my friend Heather, making up dance routines where we would twirl long ribbons on sticks. I'd run over to her house every day, eager to get started. For each of these pairs the activity is different, but in all the cases, everyone has the feeling of "Yes! Let's do it again!" They are feeling connected.

What makes the young child say, "Again!"? We know that turning a task into a game can generate that response, but what if you're not a "fun" parent? How can you create a game out of nothing? What types of games work? What if you get bored with the same old thing, time after time? Or, what if you're tired and grumpy, and don't feel like playing a game? Are there other responses that can work?

The answer is a resounding *yes*! We'll look at five different ways that young children feel connected. These can become five skills in your tool belt for transforming *no* into *yes*.

Why Five Ways?

When you read about these five ways, you will likely discover that you already use some, or even many of them. Perhaps one or two are your "standards." But, if these standard responses only work sometimes, it may be that your child would feel more engaged or connected using another path to connection.

Just as you will probably have one or two tools that feel the most natural to you, each child has one or two that feel most engaging to him or her. However, it is possible that these two only overlap partially, or not at all. If you're always making interactions fun, but your son is really longing for love and appreciation, he may reject your attempts. If you tend to want to snuggle, but your daughter squirms away when you try, it could be that she's longing for some roughhousing or funny sound effects. With five different types of connection at your fingertips, if you try one tool and it's not right for the job, you can try another, and another.

Finally, it's useful to have five different ways of connecting because sometimes a child knows exactly how he or she wishes to connect, but it's not possible or practical in that moment: perhaps your child wants to wrestle, but you've thrown out your back. Perhaps your child wants to breastfeed, but you're weaning or it's not a good time. Perhaps your child is trying to engage you in a game of chase-and-tickle, but it's bedtime. Instead of simply rebuffing your child and saying *no*, you can say *yes* to their desire for connection, but use a different approach.

WHEN YOU WANT TO CONNECT WITH YOUR CHILD, DON'T FORGET TO *S*M*I*L*E*

When a child says *no* and your first idea doesn't work, it's easy to feel at a loss. To make the categories easier to remember in the moment when that *no* appears, I've made a little mnemonic device: *When you want to connect with your child, don't forget to SMILE.* Use **S**inging, **M**ovement, **I**magination, **L**ove, and **E**xaggeration. The strengths of each of these have been well documented by early childhood researchers, and most are easy enough to do. All of them can feel silly or awkward at first, but just like using any new skill, they get easier with practice. Let's go over each of these in turn.

Singing

***Singing**, Movement, Imagination, Love, Exaggeration*

Children connect through songs and rhymes. Remember when Ashley and her mother left the house marching to the tune of *I've Been Working on the Railroad*? Well, it turns out that singing and rhymes reach children in special ways. The beneficial effects of nursery rhymes on later reading ability have been well documented,[3] but this hardly scratches the surface of all the advantages that songs and rhymes can bring. New research is showing what cultures have known for millennia: singing together promotes feelings of fellowship ("social affiliation"), emotional bonding, and the sharing of common goals.[4] This is why singing together is so prevalent in religious and military ceremonies, and even used to begin many sporting events. Singing affects even the youngest of us: live singing to babies in Intensive Care lowers their heart rates, promotes sleep and weight gain, and allows them to go home earlier than babies exposed to recorded music.[5] Even more relevant to the work of this book, adults and children moving together to music has been shown to promote helpful behavior afterward, in children as young as fourteen months.[6] In another study, four-year-olds who participated in a musical game later played together in a more helpful and cooperative manner than children who took part in a non-musical game.[7] So, sing to your children! Sing when you want their attention, sing your instructions to them, sing while they have to wait, and sing while they do the thing that you've asked them to do.

Songs can be rousing and fun for getting out the door, like the song Ashley's mom used. They can be silly, for livening up boring tasks or having to wait for something. They can be soothing and sweet for snuggling together or going to bed. Songs can instruct, let children know it's time for a certain activity, and help transitions go more smoothly. Give it a try. It doesn't matter whether you can sing in tune or not; the act itself is connecting, not the objective quality of the song.

If you are worried that you don't know many children's songs, you can sing songs you listen to on the radio, songs you remember from your childhood, or take a really common song—say, *Twinkle, Twinkle, Little Star*—and add your own words about getting out of the bathtub, getting into the car, climbing into bed, etc.* When I was a child, my mother sang a special lullaby that was "my song" (basically my name sung over and over again), and I remember as a teenager being quite shocked one day to hear my lullaby playing on the radio. My mom had not invented it after all—it was *Song Sung Blue*, by Neil Diamond! So, don't feel like you have to learn a bunch of new songs, just use what you have. They are still powerfully connecting. (I must admit that I still sometimes hum *Song Sung Blue* to myself when I'm upset.)

Songs are also great anytime a child needs to wait for something. When I have multiple children waiting for a turn to stir the batter

---

* If you want to learn more songs, I highly recommend any of the songbooks by Mary Schunnemann. They come with sheet music and a CD of her singing each one. My favorites are *This Is the Way We Wash-A-Day*, and *Sing A Song with Baby*. I also like the lullaby one.

while we're baking muffins, I'll sing *All Around the Mulberry Bush* for each child, so that the one stirring knows exactly how long his turn is, and the ones waiting know exactly how long they have to wait. If a child is waiting for me to finish washing a pan in the sink so that I can tie a cape around her neck, I'll sing *One, Two, Buckle My Shoe,* and when it's done, I'll dry my hands and help her. Children are better able to wait patiently when we sing a little song, because they feel connected to us through our singing.

Occasionally, when I've encouraged parents in my classes to sing to their children, they've been mortified to try it, only to hear their child demand, "Stop singing!" If this happens to you, it doesn't mean that your voice is terrible or that singing won't work for your child; more often it's just an acknowledgement that you're doing something new and different. Try weaving some other connecting activities into your singing: exaggeration (sing in a silly voice, very fast or slow, soft or loud, etc.), and movement (swinging them around while you sing, doing hand motions to your song, marching to the beat, etc.) are good activities to combine with singing; you'll get more ideas below.

> *While preparing dinner and wearing my five-month-old to wind her down for bed, I sang what I was doing and gave my almost-three-year-old small tasks: putting dill in a bowl and whisking the sauce, which both made him feel involved and also occupied him so he wasn't loud and disturbing the baby. What made me laugh out loud was when he climbed into his highchair and sang for his daddy to buckle him in. How nice to hear that instead of a demand! This little experience shows me how powerful modeling is.*
>
> —Jessica, mother of two†

As an early childhood teacher, I saw on a daily basis that if children weren't listening when I spoke, singing my words would cut directly through to them in a completely different way. I can still remember my first week as an assistant in the toddler classroom, trying to get ten one- and two-year-olds to come inside from the play yard; it felt like herding cats! That is, until the lead teacher started singing a *Come, Follow, Follow* song, whereupon the children were drawn to her like the Pied Piper of Hamelin. Songs and rhymes are powerful tools for connecting with children and transforming *no* into *yes*.

Movement

*Singing, **Movement**, Imagination, Love, Exaggeration*

Children connect through movement, touch, and physical fun. Remember when Ashley's mom chased Ashley around, then slung her over her shoulder? When she turned back and forth, "looking" for Ashley? When she took Ashley's hand to walk out the door? Children love vestibular stimulation (spinning, jumping, going upside down), and with good reason: physical movement literally makes children happy.[8] In addition, active movement is shown to strengthen cognition, academic achievement, behavior, and social skills![9] So anytime you'd like to avoid a power struggle, get your child into motion!

Positive touch is also powerfully connecting, as it causes our brains to release oxytocin, the "hormone of connection." When movement and touch are combined, it can elicit a powerful *yes* from children.

There are additional advantages to encouraging healthy movement, as described by Sally Goddard Blythe, director of the Institute of Neuro-Physiological Psychology and author of *The Genius of Natural Childhood*: "When a child's movement vocabulary is well-developed, she is better able not only to express herself through non-verbal means but also to understand the body language of

† All of the direct quotes in this book are real sharings from parents who have taken my classes or worked with me privately. The names of both parents and children have been changed to protect their privacy.

others. This is the beginning of empathy (which literally means 'feeling what another feels')."[10]

In my work with parents, I've seen that physical fun comes naturally to some, but for many parents it rarely occurs to them. If physical fun is not part of your everyday interactions, then give it a try. You may have a child clamoring for more—a sure sign of connection! Big movements can be connecting in a big way, so swing your daughter around when lifting her into a high chair or car seat, hang your son upside down when you've asked him to stop harassing the dog but he can't seem to, toss your one-year-old in the air when you pick her up to go for a diaper change.

Medium-sized movements are also connecting, and are less hard on your back: horsey-rides on your lap when your child needs to wait for something or someone, "wheelbarrow walking" where you hold a child's feet and she walks on her hands when it's time to go potty but she doesn't want to go, or rolling a child up like a burrito in a blanket and stacking pillows on top. All these activities feel like big movement to children but are easier on us. Chase-and-tickle games can be as big or as small as we wish, and most children love them; taking a few moments to play when a child is having trouble doing what we've asked can often restore connection.

> *Here's one of my favorite touching games for helping diaper changes go smoothly, up on the changing table:*
>
> ***All around the haystack goes the little mouse***
> *(circle his belly button with your finger)*
> ***One step, two steps,***
> *("walk" your fingers up his belly)*
> ***Into his little house!***
> *("run" your fingers into his armpit or the crook of his neck)*

And, of course, smaller touches and movements can be lovingly connecting as well: long soft strokes down the arms or body can help a child calm down or wake up. A blanket over both your heads creates a private world and can be great for helping children who need a moment of intimacy. Touching games with rhymes like "This Little Piggie Went to Market" or "Pat-a-Cake" are great to use in between multi-step tasks, like dressing in winter clothing. For one little boy who had trouble waking up from naps, I would greet each of his body parts with firm squeezes to "help them wake up," greeting each one affectionately by name as I did. When my own daughter has trouble with a transition or doing what I've asked, I often say, "Do you need a snuggle first?" She often relaxes into me with visible relief, and is usually ready to get going again in just a moment.

Movement fun also encompasses children moving themselves in different ways. Marching along (as Ashley and her mom did while they went out the door), taking giant steps, racing, tip-toeing, and hopping all get your child from point A to point B, usually with giggles and enjoyment. Combine these movements with Imagination or Singing, and you double the amount of connection. In fact, almost anytime you ask a child to *do* something and you get a "no," getting that child into motion can help melt that "no" away.

Leticia, a mother in one of my classes, shared that her nineteen-month-old hated getting dressed. The next time she asked if he was ready to get pants on and he said *no*, she said, "*No*?! Well, I bet you'll be ready after I…hang you upside down!" And she swung him upside down. He collapsed into giggles and demanded, "Again!" She said, "Yes. Let's get pants on and then we'll do it again." And that's exactly how it went.

Another mom, Angie, had been struggling with her two-year-old running away when it was time to get dressed in the morning. In working with the ideas from the class, she switched her expectations to make his running something they could enjoy together (connecting), instead of an annoyance. After each article of clothing she'd encourage him to run to the wall and back again, saying "Ready, set, go!" to send him off, then welcoming him back with a big hug, putting on another item of clothing and sending him off again. She shared that it was not only more enjoyable than it had been when she had tried to stop him from running, but actually was quicker from beginning to end, if you counted all of the time she had been spending convincing, cajoling, and threatening.

A note about hitting: In my experience, when toddlers laugh while they're hitting, run away (while laughing), or repeatedly try to touch things they've been asked not to (also laughing), these are almost always veiled requests for Movement fun. When I notice a child doing this, I respond first to their request, and then I give them a more appropriate way to ask the next time. So, I might scoop a child up, saying, "Oho! It looks like you're ready to play!" We'd play for a bit, and as I set her down I'd add, "Next time you want to rough-house, you can say, 'Rough-house, please!'" After we've been through this a few times, if she is still hitting to invite play, I'll remind her how to ask first. Responding to the desire behind an action, rather than to the action itself, is a powerful tool to help children behave in ways that everyone can enjoy. See the section below on Transforming Attention-Seeking Behaviors to avoid pitfalls in making this shift successfully.

I've talked in this section about how to use movement and touch to help children do what we've asked, but movement and touch are so important for children that it's important for us to make sure they get lots of both, throughout the day. Many parents either enjoy rough-housing *or* snuggles, but I want to encourage you to expand your repertoire! If you're worn out or have physical limitations, look for ways for your child to move while you stay fairly still: try setting up a "race track" in your yard or home and saying, "On your mark, get set, go!" each time as he runs back and forth. Reconsider whether children can jump on or off of the furniture. If you don't want them to do it all the time, give a visual to signal when it's okay, like pulling the cushions off the couch when jumping is allowed. Or, set up a "jumping stump" for them to climb up and jump off. Try setting a piece of string or a small toy on the floor and saying, "Jack be nimble,

Jack be quick, Jack jumps over the candlestick" as your child jumps back and forth. All of these ways allow you to connect with your child through movement without having to move much yourself. Additionally, keep in mind that when a child requests connection through movement you can always say yes to their desire for connection by trying one of the other elements of SMILE instead. These may not be quite as fun, though: movement, touch and physical fun can be powerfully connecting.

Imagination

*Singing, Movement, **Imagination**, Love, Exaggeration*

Children connect through imagination. Remember the little bird that flew out of Ashley's jacket sleeve? That was Ashley's mom using imagination to connect and help Ashley put her jacket on at the same time. Preschool teachers everywhere know the power of imagination and imagery in helping children do what they've asked, and it has been well-documented by research. One of the most famous studies had preschoolers stand in the same spot for as long as they could. Half were simply given the instructions to stay put, while half were told a story about how they were guards in a factory (the study was done in the Soviet Union). The four-year-olds who were given the image of being guards at their posts were able to stay on their spot more than *four times as*

> *I used imagery and singing tonight while tidying up and making dinner, and it was amazing to see how Xander responded. I initially asked him to please close the door and he ignored me, so then I said a big gust of wind was needed to whoosh the door closed and he acted upon it happily. I then asked him to bring the two little wet birds (his socks) to the fireplace so they could dry out and he did this with joy.*
>
> —Rachael, mother of one

long as the ones who were simply asked to stay still.[11] Similarly, and even more impressively, children who were asked not to eat a marshmallow on a table in front of them and were able to wait an average of only one minute were suddenly able to wait for *twelve* minutes when they were told to imagine that the marshmallow was just a picture of a marshmallow, with a frame around it.[12] Imagination is a powerful tool for helping children do as we ask, for transforming *no* into *yes*.

When you are tired it's harder to come up with engaging imagery, but just like any new skill, it gets easier with practice. If it feels challenging for you to come up with imagery in the moment, go through a typical day and write out a list of ideas that might work for your family. Here are some to help you get started:

- When cleaning up, pretend you're squirrels scurrying around to put nuts away for the winter.
- While eating, pretend your arm and spoon are a steam shovel at a construction project.
- While washing hands, let your hands be salmon swimming upstream.
- While wiping a child's face, have the cloth be a little mouse looking for crumbs she left behind.

Your son doesn't want to brush his teeth? Turn that toothbrush into a bunny that's hopping around, looking for carrots to eat. Then it can "find" carrots—in his mouth! Mmmm! Each tooth gets brushed as that bunny munches away.

I have a few hard-working standards that I pull from when I'm tired and not feeling original: mine are bunnies, mice and airplanes. I might say, "Come on little bunny, hop on over to the table to eat your bunny-food." Or my fingers can make a little sniffing mouse who can tickle, whisper instructions in a child's ear, or lead the way. Airplanes are especially useful if it's time to go somewhere and I suspect the child won't want to go, because I can make the airplane's flight pattern fun and connecting, while still actually moving toward my goal.

With newly-turned two-year-olds, start using imagery of things that they see every day: kitties and doggies, eating and sleeping. As children turn three and four and five, let your imagery grow to reflect and encourage their own imaginative journeys. For preschool-aged and older children, impromptu storytelling can help things go smoothly. Your little girl doesn't want to go to bed? Tell a story about how *you* didn't want to go to bed when you were a little girl or boy. It feels like it's taking forever to get snowpants, boots, jacket, hat and mittens on? Tell a story about the Inuit Eskimos getting ready for a dog-sled trip. Your four-year-old says he doesn't like carrots? Really? Well, has he ever heard The Story of Carrots? "Let me tell you, carrot seeds are soooo tiny that you can hold a hundred of them in the palm of your hand you can hardly see them. You sprinkle them into the ground, and each day you water them while the sun shines down, and soon…"

When we use imagination to ask a child to do something, we are more likely to get eager participation, and their *no*'s can dissolve—not because we're distracting them, but because we're taking the time to connect. Using imagination to help make your request more enjoyable will help your children learn to say yes when you ask them to do things.

Love

Singing, Movement, Imagination, ***Love****, Exaggeration*

Children connect through love and appreciation. Your toolbox of skills includes more than just fun and games: love, warmth, affection and appreciation are vital for a child's sense of wellbeing, and they are perhaps the most powerful ways that we can connect with our children.[13]

Undoubtedly, if you're reading this book you love your child or children deeply, but let me ask you: how do you convey that love to your children? Do you tell them things you love and appreciate about them *throughout* the day, or is it limited to part of the bedtime routine? When we can weave moments of expressing love and appreciation into multiple aspects of our daily routines, especially in doing things that perhaps are otherwise not especially enjoyable, those expressions can transform the quality of our interactions. For example, one mother I worked with, Mira, had a daughter who hated having her face wiped after each meal. After hearing about these five ways of connecting, Mira combined touch (an aspect of Movement) and appreciation (an aspect of Love) by taking her daughter onto her lap, snuggling her close, and then using a warm, wet cloth to gently wipe her face, saying as she wiped each part, "I love your cheek. And your chin. I love your other cheek, and your tiny button nose. I love your top lip, and your bottom lip, and I love all of you, so much," and finishing with a hug. What a difference from holding her daughter's head still while she efficiently swiped her face! This new ritual turned the end of a meal from an ordeal to one of the most special parts of their day. I was so inspired by Mira's success that I couldn't wait until my own infant daughter was a little older so I could try it with her. As my daughter grew from a baby into a toddler, I was disappointed to discover that she didn't love this "appreciation" method of face wiping at all; she far preferred funny sound effects (Exaggeration), which we'll discuss below.

You don't need to use words to convey love. Snuggles of all types are a mix of touch and love, which doubles the feelings of connection; breastfeeding falls into this category as well. When a little boy is having a rough day filled with *no*'s, or has dug his heels in especially deeply about something, I might stop, take a deep breath, muster my compassion and say, "Let me give you a big hug." I'll envelop him in my arms and just pour in as much love as I can, imagining it literally filling his tiny body. When I feel him begin to soften, I wait a*no*ther moment until my imaginary love is overflowing out the top of his head and then I lean back, making eye contact. "Ah, that's better." If he seems ready, I might ask, "Are you ready now?" or I'll just get him into motion (remembering that movement is also connecting). Sometimes that *no* comes back, although almost always in a softer way than before. In that case, I'll try to determine whether he's asking for another snuggle, or whether to move on to humor, imagination, or one of the other ways of connecting, in order to help him sit down so we can begin our meal, or get his boots on, or whatever it is that I've asked him to do. Obviously, we can't always melt away a child's *no*'s, and in those cases we have to decide when to help the child follow through anyway, or when to change our request in some way. We'll talk about that in depth in Section 2.

Remember that not all children love snuggles, but that doesn't mean that they won't feel connected through loving touch if offered in a different way. My brother shared that with his five-year-old daughter, "We do jiu-jitsu together so I can disguise my hugs." Lawrence Cohen, author of *Playful Parenting: An Exciting New Approach to Raising Children That Will Help You Nurture Close Connections, Solve Behavior Problems, and Encourage Confidence*, calls this "active cuddling."[14]

When we observe and verbalize elements in a child's physical experience, we show an appreciation that can be deeply connecting. A child doesn't like having his hair washed? Slow down and "notice" *out loud* all of the physical sensations he might be feeling: the tickly water, the cool breeze on his wet skin, the sound, feel and smell of soap in his hair, the feeling of your fingers as you massage his scalp, the drippy feeling as soap runs down and you wipe it away before it gets to the eyes, the uncomfortable feeling of leaning back into the water, then relaxing as you hold his head. When children know that we "really get it," they are more often able to trust and allow us to help them through discomfort. I use this type of appreciation a lot for diaper changes, and dressing or undressing, and sometimes for tooth brushing as well.

One word of caution: contrary to many parenting books, I suggest being careful about labeling emotions with young children when they're upset. While our intentions may be to show our understanding and empathy, it often ends up being received as judgmental rather than appreciative. If I want to let a child know that I see his emotions, I will point out physical manifestations of those feelings, instead. "You're pulling on that toy really hard." "Your hands are in fists." "You're crying." However, even these are only appropriate sometimes; often, focusing on a child's feelings of anger, sadness or overwhelm only serves to amplify them, making them bigger and bigger. Instead, when children have strong negative feelings I often keep my appreciation for their experience internal, taking a moment to feel genuine compassion, and then deciding what would help that child move through their disappointment and come out the other side. We will explore ways to help children recover from disappointment in later chapters.

Finally, we can use appreciation to connect with children by enjoying something beautiful together. I have a painting of a mama and baby above my changing table, and when I bring a child over, we'll spend a moment gazing at the painting together before I lay the child down. You could appreciate a flower blossom, a candle flame, anything really. Children themselves can often teach us lessons in appreciating beauty in unexpected places: I had one little boy who was staring at a pile of wet mulch, and when I came over to him, he looked up at me with shining eyes, exclaiming: "Miss Faith, those sticks are *soooo beautiful!*"

Love and appreciation re-establish our connection with children, and when nothing else seems to be working, push your annoyance aside and reach deep within yourself to find and generate this quality in your actions. Our own softening is often what allows the *no* to melt away as connection returns.

Exaggeration

Singing, Movement, Imagination, Love, ***Exaggeration***

Children connect through exaggeration and humor. Remember when Ashley's mom "lost" her over her shoulder, turning this way and that, saying, "Where did Ashley go," and then pretended shock when she put her down: "Hey, how did you get here?" Pretending that we don't know something obvious is extremely funny for young children, and things that are funny are connecting. In fact, anything that gets giggles shows that we're connecting with that child in that moment.

The research on humor and young children is sparse when compared to research on the other types of connection I've talked about. Humor seems to be less common in daily life as well: when I observed ten families over the course of my dissertation research on toddlers' involvement in household tasks, only one parent out of the ten families used humor to help shape her child's behavior (It worked really well, by the way).

What do toddlers find funny? Among other things, exaggerations of all types can be uproarious:

- **Exaggerate your voice**: make it fast and squeaky, slow and deep, or have a funny accent. Think about the voices you hear in cartoons—the reason they're done that way is because that's funny to children!
- **Exaggerate sounds**: Sound effects of any kind are funny and connecting. Your son doesn't want to wash his hands? Rub his hand in the water and make squeaking sound effects, a different squeak for each hand. Hilarious! He doesn't like getting his bottom wiped during diaper changes? Try making *zooooping* sounds that match your motions, alternating long and short strokes. I mentioned in the Love section that my own daughter didn't enjoy the appreciative face-wiping that another girl enjoyed; instead, my daughter dissolved into

giggles when the washcloth enveloped her hand and I made it buzz vigorously, with the vibrations wiping the food away.

- **Exaggerate effort**: Do you get a *no* when it's time for shoes to go on? Try making creaky sounds as you push, or exaggerated huffing and puffing like it's the hardest thing you've ever done.
- **Exaggerate knowledge** (or lack of knowledge): Pretending you don't know something that your child knows you do is extremely amusing. Remember, your child doesn't *actually* think you don't know; that's why it's funny. So, pretending to put a sock on a hand, elbow, or foot is likely to get giggles from the toddler crowd, and you can either pretend mock amazement or give a sly, knowing smile when they tell you that it really goes on their foot. Of course, it helps if you think what you're doing is funny, too! If you don't feel comfortable playing the fool, grab a stuffed animal and have Teddy Bear be the one to not know how things go.

Humor can be enormously connecting when it is shared. When a child says *no* and we respond with humor, that *no* can often dissipate quite quickly. Not because we are distracting them or tricking them, but because we are rekindling our sense of "us." Any time you use funny voices, sound effects, or pretend you don't know something, those *no*'s melt away as the two of you connect.

If you use humor and a child responds with anger instead of giggles, she is telling you that she's longing to connect in a different way: most often, anger at humor means that he or she is longing for love and affection. With that cue, drop your funny voice, make eye contact, look for understanding and offer love.

Likewise, sometimes children try to connect with us by doing something that *they* find funny, but it doesn't go over well with us. Some common examples for younger toddlers include running away, or hitting us and laughing. For older toddlers, it might be a social taboo, like talking about poop. When children do these things we tend to get serious, but this often leads to meltdowns because children feel misunderstood: they were getting funny, and we got mad. Get serious if it's a safety issue, but otherwise respond by offering a more appropriate type of humor instead. I've had great success with turning potty humor into rhyming humor: if Dion says his lunch is poopy, I might say, "Really? It looks more like it's Goopy. Or maybe Shoopy. No, it's…" I give him a chance to contribute, then it's my turn again, "…Loopy!" Try turning running away into funny movements: jumping, lumbering, spinning. Turn hitting into tickles. In this way, you're responding to their intent, while transforming the action into a form that both of you can enjoy.

Want to develop your sense of fun and humor with your child but don't know how? I highly recommend the book *Playful Parenting* by Lawrence Cohen (I've listed it in the notes at the end of the chapter). He offers hundreds of examples and ways of being more playful with children from toddlers to teens.

When to Use S*M*I*L*E

You certainly don't need to wait until your child says *no* in order to use these techniques. In fact, if you incorporate them into your requests in the first place, you're much more likely to get the *yes* you're looking for. But, once that *no* appears, then remember, *most of the times that children say* no, *what they're really saying is, "I don't feel as connected to you right now as I wish I did."* Stop, take a moment to connect, and use those connecting activities to help your child do what you've asked. You can tell if it's working because you see her eyes light up; or because he's giggling; or because he says, "Again!"; or because she melts into you. At bottom line, you can tell these connecting strategies are working because the *no* disappears and the two of you are on the same team again.

If you're wondering which types of connecting activities you should use, the answer is: All of them, of course! Ashley's mom used four out the five in the few brief moments it took to get ready to walk out the door. Combining two ways of connecting (Singing with Movement, Movement with Imagination, Imagination with Love) can amplify the connection. Try them all, and see how your child responds. In my online class, I recommend that parents spend five days and focus on a different element of SMILE each day. Sometimes children surprise us with the strength of their yes. You may discover new ways of connecting that deepen your relationship and really change the dynamics between the two of you.

OVERCOMING YOUR RESISTANCE

Perhaps this is all making a lot of sense, and you can't wait to put this book down and try some of these new approaches. On the other hand, perhaps you're feeling a bit of resistance. "This is all well and good," you might be thinking, "but isn't doing something fun when my child says *no* just rewarding bad behavior?"

To that, I answer an emphatic *NO*. This is not rewarding bad behavior; this is being responsive to our children's needs, so that they can be responsive in return. If a toddler was having a meltdown because he was hungry, we wouldn't say, "Well, mister, fat chance that you'll get any food now, with an attitude like that!" No, we would give that child what he needed, because we know that he can't be his best self when a vital need is not met. Likewise, we wouldn't withhold sleep from a child who's having a meltdown because she's too tired; that would be ridiculous. When we give children what they need, then they are better able to be their best selves. With a lack of connection, just like with hunger and fatigue, we respond first to the need, and *then* we address the behavior.

Another reason that responding to a *no* with connection isn't rewarding bad behavior is that the game is not the end. When a child says *no*, we don't just offer her fun and then do the thing ourselves; we offer the game in order to help her move from *no* to *yes*. We support her and help her follow through with what we've asked. We are getting buy-in for our demands, by combining high demandingness with high levels of warmth.

Sometimes, a child is happy to play the game, but then *no* comes back when we move toward actually doing what we've asked. Sometimes, we can't transform that *no*, either because we can't figure out how to connect in that moment, or we don't have time, or because in that instance the *no* was not a request for connection. In those cases, we need to decide: do we drop our request, do we work on convincing them, or do we insist that they do what we've asked, even though they don't want to? For an in-depth look at these options and when to choose each one, see Chapter 4: When We Can't Figure Out How to Connect.

Transforming "Attention-Seeking" Behaviors

We don't want to fall into the trap of having a child display negative behaviors in order to get positive attention from us. There is a way to prevent this from happening that is simple in theory but more difficult in practice: if they start using a negative behavior to ask for connection, simply *teach them* a better way to ask, then be sure to respond whenever they ask in this new way.

Let's say Ruby is whining to get attention. Rather than ignore her, you can give her the attention she needs: "It sounds like you need a snuggle. Let me dry my hands and we can sit down on the couch for a moment or two." You respond to her whining in this way two or three or five times, stopping what you're doing each time for a snuggle. When she starts to expect that her whining will get this response, you shift your response slightly: the next time she whines, you say, "Do you need a snuggle?" She knows from experience exactly what that means, and she nods. You can respond, "Oh, okay. You don't have to whine to get a snuggle. You can just say, 'Snuggle, please?'"

Simple, right? Simple in theory, difficult in practice. It's difficult in practice because this only works if we respond *just as* consistently to the new way of asking as we did to the annoying behavior. You may not think, sitting on your couch (or wherever you're sitting while you read this), that this would be hard. In reality, however, we *always* respond with emotion (engagement) when a child is annoying or doing something we've asked them not to, but we only *sometimes* respond with emotion (engagement) when they ask politely. When they politely say, "Snuggle, Dada?" or "Tickle?" or "Chase, please," we sometimes say yes, but it can be tempting to say, "I'm busy," or "in a minute," or "not right now." When that happens, your child will quickly revert to the old, guaranteed method of getting you to engage immediately, by hanging from your leg and whining, by sticking his hand in the dog's water, or by hitting you and running away. We can get them to change the way they ask for engagement/attention/connection, but in order to make it happen, we have to be just as consistent as we are when they poke us emotionally. Remember, we don't need to connect deeply at every moment, but we do need to take a moment to connect every time they need it. So, wipe your hands or put down your phone and take a moment to really connect.

The Power of Rituals

When you use these ways to connect, and when you succeed, chances are you'll start hearing the words, "More!" "Again!" or, "Let's do it again!" When this happens, say, "Yes!"

You might say yes and do the appreciated action again, right away. You might say yes and do something a bit different that's still connecting. Or, you might say, "Yes! We'll do that again the next time we get our shoes on/get out of the bathtub/come to the table." When you can repeat certain connecting actions every time you perform a given task, the result can be especially sweet. If you always swoop your child up and swing her around in a circle before you put her in her high chair, and she loves it every time, then soon it will go from being a connecting activity to being a ritual. "Again!" "Yes!" you reply. "We will do this again at our next meal." When that next meal comes, that little girl is eagerly awaiting that swoop, and she squeals with glee when it comes. You have created a ritual.

Rituals are extra-connecting because they are enjoyable in the moment, *and* they carry the weight of past moments of connections with them. They provide established times to pause and connect with your child. And, even if you are not feeling especially connected with your child in a given moment, the momentum of past connections forged by that ritual will help your child say *yes* again. Momentum will not carry you forward forever, but it can provide a buffer until you are able to take that nap, pass that work deadline, or otherwise renew yourself and your connection with your child.

Weave connecting rituals into as many parts of the day as you can: your getting-shoes-on ritual, your cleaning-up-from-lunch ritual, your tooth-brushing ritual, etc. After awhile, you can just start to sing the song or use the funny voice, and your child will run for her shoes without you having to say anything else.

If you use the funny voice and your child makes a beeline to hide under the coffee table instead of going for her shoes, she is telling you that she doesn't actually find the funny-voice routine funny. It's not getting that feeling of, "Yes! Let's do it again!" Go back to SMILE and try one of the other four ways: getting into movement, perhaps, or giving a sweet leg massage once each shoe is on.

Once you find a ritual that works for both of you, it may be effective for a week, or a month, or a year, but it's likely that eventually your child will stop responding. When that happens, he's saying, "This doesn't feel connecting anymore." Sometimes, it's just that you've let the ritual itself do the heavy lifting, and when you bring your attention back to it, the activity is suddenly fun again. Other times, your child has outgrown that activity and is ready for a new one. In that case, remember to SMILE and find an alternative way to connect. If you hear "Again!" then perhaps you'll have a new ritual in the making.

In order to create a life that you and your child both love, you need to be doing things that you both enjoy throughout the day. Figuring out what makes your child say *yes* is a good first step, and using those clues when you are asking your child for compliance will help set positive habits in place, promoting connection instead of conflict. The next time you tell your child that it's time to do something, and she says *no*, remember what this really means: "Our relationship is important to me, Mom. Let's take a moment to connect first, and then I'll be happy to work with you."

KEY POINTS‡

The Big Ideas in *Being Responsive to Children: Don't Forget to S*M*I*L*E!*

The vast majority of the time that children say *no,* what they're really saying is, "I don't feel as connected to you as I wish I did right now."

If you want to connect with your child,
don't forget to **SMILE**!

SINGING (and rhymes)
Songs can be silly, they can be soothing, or they can be rousing. Sing songs from your childhood! Make up words and sing about what you're doing to the tune of your favorite rock song, or *Twinkle, Twinkle.*

‡ For a printable version of this chapter's Key Points, visit joyfultoddlers.com/smile-printout/

MOVEMENT (and touch)
Swing your child around! Hang her upside-down! Run races! Wheelbarrow walking, flying like an airplane, bouncing on your lap (love those horsey rides), stroking his arms, his hair, his back are all fun or loving touch. Give hugs. Play touching games like "This Little Piggy Went to Market," or "All Around the Haystack."

IMAGINATION (and more imagination!)
Ask your child to be "quick like a bunny," "quiet as a tiny little mouse," "strong like a bulldozer." Instead of cleaning up, ask your little squirrel to put all of the nuts into their spots, because winter's coming!

LOVE (and appreciation)
Give hugs. Give kisses. Make eye contact and smile. Tell your child how much you love her, in detail! "I love your sweet cheeks (kiss, kiss). I love your nose (kiss)." Appreciate your child's physical experience and describe his sensations. Finally, if you can't figure out how to connect, get interested: "What's going on?" Listen to understand. This is a type of appreciation, too.

EXAGGERATION (and humor)
Make everything bigger, heavier, sillier. Talk in funny voices. Make up sound effects. Pretend you don't know how things go. Pretend that *you* want it even more than they do! Be silly and have fun. Combine it with singing or movement or exaggeration or love for extra power!

ENDNOTES, CHAPTER 2

1 For a good overview of her research, see Dweck, C.S. (2008). *Mindset: The new psychology of success.* Random House Digital, Inc.

2 Brooks, R., & Goldstein, S. (2004). *Raising a self-disciplined child: Help your child become more responsible, confident, and resilient.* McGraw-Hill Professional, p. 51.

3 Dunst, C. J., Meter, D., & Hamby, D. W. (2011). Relationship between young children's nursery rhyme experiences and knowledge and phonological and print-related abilities. *Center for Early Literacy Learning,* 4(1), 1-12.

4 Dissanayake, E. (2006). Ritual and ritualization: musical means of conveying and shaping emotion in humans and other animals. In S. Brown & U. Voglsten (Eds.), *Music and manipulation: On the social uses and social control of music* (pp. 31–56). Oxford and New York: Berghahn Books.

5 Loewy, J., Stewart, K., Dassler, A. M., Telsey, A., & Homel, P. (2013). The effects of music therapy on vital signs, feeding, and sleep in premature infants. *Pediatrics,* 131(5), 902-918.

6 Cirelli, L. K., Einarson, K. M., & Trainor, L. J. (2014). Interpersonal synchrony increases prosocial behavior in infants. *Developmental Science,* 17(6), 1003-1011.

7 Kirschner, S., & Tomasello, M. (2010). Joint music making promotes prosocial behavior in 4-year-old children. *Evolution and Human Behavior,* 31, 354–364.

8 Williamson, D., Dewey, A., & Steinberg, H. (2001). Mood change through physical exercise in nine-to-ten-year-old children. *Perceptual and Motor Skills, 93*(1), 311-316.

9 Lees, C. (2013). Effect of aerobic exercise on cognition, academic achievement, and psychosocial function in children: A systematic review of randomized control trials. *Preventing Chronic Disease, 10.*

10 Blythe, S. G. (2011). *The genius of natural childhood: Secrets of thriving children.* London: Hawthorn Press, p. 7.

11 Manuilenko, Z. V. (1948/1975). The development of voluntary behavior in preschool-age children. *Soviet Psychology, 13*(4), 65-116.

12 Moore, B., Mischel, W., & Zeiss, A. (1976). Comparative effects of the reward stimulus and its cognitive representation in voluntary delay. *Journal of Personality and Social Psychology, 34*(3), 419.

13 It was not always taken for granted that love and affection were important. For a fascinating description of how scientific opinion changed, read Blum, D. (2011). *Love at Goon Park: Harry Harlow and the science of affection.* Basic Books.

14 Cohen, L. J. (2008). *Playful parenting: An exciting new approach to raising children that will help you nurture close connections, solve behavior problems, and encourage confidence.* Ballantine Books.

CHAPTER 3

Teaching Children to Be Responsive: Cultivating a Habit of Yes

This chapter explores ways to get buy-in from children and help them respond positively to our requests without having to make everything fun all the time. It looks at the idea that saying *yes* could become a habit, and discusses ways to develop a "Habit of *Yes*" by changing the way we speak (using positive language), changing the way we think (assuming positive intent), and changing the way we act (helping them get started).

The previous chapter looked at how to shift the energy when children say no to us. But, wouldn't it be great if they didn't have to say no in the first place? The last chapter suggested weaving connecting activities into everyday tasks, and that is certainly a good idea. However, many parents I work with are exhausted by even the *thought* of making every request fun and engaging. While using the elements of SMILE is an effective skill that gets easier with practice, you may be wondering, *can't I just ask my child to do something and have him say, "Okay, Mama," or, "Okay, Daddy?"* Is this just a fantasy that we need to give up on until our children are older?

I have good news for you, and it comes in two parts. The first is that we don't have to bring out a dog-and-pony show every time we ask our children to do something. The elements of SMILE definitely help children feel connected, and we can use these when we suspect a child will not be interested in doing what we want, or when they let us know (through their actions or by saying no) that they need an extra dose of connection. However, we don't have to feel deeply connected at every moment in order to have a positive, healthy, mutually responsive relationship with our children in which saying *yes* to us is the norm rather than the exception. Instead, we can set ourselves up for success through the language that we use (how we talk), the assumptions that we make (how we think), and the actions that we take (how we act). That's what this chapter is about.

The second part of the good news stems from a research project examining compliance and power struggles between young children and parents over several years. The study found that overall, "initial compliance leads to future compliance and initial resistance leads to future resistance."[1] Although that last bit may sound rather ominous, it's really saying that relationship patterns continue over time. This may not feel like great news for you if you're currently in a negative pattern with your child, but it is, because it means that the effort of teaching children to respond quickly and positively to do what we ask can have lasting results. I like to say that the work we do with children is "front-loaded": if we put the work in now, we will reap the benefits for a long time. Changing established habits can be challenging, but once we put new habits of respectfulness and helpfulness in place, those new habits will become what feels easy and right. I learned many lessons about teaching children how to be responsive in my early years as a toddler teacher. Let me share what I discovered so that you can use them, too.

REAL HELP FROM THE LITTLE RED HEN: MY EXPERIENCE IN THE CLASSROOM

It is my second year teaching in the LifeWays toddler class at a sweet Waldorf preschool in Colorado, and I am looking for a new story to tell. The children never seem to get tired of "The Three Little Pigs" and "Goldilocks," but I am certainly ready for a change.

I try to think of an appropriate tale, and come up with a great idea: the story of "The Little Red Hen." The story has lots of repetition, and our class makes bread together regularly—just like the Little Red Hen. This could be perfect! Over the next few nights I read the story through quite a few times, then I start telling it to the children.

"Who will help me knead the dough?" said the Little Red Hen.

"Not I," said the dog.

"Not I," said the cat.

"Not I," said the duck.

"Then I will do it myself," said the Little Red Hen. And she did.

I tell the story, and an uncomfortable feeling develops in my stomach. I push through, feeling increasingly uncomfortable as the story progresses. The next day I tell it again and it feels just as bad. I'm not sure why, but I am positive that I can't tell this story.

I abandon "The Little Red Hen," find another story to tell, and life moves on, but my discomfort with the story sticks with me. Why had it felt so strange? This was "The Little Red Hen," a classic children's tale! Finally, it dawns on me: I don't want to tell a story about the consequences of saying no when someone asks for help, because I don't even want to bring up the possibility that the children might say no to me when I ask *them* for help. The toddlers in my care are an eager and cooperative bunch, and I want it to stay that way! I refuse to tell them a story, day after day, about animals that say *no*; I want the children to say *yes*! I don't want to have to convince a child each time we need to do something. I don't want negotiations. I don't want them to have to think about consequences and *decide* to say *yes*; I want them to say *yes* eagerly, joyfully. I want *yes* to be their automatic response. I want them to have a *Habit of Yes*. In italics, with capital letters.

(I didn't know it at the time, but there has been research that unexpectedly revealed a group of children watching "educational" TV shows displaying significantly more social aggression than other children. The researchers surmised that young children "learn from each of the behaviors shown" in a given TV show, meaning that the conflict was just as informative as the conflict resolution.[2] My hunch about "The Little Red Hen" was a good one.)

After several months of conscious effort to cultivate a Habit of *Yes* with the children, I find that our days are going significantly more smoothly. There are fewer struggles, and the children seem to float through the day being successful, helpful and enjoyable. I find that I am enjoying them in a whole new way. I am busy patting myself on the back when I have an epiphany: this new ease isn't because the children are different. The reality is that *I* am the one who has changed, and the children are merely responding to that. The person I've transformed through my hard work is none other than myself. Just like the children, I can now float through the day being successful, helpful and enjoyable. I, like the children, have developed the Habit of *Yes*. I will tell you what I learned about myself.

DEVELOP A HABIT OF *YES* BY CHANGING THE WAY YOU TALK

Use Positive Language: Say What You Want

My first realization was that if I wanted the children to say *yes* without having to think about it, I needed to word my requests so that the preferred answer would always be *yes*. With this in mind, I focused on telling the children what I *did* want them to do, rather than what I didn't. Instead of saying, "Stop banging your spoon on the table," I'd say, "You can use your spoon to take a bite." Instead of saying, "Don't throw the sand," I'd say, "You can put that sand into a bucket." Instead of saying, "We don't grab," I'd say, "You can find a toy that *nobody* is using." In phrasing things in this way, the children didn't have to stop doing something and come up with an alternative on their own; instead, they could just say *yes*. Saying exactly what

I wanted set them up for success, and made it easier for them to respond quickly and positively to me.

The idea—of saying what I wanted and not saying what I didn't—seemed simple, but the reality of doing it was actually quite challenging. It seemed to be a sort of "ninja" move that you hardly notice when someone else does it, but often seems just out of reach when the need arises. To assert a correct action was especially challenging to remember in the moments when I needed something to change quickly: the phrase "Stop it!" came so automatically to my lips. I had to practice and work on this for a long time before it came anywhere close to feeling natural.

For example, one spring day my toddlers and I were looking at the baby chicks visiting our play-yard in a collapsible playpen. I glanced to my left and noticed two-year-old Janna leaning hard against the playpen to peer over, making it bow in to the point of possible collapse.

My immediate thought was to say, "Stop leaning against the playpen." However, I stopped myself before I opened my mouth, committed to practicing this new technique.

My next thought was to say, "Be careful." But I knew that wasn't quite right either. Although taking care was what I wanted her to do, I knew it wasn't specific enough, since "careful" means something different in every situation: being careful touching the cat is different from being careful carrying a bowl of soup, which is different from being careful leaning against a collapsible playpen. *Gah*! Time was running out! Think!

What did I actually want her to do? I took a deep breath, and it came to me: "Stand up straight and tall," I told her.

As soon as the words were out of my mouth, she popped upright, letting go of the playpen.

Wow...it felt like magic! She didn't have to think about it, she just did what I asked. I was cultivating a Habit of *Yes*. As I got better at being able to tell children what I actually wanted them to do, I was amazed again and again at how effective positive language can be in helping children do what I ask without them even having to think about it.

In using this positive language, I wasn't any more permissive than I had been before; if Janna had not stood up straight when I asked her to, I would have shown her exactly how she could touch the playpen, saying, "It's important to touch it gently," or, "Just look over the top." If she still couldn't resist leaning, I would have picked her up to look over, or helped her move on to another activity. My boundaries and my expectations were clear. In fact, I discovered that my boundaries and expectations were even more clear in telling children how it's appropriate to act, than they had been in telling them to stop this, or don't do that. Clear and effective, this methodology helped the children learn to be responsive to me.

Why is positive language so powerful?

One of the reasons that this positive-language technique is so effective is that we all think in images, and the modifier "Don't" means hardly anything to the image-producing part of the brain. To prove this point, let's do a quick experiment right now. What image comes into your head when I say, **"Don't run out into the street."**

Close your eyes for a moment if you need to. What image is there? Someone running out into the street, wasn't it?

All right, now for the second part of the experiment. This time, what image comes into your head? **"Please walk straight along the sidewalk."** A much different image, isn't it? Words create images in our heads, and modifiers (like "Don't") barely touch those images. It takes intellectual effort to apply the modifier to the image. If this is true for us adults, who have decades of experience with modifiers, how much stronger must it be for young children, who are just starting out? If we want children to do what we've asked, the most effective way is to create and share an image of what we wish they were doing, and then help them respond quickly and positively.

The main reason I use positive language is that it is *by far* the most effective way to get children to do what I want with the least amount of effort. However, there are other reasons I use it, too. "No," "Stop," and "Don't" absolutely have their place in our vocabulary, especially when needing to get a child's attention quickly: in a situation of danger, for example. But, when we over-use these words, they lose their impact and effectiveness. Children start to tune us out, and we then have to use a harsher tone to get their attention. In developing a mutually responsive relationship, we want all of our words to count, the first time we say them.

Next, we want to limit our own use of "no," "stop," and "don't" because we don't want our children to start using those phrases with us! Remember that children learn through imitation, so use phrases that you would be happy to hear coming from your children's lips. This goes beyond *no* as well. If you don't want your child to say "Move it" or "Watch out" when they would like you to move, then make sure that you say "Excuse me" when you'd like them to move. If you want your child to say "please" and "thank you," make sure that you are doing so each time you ask him to do something as well.

Most importantly, the use of negative language affects who our children become. In her book surveying the research on how children gain self-control, Martha Bronson points out, "Although [toddlers'] ability to act independently is growing and their desire to do so is growing even faster, toddlers are still very dependent on caregivers. They judge their own behaviors largely by the positive or negative reactions of others and look for cues from them ('social referencing') when they are uncertain."[3] Studies of identical twins raised apart have shown that about half of our personality is determined by genetics (nature), while fully half is determined by experiences we have in life (nurture).[4] With young children, the vast majority of their experiences revolve around us. How we react to our children, and the behavior we model, matter.

I didn't know all these things when I was a new toddler teacher; I simply used positive language because it was the most effective for getting children to do as I asked the first time. Easily said, challenging to do. For me, several months of conscious practice were required before the practice came easily, and probably a year before positive phrasing became my natural response. As I practiced, I gradually developed some tips that helped me to be successful. I will share those with you, here, and perhaps your practice can go more smoothly than mine did.

Be Specific!

As I hinted in my story about the girl with the chicks, I learned to avoid using phrases that mean different things in different circumstances. One of these nebulous phrases is "be careful," which means a different action in every circumstance. Other such phrases include "watch out," and "use your words." Be specific in expressing what you want! If Ethan is heading his bike toward his friends, rather than saying, "Watch out," try saying, "Please go around your friends." If Emma is climbing recklessly, swallow your, "Be careful" and try, "Make sure each foot is solid before your next step." If you want Liam to say, "Can I have a turn," don't say, "Use your words"; instead, tell him, "You can say, 'Can I have a turn?'" Children often are happy to be responsive to us if we let them know exactly what we'd like. When we use ambiguous phrases, we're counting on children to guess correctly what we mean in this particular context. Correct guessing depends on having a body of prior experiences, being able to recall those experiences on demand, and quickly sorting through them to figure the probability of getting the right answer for this situation. Quite a tall order for this little being whose brain is just developing the capacity for memory! Be specific.

I discovered that I could also use the technique of creating specific images to shape positive behavior before the opportunity for something undesirable arose. Upon returning with my group of toddlers from a visit to the grandmas and grandpas in the nearby assisted-living home, I might say, "When I take you out of the wagon, you may take your bags straight to the door and sit on the step until I come open it." Then, when I got to the door, I'd provide a new image: "When I open the door, we'll go right to the boot place and take off our wet boots." Being specific like this provides an image for children to live in to, and makes it easy for them to say *yes* with their actions.

If I could anticipate that a child might have trouble doing what I was about to ask, then I'd take the time to weave one or more of the elements of SMILE into my image: "When I open the door, I'll need every little mousie to scurry straight to the boot place to take off their wet mousie-boots." If the interest still wasn't quite high enough for me to feel confident of success, I'd develop the imagination a bit farther before proceeding: "Where are my little mice? Oh, Max looks like a little mouse! So does Sammie. Do any of my mousie friends want a nibble of mouse-cheese?" I'd offer pretend nibbles of cheese to each mouse, and perhaps show them how to scurry, and when I felt like they were ready, I'd remind them again about the boot place and then open the door. Off those little children would scurry. Remember from the last chapter, using imagery helps children to be able to control their actions. Being specific and using imagination are not mutually exclusive; rather, they can reinforce one another nicely. I didn't need to use imagination every time, just when I suspected that my clear image of what I wanted might not be enough. Often, simply *saying* what we would do worked quite nicely.

Respond to Their Urges

In order to suggest things children could say *yes* to easily, I was most often successful when I'd take a moment before speaking to look behind the behavior to try and understand their urges. For example, if Caitlyn was throwing blocks, I'd make a quick assessment: which seemed more important to her, interacting with the blocks, or the act of throwing? Depending on the answer, I'd either emphasize what she could do with the blocks, or I'd emphasize what she could throw. Even with a newly-turned one-year-old, the question, "What *can* you throw?" will often lead to an eager child running over to the basket of soft balls that are sanctioned for indoor throwing. For older children, or if I didn't have time to assess, I might offer both options: "Those blocks are for stacking. Will you stack them, or find something to throw?" Then, I would help the child follow through, perhaps by starting to stack some blocks myself, or by picking up another toy more appropriate for throwing.

Responding to urges rather than simply addressing behaviors is helpful for curbing rambunctious behavior as well. If Mason is yelling gleefully in the kitchen, ask yourself which seems more important, the act of yelling, or being in the kitchen? If it's the yelling, where *can* he yell? Outside? In the bathroom? Into a pillow? There needs to be somewhere or some way that our children can do the things they feel compelled to do. If he wants to stay in the kitchen with you, then he needs to find something new to occupy him. You can help him do that, too. "If you'd like to stay in the kitchen, I'll need you to speak softly. I'm about ready to wipe the table…can you find some cloths for us to use?" Remember, getting children into motion can help shift the energy almost immediately.

With older preschoolers, their play can sometimes become big or wild. In these cases, I would still respond to their urges by giving their imaginative play a direction that could work for everyone. I remember one of the first times I observed (as an adult) in a Waldorf kindergarten: a group of four-year-old boys were playing that they were wild dogs, running around and wreaking mayhem on the other children's play. The teacher looked at them with interest and said, "Oh! but you're all inside; you must actually be *pet* dogs. Each dog should have an owner and a leash." The boys immediately engaged in a heated discussion with one another over what they could use for leashes, and who got to be the owners and who would be the dogs. This teacher responded to their urge for deep, imaginative play, but shaped it in a way that everyone could enjoy it.

Don't Get Stuck in a Rut

With a few children I found myself repeating the same requests over and over: "Please keep the sand in the sandbox." "Please talk in a quiet voice." "Please use your walking feet." I discovered that these "please dampen yourself down" requests were often less effective than I wished. Every time I repeated a request, the child became slightly less responsive to it. In my efforts to create a Habit of *Yes*, I wanted children to become *more* likely to do what I asked, not less likely! I discovered that when I switched tactics by suggesting something silly or unexpected, the children's responsiveness would go way up. Instead of endless requests for walking feet, I'd suggest hopping like a bunny or crawling like a kitty-cat. Instead of another call for inside voices, I'd suggest whispering, singing, or speaking with a funny accent; or I'd just do those things myself and the children would joyfully join in. Instead of reminding children yet again that sand stays in the sandbox, I might say, "Oh, that sand will be so sad to be apart from its brothers and sisters. It needs to stay home! What else could you find for your pot?" Humor and imagery are both powerful tools in stimulating connection and the desire to say *yes*.

When a child is annoying someone else, an unexpectedly successful technique is to suggest that they do that same action to themselves, instead: "You can put sand on your own head." "You can pull your own sleeve." "You can poke yourself!" I'm not sure why this works, but it often does. Younger toddlers try it and look slightly puzzled; older preschoolers think it's hilarious and laugh as they try. Humor shifts the energy and allows everyone to move on to something different.

Ask Your Child for Alternatives

Sometimes, I'd tell a child what I wanted him to do, but I wouldn't get easy compliance. He might ignore me altogether, launch into an elaborate explanation of why he *needs* to be doing this particular thing, or he'd veer off and do something completely different. If a child ignored me or launched into an impassioned speech, my response was the same either way: I'd invite the child's solution. "What *can* you do?" Occasionally, a child might need a little more guidance: "What *can* you do that still keeps our floor dry?" "What *can* you do that keeps our toys safe?" "What *can* you do that's as quiet as a mouse?" Brooks and Goldstein share: "When parents communicate to their children that the children have within themselves the ability to find ways to succeed and solve problems, the children are more likely to incorporate and apply this integral ingredient of a resilient mindset."[5]

Other times, I'd give a child something to say *yes* to, but he'd deliberately do something different than what I'd suggested. Perhaps I'd said, "You can pour sand on yourself," and he started pouring it in the bucket instead. Or, "Please touch gently," and she hid her hands inside her sleeves. Far from being negative, these are fine examples of children being responsive: responding quickly and positively, even though they're not doing exactly what I've asked. In those cases I'd simply acknowledge that they've found an acceptable alternative: "That works, too."

Consistently using positive language didn't happen overnight for me, or even in a week, but with attention and practice it began to come more and more easily. Eventually, I didn't have to think about it at all; that was just how I spoke. When I was able to use positive, *yes*-oriented language, I found that my interactions with the children went significantly more smoothly. I was able to set clear boundaries without saying "Stop" all the time, and the children were able to be responsive to me without having to stop and think about what I wanted. We were well on our way to developing that Habit of *Yes*.

DEVELOP A HABIT OF *YES* BY CHANGING THE WAY YOU THINK

Assume Positive Intent

Saying what we want, rather than what we don't want, will take us a long way toward establishing that Habit of *Yes* in our children. However, the way we speak isn't the only thing that helps our children become enjoyable little people to be around: how we think affects our children's actions too.

Back in my second year of teaching in the toddler room, I wanted the children to feel that saying *yes* to me was easy and natural. I wanted them to feel like they did it all the time, that we were in a mutually responsive relationship. One of the ways I did this was by making the conscious decision to assume that **children want to be enjoyable and helpful**. Like using positive language, this is a ninja move, because it can be subtle but also powerful. Remember Chapter 1, where we talked about the universal needs for connection, competence and contributing? Being enjoyable and helpful takes us a long way on that path. We'll talk a lot more about how to let children actually help in Part IV, but for now, even just recognizing that children *want* to be enjoyable and helpful can transform our interactions when the things children are doing don't seem especially enjoyable or helpful in the moment.

I discovered that when I was able to assume positive intent, I was often able to transform borderline behavior into something that actually *was* more enjoyable. If I was folding laundry and little seventeen-month-old Tal threw the washcloths into the air, instead of just saying, "You can put it down gently" (good, positive language), I would assume helpful intent: "Thank you for these washcloths! Can you find another one for me?" When he did, then I shaped the behavior even further: "This time, you can put it right here," and I'd pat my lap.

When we were eating and two-and-a-half-year-old Jackson started making loud droning noises, better than saying, "Please talk softly," or, "Why don't you take a bite?" I'd assume positive intent: "It does seem like it's time for a song, doesn't it, Jackson? Let's sing together," and we'd sing *The Wheels on the Bus*, or *The Muffin Man*, or *Three Little Ducks*. I assumed that the children wanted to be helpful and enjoyable, and I gave them a little nudge to make it so. This made it possible for them to be helpful and enjoyable in actuality.

I found it easy to assume positive intent with most one-year-olds, and I still did a pretty good job with the two-year-olds, but the older the children got, the harder it became for me to attribute positive intent to annoying behavior. As I left the toddler room and started teaching a mixed-age group with children ages one-to-five years, I found myself challenged in my decision to assume positive intent; I felt like those older children "should know better." I felt as if I should have to ask them to stop an annoying behavior only once or twice, and they should just stop. Unkind behavior especially would get under my skin. If I looked over at a couple of four-year-old girls, and saw Raina grab a toy from her friend, shout, "Go away!" and stomp off, I would feel a sharp spike of judgment. Yikes! What positive intent could I possibly attribute?

After struggling with my own negative feelings for a bit, I decided to renew my vows and assume positive intent, even with the older children. I chose to believe that children *of all ages* want to be enjoyable and helpful. If it's not possible for Raina to be friendly at this moment it's not because she is a bad child, or that everyone wants to be enjoyable and helpful but her. Instead, I reminded myself that children ask for what they need, even if they don't use the techniques I wish they would. So I would try to ask myself, *what underlying need is this little girl trying to express*?

In the moment that a child is unkind I might not have much time to think about the answer to that question, as some sort of response is needed immediately. In Raina's case, I went with, "It looks like you're telling us you need a break right now." I kept an eye on things, and after she had played alone in the corner for a few moments I went up and put a warm hand on her back (connecting through touch), then reflected to her, "It's okay to need a break, but it's not friendly to grab toys or to yell. Maybe you could find another toy to give to your friend so she knows that everything's okay." Raina looked intrigued, but couldn't bring herself to do it. "Would you like me to do it for you?" I asked. When she nodded, I said, "Sure. What toy would you like to give her?" She pointed to a random toy and I picked it up and offered it to the other little girl on her behalf.

In this interaction, I was acting out of the consciously chosen belief that Raina actually wanted to be kind and enjoyable, even if she didn't have the ability to do it on her own. I was willing to give her as much support as she needed to be enjoyable in reality, even if I had to do ninety percent of the work. After a year in my program, Raina did in fact gain the ability to be kind, enjoyable and helpful, although I still needed to step in to remind and support her on a regular basis.

Expecting children to be kind and helpful can be beneficial in more ways than one. Remember Grazyna Kochanska, the researcher who has done so much on mutually responsive orientations between parents and toddlers? One of her studies looked at the types of demands mothers made on their two-year-olds, and then followed up at age five, to see how things were going. Kochanska found that mothers who expected "competent action" at age two went on to have children with fewer behavior problems at age five. She highlighted that, of the different types of "competent actions," expectations of kindness and helpfulness were the most relevant (rather than being independent, for example).[6]

Overcoming Our Resistance

Assuming positive intent can be challenging for a variety of reasons. One is that it can confront our unexamined mindsets about why children act the way they do. These can be deep assumptions that we have held for a long time. I remember talking about consequences and discipline in a workshop I led. One father kept asking about what I would do in this situation or that situation. After about five scenarios, he burst out, "But when do you punish them?" Although he could see that consistent redirection was effective, and that helping a child develop empathy was more likely to help a child feel remorse for his or her actions than punishments were, he still had trouble letting go of that mindset that being "bad" should result in a punishment.

Another challenge to assuming positive intent is that it forces us to think from the child's perspective, rather than just reacting. Another person's perspective is much easier to see from a distance than when one is the recipient of annoying or negative behavior. Recognizing a three-year-old's positive desire to gain competence when he refuses to relinquish the car keys, as he tries again and again to unlock the doors, is hard to do when you're trying to get to play group on time. To take a deep breath, say compassionately, "You really wish you could be the one to unlock the doors, huh?" and then calmly decide what will work best, in that moment, is a lot harder than just reacting.

I truly believe that we all (you, me, and the other readers of this book) do the best we can in any given moment. Sometimes, our best isn't that great. In some areas our not-so-great actions are deeply entrenched, but in many others all we need is a reminder to be our best selves, and our interactions can shift almost immediately. Has this ever happened for you? I see it in my workshops and coaching practice all the time: a gentle reminder can be quite powerful. Just as this is true for us as parents, it's true for our children as well. When we expect our children to be enjoyable and helpful, then we're more likely to give them those gentle reminders to be their best selves. Children tend to live up to our expectations of them. Do you expect your child to be helpful and enjoyable? If not, try changing your expectation first, and it will be easier for their actions to follow.

Sometimes, finding any positive intent or even a silver lining feels impossible. Sometimes children are clearly pushing boundaries, engaging in negative attention-seeking behaviors, or doing things that they know will make us angry. Even in those cases, remembering that children generally want to be enjoyable and helpful can turn things around: rather than getting angry, we can get curious. We can think, *normally you're enjoyable and helpful. This is so out of character for you; what's going wrong?* Then we can look at the child and ask, with real interest and care, "Hey, what's going on?" Chances are good that the child won't be able to tell us directly, but having someone respond with compassion and interest rather than anger can still defuse a situation and help children remember their best selves. If these severely negative actions are regular and not an exception, then the child may be trying to send a message in the only way that he or she knows how; we'll go into that in Chapter 5. Regardless of how frequently or infrequently negative interactions happen, though, consciously choosing to assume that children want to be enjoyable and helpful can shift our actions and help them become enjoyable and helpful in reality.

DEVELOP A HABIT OF *YES* BY CHANGING THE WAY YOU ACT

Help Your Children Get Started

No matter how positively I thought about the children, and no matter how skillfully or positively I framed my requests, there were still many times each day as a toddler-teacher that my requests fell on deaf ears. This was not necessarily because the children were being defiant, but simply because they were busy doing other things. Especially when they were having fun, my words just seemed to wash over them without sinking in. I realized that if I wanted *yes* to be a habit, then it had to become automatic, happening as close to every time as I could manage. I recognized that for this to happen, if children didn't do what I asked right away I would need to help them get started. Ideally, I wanted to help them get started in a way that would make them *more* likely to say *yes* to me in the future, not less likely. I wanted saying *yes* to be a positive experience.

After some experimentation, I discovered that saying what I wanted in a louder voice was not very effective: if a child didn't do something the first time I asked, then repetition rarely changed much except my level of frustration. I discovered that long explanations about *why* I wanted them to do as I'd asked were largely ineffective as well: the younger toddlers ignored me, while the older ones got good at explaining back why they actually *didn't* need to do what I asked. I discovered that getting stern and counting to three, or telling them that they needed to do it "right now," sometimes worked in the moment but mostly only when I got mad, which was actually the opposite of what I was trying to achieve: I wanted them to say *yes* automatically, not just when I was angry.

Finally, I realized something that in hindsight seems rather obvious. I realized that for young children the world is a full-on sensory experience. If they are immersed in the sights, sounds, smells and other aspects of their experiences, then of course words coming from outside are just a small aspect of their sensory input. I realized that if I wanted to change a child's direction, then I needed to get into his or her experience in order to steer the ship. With this realization, I discovered that if a child didn't do what I asked the first time I said it, then the thing most likely to help them get going was for me to get up and help them physically. Just like Newton's first law of thermodynamics, a child in motion tends to stay in motion. More often than not, I simply needed to help a child get started in the right direction and suddenly the child who had been ignoring me would be happy to do what I'd asked.

So that's it: I would ask them once. If they didn't do it right away, then I'd say, "Can you do it on your own, or should I help you?" I'd wait for a beat, and then I'd get up and help them physically. Sounds simple, right? Largely, it is. Simple *and* effective. Unfortunately, I hated it! I hated hauling my adult body up and down all the time. I was often busy with another child or several other children. Even today, after years of seeing how effective helping them get started can be, it still feels so much easier to talk than to get up. But I saw how much more effective physical help was, and I was determined to help the children in my toddler class to develop the Habit of *Yes*, so I put a lid on my "personal pity-party" and just did it. I stopped saying things again in a louder voice. I stopped explaining *why* they needed to do the thing I'd asked. I stopped telling them that they needed to do it "right now," or that I needed them to be a big boy or a big girl. I stopped counting to three. At that moment of realization, I committed to doing one thing if my request fell on deaf ears: to go over to them and help them physically. Young children live through the will, and are happiest in motion. I incorporated imagination and humor when I could, but the physical nature of my help was the key.

Sometimes, the only physical help that is needed is to point children in the right direction. More often, it means taking them by the hand, and sometimes it means swooping them up and flying them over like an airplane. I will give each child as little or as much help as he or she needs, reassessing at each point. If physical help alone is not enough, I will weave in the elements of SMILE. But, regardless of whether I use the elements of SMILE or not, I try to ask a child once, then say that it looks like they need help, and then get up and help them physically. Each time that we repeat ourselves without moving into action, we are simply teaching our children that they don't need to actually do what we've asked until we get annoyed. Why not teach them that they need to do it the first time? As the children learned that I would *always* follow through immediately, the Habit of *Yes* grew.

Here's an example of how this might look: I've asked Ashton to take his bowl to the counter, and he ignores me. I say, "Can you take your bowl by yourself, or should I help you?" He continues to ignore me. I start by walking over and pointing his body in the direction of the table. That's not enough this time, so I take him by the hand and walk him back to the table. That's still not enough this time, so I take his hands and wrap them around his bowl, giving him "hand-over-hand" help.

It's important to pause right now and point out that my physical help is not punitive; on the contrary, it's as connecting as I can make it. If bringing Ashton to the table to take his bowl is met with a sullen response, I realize that I need to bring in one or more of the elements of SMILE to help him say *yes* to my request. I quickly think of *I* (Imagination) and say, "You be the baby elephant and pick up your bowl with your trunk." I wait a moment, but he doesn't get started, so I give hand-over-hand help, wrapping his hands around the bowl. I say, "Come on, baby elephant, let's galumph to the kitchen." I wait another moment, to give him a chance to galumph to the kitchen on his own. He doesn't, so I move directly behind him with my hands still over his, and start taking baby elephant steps that sway his body back and forth. As we go to the kitchen together, I say, "Lumpety-lumpety-lump." Now I'm using both *M* (Movement with touch) and *E* (Exaggeration) in addition to the *I* (Imagination). As long as I'm not angry while I'm doing it, the vast majority of children will be giggly and happy by the time the bowl gets over to the counter. The next time, he might be able to take his bowl on his own, remembering how fun it was the day before, or he might request the same connecting fun: "Let's be a baby elephant again." That day, perhaps I can just narrate the baby elephant story while he does the motions all on his own, or perhaps he'll need the additional connection supplied by touch.

Oh gosh, you say. *I thought this chapter was about not having to use the elements of SMILE every time.* Yes, you're right, I did say that. When we use positive language, assume positive intent, and physically help a child get started, we are setting ourselves up for success and are less likely to get that *no* in the first place. Remember the study that concluded, "Initial compliance leads to future compliance, and initial resistance leads to future resistance." The more often we get that *yes*, the more likely we are to get it the next time, and the time after that. We are creating a Habit of *Yes*.

No matter how much we set ourselves up for success, however, we won't get that *yes* every time. If we don't get it, then it's time to bring out those elements of SMILE again. We swallow a sigh, and remind ourselves that the work of using SMILE is "front-loaded" in that it often saves us work in the end by avoiding the cajoling, threatening and possible meltdowns that come with power struggles. As we work to make what we've asked enjoyable, perhaps we actually start to enjoy it a little bit ourselves.

Our attitude matters, and helping our children with a smile whenever we can has lasting effects on children's abilities to develop self-control. Another study by Kochanska, in 1995, found that the more frequently a mother and toddler shared positive expressions and body language, the more likely the child would be able to resist touching the attractive objects that mother had asked them to avoid. This was true when mom was in the room, and remained true when she left the child alone with the attractive object.[7] Being friendly, even (or especially) when we are correcting a child's behavior, matters.

When Nothing Works

What do we do when we've pulled out all the stops, and nothing works? Perhaps these last few chapters have already made a big difference for your relationships with your children, but nothing works all the time. What do we do when we get a hard *no* that won't budge, or a complete meltdown? Or, perhaps you and your children are stuck in a negative cycle of resistance, defiance and meltdowns, and pulling out baby elephant imagery doesn't even scratch the surface.

Perhaps imagery works when you use it, but you find that you have trouble reaching that part of yourself because you get angry at your children and don't *want* to make things fun for them when you're angry. Perhaps you find yourself yelling more than you want, and you don't know how to break the cycle.

If any of the above applies to you and your children, then go on to Part II. Chapter 4 looks at what to do when we normally can connect, but it's just not working in this moment. It addresses the questions: When do we insist that our children do as we've asked? When do we try to convince them to change their minds? When do we drop our requests? Having an inner road map of when to choose each approach will help us deal with those hard *no's* with equanimity. Chapter 5 looks at the issue of regular tantrums—how they are a symptom of a relationship out of balance, and what possible messages our children may be trying to send through their behavior. We ask, "Do they need stronger boundaries, or more affection? More structure, or less?" That chapter will give step-by-step instructions of how to find the answers to these questions. Chapter 6 addresses dealing with our own anger. How do we keep from losing our cool? What can we do once we've lost it? How can we repair a broken connection with our child? What resources are available for dealing with our anger so we have a better chance of responding to our children's actions as they are, rather than seeing them through layers of past hurt or frustration?

In attempting to use positive parenting techniques, we can easily fall into the trap of thinking, *If I could just be responsive enough and loving enough and good enough, then my child would never have meltdowns and I would never get angry and we would never get stuck in power struggles.* This is a fallacy. We are all just human, with good days and bad days, good moments and bad moments. How we recover from our falls, and how much we learn from the tough times, show our true mettle. Read on, gentle reader.

KEY POINTS

The Big Ideas in *Teaching Children to Be Responsive: Cultivating a Habit of Yes*

Parent–toddler relationships are healthiest when they are *mutually responsive.* We can support children in learning how to be responsive to us by cultivating a **Habit of *Yes*.** Ways to do this:

Give Them Things to Say *Yes* To:

- Say what you *do* want rather than what you don't
  "Walk straight along the sidewalk," rather than "Don't run out in the street."
- Be specific
  "Make sure your feet are solid before each step."
- Respond to their urges
  Which is more important, using the blocks, or the act of throwing?
- Don't get stuck in a rut
  If you're repeating the same requests often, infuse humor or imagination.
- Ask your child for alternatives
  "What can you find to do instead?"
- Assume positive intent
  Actively assume children want to be enjoyable and helpful, then nudge their behavior in that direction.

Help Your Children Get Started:

- Ask once, then say, "Can you do it on your own, or should I help you?" and then get up and help physically.

- Your help is not a punishment; it is a chance to reconnect; saying *yes* to you should be enjoyable.

Remember: Teaching young children to be responsive to us teaches us to be more responsive to them as well.

ENDNOTES, CHAPTER 3

1. Lepper, M. R. (1983). Social control processes and the internalization of social values: An attributional perspective. *Social Cognition and Social Development*, 294-330.
2. Ostrov, J. M., Gentile, D. A., & Crick, N. R. (2006). Media exposure, aggression and pro-social behavior during early childhood: A longitudinal study. *Social Development*, *15*(4), 612-627.
3. Bronson, M. (2000). *Self-regulation in early childhood: Nature and nurture*. Guilford Press, p. 67.
4. Polderman, T. J., Benyamin, B., De Leeuw, C. A., Sullivan, P. F., Van Bochoven, A., Visscher, P. M., & Posthuma, D. (2015). Meta-analysis of the heritability of human traits based on fifty years of twin studies. *Nature Genetics*, *47*(7), 702-709.
5. Brooks, R., & Goldstein, S. (2004). *Raising a self-disciplined child: Help your child become more responsible, confident, and resilient*. McGraw-Hill Professional, p. 134.
6. Kuczynski, L., & Kochanska, G. (1995). Function and content of maternal demands: Developmental significance of early demands for competent action. *Child Development*, *66*(3), 616-628.
7. Kochanska, G., & Aksan, N. (1995). Mother-child mutually positive affect, the quality of child compliance to requests and prohibitions, and maternal control as correlates of early internalization. *Child Development*, *66*(1), 236-254.

PART II

Maintaining Connection Through Tantrums and Meltdowns (Theirs and Yours)

CHAPTER 4

When We Can't Figure Out How to Connect

This chapter discusses what to do and what to avoid when we get a hard *no* that we can't transform using the elements of SMILE. When do we drop our requests, when do we try to explain and convince, and when do we insist that the child does what we've asked, even if they don't want to? When are rewards and punishments appropriate? Each is explored and suggestions for appropriate use are offered.

The mindsets and techniques shared in Section 1 can help minimize tears and tantrums, but they won't eliminate them. No matter how connected we are with our children, we are still separate individuals with separate desires, fears and aspirations. We all have to learn to recover from disappointment when things don't go our way, and tears don't mean that you're "doing it wrong" or are inadequate as a parent. You have what your child needs, whether that ability is easy to access or still feels hidden. You are enough. Parenting well requires skill, but it's not a skill that we have to have perfected at this moment. Rahima Baldwin Dancy, in her book *You Are Your Child's First Teacher*, gets to the heart of it: "We will be better off if we can give up the idea of perfection in parenting. Parenting is a process of mutual growth, during which parents and children grow on different levels through their interactions and through the elements they bring into one another's lives."[1] She goes on to suggest that perhaps it is seeing us strive and grow that best serves our children. (As her daughter, I can agree with this from experience!)

No matter how skilled we are, there are times—many times—perhaps many times each day!—when our children will want different things from what we want, and no amount of singing or imagination or tickle-games or humor or affection will change that. We know that authoritative parents are high on warmth and high on demandingness. We spent Chapters 2 and 3 looking at how to get buy-in from our children so it's easier for them to say *yes* to our requests and demands. But, no matter how connected we are to each of our children overall, we will not always be able to get our children to agree with what we ask. When that happens, then what?

The short answer is that it depends: it depends on the type of request, how tired we are, how tired our children are, what our goals are, and more. This chapter will go over what works best, and when. It will look at how each of four options can simultaneously support the Habit of *Yes*, and strengthen the quality of your relationship with your child. We will also go over traps to avoid in each of these options. Our goal is to promote a mutually responsible relationship, and how we act when we can't agree is important.

This chapter focuses on what to do with a child who is usually (or at least often) happy to go along with your agenda, but in this moment you can't get him to go along with what you've asked, perhaps because he's hungry, tired, or having a *really* good time doing something else. Or, maybe you are the one who is tired, hungry, or in desperate need of a break from your little darling, and you can't find it in you to make your request enjoyable. The next chapter will look at what to do with intractable defiance, or regular, on-going meltdowns and tantrums. In those cases, your child is trying to send you a message, and your response needs to be different in order to figure out what the message is. In Chapter 6 we'll consider how to deal with frustration and adult anger. For now, let's begin with the first scenario: when your generally enjoyable child is having a rough time and you're unable to connect *in this moment.*

TRYING EVERYTHING: Isaiah's Story

Let's say that Isaiah is exactly the age that your child is. Isaiah comes in, takes off his jacket, drops it on the floor, and heads for the play area. I start with a simple request: "Hang up your jacket, please." If that doesn't work, I get his attention and feign horror at this coat lying on the floor (Exaggeration). If that doesn't work, I get up to help him get started. If he *still* shows resistance, I might make it extra fun by picking him up and lowering him headfirst toward his jacket like a crane (Movement/touch plus Imagination), complete with sound effects. If I don't have the energy for that, I might take his jacket and throw it over his head, saying, "Hey, where'd Isaiah go?" (Movement plus Exaggeration). If he pulls the jacket off and angrily throws it down, I switch gears and get curious: Why is it so hard for him to feel connected right now? I kneel down and look at him with real interest. "Hey, sweet boy. What's going on?" (Love/appreciation; I'm appreciating his experience). Then, I'll listen to whatever he has to tell me. Depending on his age, verbal abilities, and level of tiredness, he may have a lot to say, or a little. I listen as thoughtfully as I can, taking a moment to really connect with my compassion and empathy. If he seems like he wants a hug or a snuggle, I'll give him one.

Many times, this love is enough to melt away the resistance, but not always. If the energy has shifted enough, then I can pat myself on the back for being one step closer to a mutually responsive relationship. All of that effort was worth it! But, let's say on this particular day with Isaiah, the *no* doesn't go away. What happens now? I take in the information that Isaiah has offered me through his words, body language, and my knowledge of his abilities, whether he skipped a nap or didn't eat much for breakfast, and then I wonder/figure out what to do. At this point, I have four options:

1. **Explaining and Convincing**: I can explain why I'm asking him to hang up the jacket, and engage in discussion until he changes his mind, or until I give up/switch to one of the other options.
2. **Making Him Do It**: I can insist that he complete the task, and help him follow through, either kindly or angrily.
3. **Giving In:** I can drop the request, and either hang the jacket up myself or let it remain on the floor.
4. **Bribes and Threats**: I can offer a reward for doing what I've asked, or threaten a punishment if he refuses.

FOUR OPTIONS EVALUATED

Option 1: Explaining and Convincing

In considering the story of Isaiah, maybe your first response would be to say, "Now, Isaiah. You really need to pick up your jacket and hang it up. How would it be if we all left our things on the floor? Everyone needs to do their part, right? Come on, let's go, okay?"

This option of explaining why we're asking them to do something, and inviting discussion about it is *so* attractive. It's what most parenting books *and* many books on communication suggest; explaining and convincing is the approved technique in our culture for parents who don't want to be considered authoritarian (low warmth and high demandingness). Diana Baumrind herself, who developed the idea of the authoritative parent, suggested that explaining and convincing, and engaging in discussion, were important aspects of authoritative parenting. The problem with this is that many people fail to take child development into account first. Even Baumrind admits that the level of discussion should depend on the child's stage of development. Thirty years into her work she explained her stance in more detail: "Because the preschooler's social-conventional reasoning is limited, toddler compliance is most effective when the adult briefly explains the rule, and provides a consequence if the child persists in disobeying."[2]

For toddlers and most preschoolers, explaining and convincing is not only generally ineffective (because their brains are immature), it also has some possible side effects that most parents would prefer to avoid. When we explain and explain, and work to convince Isaiah that he should actually pick up that jacket, even though he doesn't want to, a couple of things are happening.

First, we are addressing emotion with logic, which is rarely effective even in cases where a person's brain is fully developed.

Secondly, children learn through imitation, so our actions are actively cultivating his desire and ability to explain to us in return why he *shouldn't* have to do something, even though we've asked. Susan Stiffelman, author of *Parenting Without Power Struggles: Raising Joyful Resilient Kids While Staying Cool, Calm, and Connected,* refers to this type of exchange as "The Two Lawyers." She says, "This is where power struggles take place, with each side debating the merits of its position, and the most committed—or least exhausted—prevailing."[3] This technique does little except give children practice at saying *no.*

Thirdly, when we engage in discussion with Isaiah about why we want him to do what we ask, and why he doesn't want to, what we're actually doing is extending the feelings of disconnection. The longer the discussion goes on, the longer those negative feelings are drawn out and dwelt upon. As dueling lawyers, we're not on the same team; we're on opposite teams. In working to create a mutually responsive relationship, we want to be on opposite teams for as few minutes per day as possible. Allowing children to be disappointed, and then supporting them to move on, can put parents and children on the same team for more of the time.

As toddlers grow into preschoolers and become more verbal, many parents feel increasingly uncomfortable insisting that their children do what they've asked if they don't want to. Many parents are aware that being inconsistent and changing their minds as soon as a child gets upset is not a best parenting practice. However, it pains them to be the cause of upset and they don't want to be a dictator, so they start engaging in longer and longer discussions, trying to get their children to agree with what they've asked.

If that feels similar to what you're experiencing, I'd like to suggest an alternate way of looking at the situation. Although our ongoing discussions stem from a desire to be kind, if we refuse to move on until children give up their feelings on the issue, we're not really being kind. Arguably, we're actually being *more* controlling, because not only do they have to *do* what we want, but they can't even *feel* the way they want about it, either! I'm not suggesting that we ignore our children's feelings; quite the contrary. I'm simply suggesting that explaining and convincing are not the best ways to help preschoolers manage their feelings. Connecting through singing, movement, imagination, love and exaggeration are much more effective.

One more thought before we move on, because I have worked with parents of both toddlers and preschoolers who tell me that explaining works for them. Likewise, I've had parents who insist that their children will listen only when they get mad and yell. In both cases, I don't think the logic (or the volume) is convincing the children. Rather, children learn how long they can ignore us, what our signs are that we're "serious," and when what we've said is non-negotiable. For some parents, that sign is an angry edge on the voice; for others, it's using the "explaining voice." The question is, then, how can we let children know that we're "serious" without having to get angry or engage in endless discussions? Although letting children know that we're "serious" in a new way is a challenge, it *is* possible, and the secret ingredient is consistency.

In my preschool class, I unconsciously developed a seemingly innocuous phrase that I used only when the answer was non-negotiable: "Not today." I didn't even realize this until I noticed that whenever the children in my program asked if they could do something and I answered, "Not today," they would accept and move on without any debate or discussion. Thereafter, I started consciously adopting more phrases that always meant what I said. At the beginning, I'd get push-back and testing, but gradually the edges would wear off and the phrase would be accepted without question because the children knew that I was serious.

Option 2: Making Them Do What We've Asked

When I've taken my best shot to connect with a child and to melt away the *no,* and when I've tried different tools in my toolbox, but nothing seems to be working, then I need to make a decision: do I "make them" do it, or do I drop the request?

In general, I try to drop my requests as infrequently as possible, especially after I've put as much effort as I did with Isaiah and his jacket. Remember, I'm trying to cultivate a Habit of *Yes*. Occasionally, I will realize that I'm being unreasonable and the better option really is to drop the request; we'll look at how to recognize that, as we continue here, and then how to handle it gracefully. But, most of the time I will insist, as kindly as I can, and I will follow up with as much support as they need.

If you are a parent who prefers to explain and convince, and you have a hard time with the idea of "forcing" a child to do something if they really don't want to, I would like to share this: When we don't insist that children do the things we've asked unless they want to, we are sending them the message, *"You should only have to do things that you feel like doing."* However, giving them this message does them a great disservice. The brain research on executive function (higher-level thinking and decision-making) shows that people who do the best are *not* those who only do what they feel like doing. The people who do better in school, who are less likely to do drugs or get pregnant as teenagers, who are more likely to do well in their careers and their marriages, are the people who can resist temptation and do the right thing, even when they don't feel like it.[4] While executive function can be strengthened at any age,[5] levels of self-control in childhood are highly predictive of future success in these areas.[6] Teaching children to act responsibly, whether they feel like it or not, will serve them well.

One objection I get when I present this idea is that parents don't want their children to simply follow orders or do what everyone else is doing; they want their children to be able to question authority and do the right thing. Part of the confusion comes from the phrases we use as adults, about "following your gut" or "doing what feels right." For the young child, what "feels right" is to get what they want. That internal compass of right and wrong, which we have as adults, is developed through our formative experiences; especially those in the first six or seven years of life, when we soak in how the world *should* be from our parents, siblings, and teachers. If we want our teenagers to stand up when others treat people unkindly; if we want our young adults to honor their obligations and speak up when others don't; if we want our adult children to be able to manifest their aspirations, we do it by insisting on age-appropriate *right behavior* from a very early age. Practicing the act of hanging up his jacket even though he doesn't feel like it doesn't turn Isaiah into an adult who doesn't question what he's told, it helps him grow into an adult who can put in the hard work to make his dreams become a reality.

Instead of trying to explain and convince, I take a deep breath and call on my inner authoritative parent: remember, high warmth *and* high expectations. With little Isaiah I will say, as warmly as I can manage, "It looks like you need some help hanging your jacket up." Then I will help him.

How to Help Children Do Something They Don't Want to Do

One way to support a child in doing something even though they've refused is to **make your request smaller**: Children often say *no* when they feel overwhelmed or incapable in that moment. Making a request smaller, or altering it some way, is often an effective type of help. For younger toddlers, starting out with "Where is your jacket?" can help get the ball rolling. For older preschoolers you might say, "Here, you pick up one sleeve and I'll pick up the other." If you then weave in a song or a bit of imagination, things might pick up again.

Another way to provide support is to **give hand-over-hand help**. This lets children feel in their bodies how to do things that perhaps they didn't feel capable of a moment before. It also lets children know that we're serious and they really need to do what we've asked. If my attempt at hand-over-hand help is met with anger, this is almost always because a child needs some L (Love/affection) first.

Of course, my help will vary depending on what I'm asking a child to do. If he's digging in his heels and refusing to go upstairs to brush teeth, I will carry him. If he's picked up my cell phone and refuses to put it down when I ask, I will say, "You can put it down, or I will put it down for you." If he's refusing to put his pants on in the morning I might say, "I will hold you here on my lap until you're ready." Sometimes a "Do you need me to do it, or can you do it on your own?" leads to a child suddenly pleased to do it on his own. Other times he might be glad to get some help, and still others it may lead to a catharsis of tears.

When I make a child do what I've asked I'm not angry, and my **matter-of-fact response** is not a punishment. If I can connect, I do. If not, I help. This doesn't mean that I don't share in an age-appropriate way why we need to do the thing we're doing, but I don't expect my explanation to change the child's feelings on the issue. We do the task together, we move on, and we reconnect a bit later.

You may be asking yourself the $64,000 question right now: *how do you keep from getting angry?* This subject of your anger, and how to avoid it when working with children, is vitally important. I will consider it at length in Chapter 6.

Option 3: Give In and Withdraw a Request

Let's get back to Isaiah and the jacket, which is still on the floor. I've already put in quite a bit of effort to work on his Habit of *Yes*, but it doesn't seem to be working. My pretend horror doesn't work. My playfully throwing the jacket over his head is met with anger. My love and appreciation do result in a softening, but not a *yes*. If I am at my best, I will step back for a moment to think of what this child needs. Normally, a softening leads to a willingness to do what I've asked, but not this time. Did he have an especially busy day? Is he going through a growth spurt? If he's a child in my care, is something big going on at home that I don't know about? I am unsure, but I sense that he's feeling overwhelmed in some way, and so I look at him kindly and say, "I can tell that you're not ready to do it now. Why don't I do it for you, this time."

But wait! I hear you say. *Aren't you just caving in?* The answer is, it depends. Offering to do it for him because I understand that he's feeling tired or overwhelmed is much different from "giving in." Such letting go comes from a place of connection, and my doing it is a gift. I might set up this response as a one-time thing by creating a picture of him being able to do it again soon: "I bet next time you'll be able to pick up your jacket on your own again."

I suggest dropping a request in two cases:

- First, when the child is truly unable to do the task.

- Second, when you've gotten yourself in over your head.

In those instances, it really is okay to change your mind, as long as you're explicit about it: "Oh, I didn't realize that would be too hard for you. You can just put it down and I'll deal with it later." Or, "Wow, I didn't realize how important this was for you. I've changed my mind; you don't have to do it this time."

Even when we ask a child to do something and we change our minds because of his big reaction, we're not necessarily "giving in" to him. Rather, we are taking his opinion into account and making up our minds, as good leaders do. This may feel like a semantic difference, but it's not. Feeling certain that you're in charge, and taking someone's feelings into consideration, is vastly different from giving the decision-making power over to a young child. However, do note that I make this dropping of my request a real exception, rather than the norm. Instead of dropping altogether, I prefer to modify my request to make it more achievable, and I make sure to get the child into motion, to use imagination, or to pour in some love, etc.

Some Thoughts on High Expectations

When my husband and I first met, he loved to ask me questions about child development and "what would you do" scenarios. In one such discussion, he naïvely said, "Isn't just having high expectations the key to having children behave?" I laughed, and said, "Well, having high expectations is important, as long as they're not unrealistic." "Oh," he replied. "Well, how can you tell the difference?"

I was completely stumped by my husband's question. Realistic or unrealistic? How *can* you tell the difference? Knowledge of child development helps, although some children are much more capable than others. After mulling it over, I came up with this: a high expectation is something that you know a child is capable of doing with your help or support, *and* you're willing and able to provide that support. An unrealistic expectation is something that a child cannot do even with your support, *or* something that you're not willing/able to help them with.

Using this model, let's look at Jamal who is twenty-two-months old and new to my play program, Rainbow Bridge. He is not used to sitting at the table through the meal, but I have high expectations, and I expect him to sit at the table until we blow out our candle and wipe our hands. Because of my high expectations, when he gets up, I help him sit back down. He gets up again, and I help him sit back down. This happens four or five times, and he starts to get upset. I sing a song that he knows, which he's happy to listen to, and then I end the meal, a bit earlier than I otherwise would have. With my help, he has succeeded in sitting at the table for the entire meal! At the next meal, he tries to get up only twice, and soon he's happily sitting through every meal. I had high expectations, and with my support he was able to meet them. However, if I had not had the patience to sit him back down every time, or had a baby in my lap or other duties that prevented me from being able to sit him back down every time, then my expectation for him to sit through the entire meal would have been unrealistic.

This double component of high expectations (his capability, my willingness) is important to keep in mind. We often mistakenly think that if a preschool-aged child is *capable* of doing something, then she should be able to do it...whenever we ask her to. Unfortunately, just because your four-year-old is capable of putting on every item of clothing, this doesn't mean you can simply ask her to get dressed while you go downstairs to fix breakfast. Chances are you would go upstairs ten minutes later to find her clothes still lying on the bed as she plays with her fire engine. Even if you stay with her, even though she's *capable*, at this age she will only be *able* to manage by herself sometimes. Some days those clothes zip right on, and some days you will be helping with almost every piece. Self-control is a developing skill, and its development is not completely linear. How competent our toddlers or preschoolers are, on a given day, depends on how fresh they are, how distracted or distractible they are, how distracted *you* are, and many other factors that we can only guess at.

Finally, we need to remember that young children live in a different world from the thought-driven world we inhabit: toddlers live in a world of sensation, while preschoolers live in a world of imagination and play. This is their natural heritage, even if you haven't been "encouraging" it. Both toddlers and preschoolers have a different experience of time than we do, and are not goal-oriented like we are. All of these factors combine to mean that, just because a child is capable of doing something he will be able to do it on command. Having high expectations of your child means that you must have high expectations of yourself, as well.

When Not to Give In

While children often say *no* because they're asking for connection, when they don't respond to our efforts to connect, something else may be at play. The process of individuation gains momentum in the toddler years, and is marked by children's use of the word "I." Before that time, they refer to themselves by what they have heard: "Max do it" or "Shana's toy." This change in consciousness around the age of two and a half is monumental for the child. As a child discovers that she really, truly is separate from you, this can often seem overwhelming and can bring up the vital question: "If I'm separate from my mom (and everyone else), then where is my place in the world and what is my relationship to those around me—especially mom?" Some children react to this question by becoming clingy and going through a "shy" period, others respond by becoming suddenly aggressive with others, but many respond by becoming bossy and demanding.

We, as the adults who love these little beings intensely, see their individuality emerging and we don't want to "squash" them. We want them to be happy, and we're used to doing what they want, so when they start making unreasonable demands, we go along with it. We figure that it's "just a phase"—the "Terrible Two's," right? We still try to say *yes* to them all the time, even when it's uncomfortable. Then, we become exasperated that they're still not satisfied. What's going on?

Imagine that, when young children are demanding, they are asking (in the only way they know how) *what their place is* in relationship to you. In this case, what they long to hear is *not* "I love you and I'll put up with your unreasonable demands." Rather, what they long to feel from you is: "*You are separate from me, but you are part of the family. Your place in the family is the child, to explore and grow and help. My place in the family is the parent, to guide, protect and love. I will help you find your place in the world, now and as you grow. You will not have to figure that out on your own. You are not in charge.*"

Experiencing that they're not in charge is both a disappointment and a relief to children. It's a short-term disappointment, and a long-term relief. That's why it's so hard for us to tell, in the moment, what the right thing is for them, because they whine and cry and are desperately disappointed when we don't give in to their demands. But, at the same time that it's disappointing, it's also reassuring. We're giving them the message, "I am in charge…I am the parent." When they get that message enough, they can relax and stop feeling overwhelmed, or that they need to control things all the time. They don't have to continually push the boundaries to test for who's in charge. They can relax into the rhythm that you set for them, and be happy to explore and grow and help: the child's place.

In a mutually responsive relationship we respond quickly and positively, but we don't do everything a child asks, especially when that ask is really a demand. The Second Great Parenting Task of the toddler years is to be responsive to children's needs rather than reacting to their whims. We can tell when children are asking for clarity by their tone: when we correct their ways of asking do they respond sweetly, or do they become even more demanding and irrational?

Option 4: Bribes and Threats

Most of the parents I work with in my counseling practice tend to start out with explaining and convincing, and when that doesn't work, they resort to bribes and threats in a last-ditch effort to get their child to initiate doing what they've been told. Some of those parents punish, while some yell and threaten, but rarely follow through. Others offer rewards or other enticements.

If you grew up with parents who used punishments as their main parenting tool, then, when little Isaiah refuses to pick up his jacket when you ask him to, your first response might be, "If you don't pick up your jacket, then you won't be able to play with your train for the rest of the day." *Well,* some of you might ask, *what's wrong with that? Isn't this an example of holding a firm boundary?*

The problem with punishments is that when children are punished they don't think, "Wow, Mom has a point. Not being able to play with my train is really making me think about how important it is to hang my jacket up." No, indeed. What's more likely to be going through his mind is: "That's not fair!" "She's so mean." "When I'm as big as her, then everyone will have to do what I say, too." When we punish children, we are likely to get short-term compliance, but that is because children are avoiding the punishment, not because they now agree with the rule or norm that they broke.[7]

What about just threatening to take the train away, but not actually carrying through? Unfortunately, parents who make threats that they are not willing to follow through on tend to lose their children's trust. Children will then ignore their parents as they make more and more empty threats, until these poor parents either end up losing their cool, or giving up altogether. Threats and punishments are not effective parenting practices.

Sometimes, certainly, consequences *should be* enacted. It is fine to let a child know that he won't be able to have the snack if he refuses to wash hands. Or, if your three-year-old dawdles and refuses to brush teeth and get into her jammies, she can be reminded that the time for reading a story may run out. But, rather than stating these as threats ("If you don't brush your teeth now then you won't get a story"), you can let her know that you're on her side ("Oh, no, our time for bedtime is running out! We need to be quick like little bunnies if we want to still have enough time for a story."). Then, if she still drags her feet and the time for story is all used up, instead of being self-righteous, we can be sad right along with her. "I wish there were still time for story, too. Tomorrow we'll have to be a bit speedier and make sure that our time isn't all used up."

Bribes are also a common alternative: "Isaiah, hang your jacket up and I'll give you a sticker/treat/time on the iPad." That will get the behavior you want pretty quickly, right? Well, only obliquely, because offering rewards teaches children to try and get more rewards, which isn't exactly what we're aiming for. And, it gets worse—sometimes, rewarding actually does the opposite of what we hope for: research shows that when people are offered rewards for doing tasks, it lowers the perceived value of the thing they do to get the reward. This is referred to as the "overjustification effect." Even worse, this effect seems to be larger for children than it is for adults.[8] (For an interesting and easy-to-read overview of the research on rewards and different types of praise, search the Internet for the article "How Not to Talk to Your Kids: The Inverse Power of Praise" by Po Bronson. For a more in-depth look, read the book *Punished By Rewards: The Trouble with Gold Stars, Incentive Plans, Praise and Other Bribes,* by Alphie Kohn.)

On the other hand, there are times when rewards are exactly what's needed. One of these times is for situations where the "perceived value" of some activity really couldn't go any lower, and is unlikely to rise: for example, getting shots at the doctor's office. A slightly murkier area for the beneficial use of rewards is when a child refuses to even try a task or activity that we want them to value—for example, a child who absolutely refuses to even sit on the potty, or let a certain type of food pass his lips. Older children, too, can decide that they're bad at something or that they hate something, without even trying it. Rewards can lure a child into getting started, with the hope that they will enjoy themselves and start doing the activity without the rewards. Whether this goes well depends on the activity, the reward, the child, and your interactions. Approach with caution and use as a last resort.

HOW TO KNOW WHEN THE BALANCE IS RIGHT

In my efforts to foster a mutually responsive relationship, I can generally tell in which areas I'm falling short by how the child tends to respond when I ask him to do something and he doesn't want to do it. If he often tries to convince me that he shouldn't have to do it, then that tells me I'm explaining and convincing too much. If he's throwing tantrums and letting his emotions get big and out of control, that tells me I've been withdrawing my requests too frequently and not insisting often enough. (It is also possible that he's trying to send me another message; we'll look at common messages in the next chapter on tantrums.) When we're experiencing *lots* of episodes of me having to "help" him and neither of us is enjoying it, then I'm forgetting to make things fun/connecting/enjoyable.

Of course, no child will want to do what I ask of him every single time. But I know that we're striking a good balance when I get a refusal and I say, "It looks like you need some help," and the child either jumps up to do what I've asked, or is happy to do it when I add a song or a game or a smile.

KEY POINTS

The Big Ideas in *When We Can't Figure Out How to Connect*

If at First You Don't Succeed, Try, Try Again

- Remember, the work is "front-loaded" and will pay off later.
- A child who gets angry at humor or imagination is almost always asking for love and affection.
- Pause for a moment and pay real attention. Ask what's going on and listen with real interest.

When to Explain and Convince: *Avoid It!*

- It's not effective: you don't change emotion through logic, especially for someone with an immature brain.
- As children grow they're likely to turn into "dueling lawyers," which extends feelings of disconnection and makes it harder to recover.
- Let them know that you're "serious" in a different way. Be consistent with it.

When to Make Them Do What You've Asked: *Most of the Time*

- Make your request smaller.
- Give hand-over-hand help.
- It's not a punishment.
- Remember, your goal is high expectations *and* high warmth.

When to Withdraw Your Request: *Occasionally*

- If your child can't do what you've asked: they are too tired, overwhelmed, or you realize that what you asked is not reasonable. Do it for them as a gift from your heart.

- If you can't help them follow through: you're too tired, overwhelmed, or have your hands full. Be explicit that you've thought about it and changed your mind.

Bribes and Threats: *Very Infrequently*

- Punishments tend to make people feel resentful and only do what you want when you're present to enforce it.
- Rewards lower the intrinsic value of the thing that was done to get the reward.
- Times when rewards are appropriate:
  - When the intrinsic value of the request is very low: e.g., getting shots.
  - To get them to try something they currently refuse.

How to Know When the Balance Is Right

When you ask a child to do something, what's a typical response?

- She tries to explain why she shouldn't have to:
  - You're explaining and convincing too much.
- She throws a tantrum or has a fit:
  - You're withdrawing your request too frequently and not insisting often enough.
- It feels like you're constantly making her do things and it's exhausting:
  - You're forgetting to use positive language and/or make things connecting. Re-read Chapters 1 and 2.
- You say, "It looks like you need some help" and your child jumps up to do what you've asked:
  - Things are in balance. Good job!

ENDNOTES, CHAPTER 4

[1] Dancy, R. B. (2014). *You are your child's first teacher: What parents can do with and for their children from birth to age six* (3rd ed.). Ten Speed Press.

[2] Baumrind, D. (1996). The discipline controversy revisited. *Family Relations*, 405-414, p. 408.

[3] Stiffelman, S. (2012). *Parenting without power struggles: Raising joyful, resilient kids while staying cool, calm and collected.* Simon & Schuster, pp. 9-10.

[4] Baumeister, R. F., & Heatherton, T. F. (1996). Self-regulation failure: An overview. *Psychological Inquiry*, *7*(1), 1-15.

[5] Diamond, A. (2013). Executive functions. *Annual Review of Psychology*, *64*, 135.

[6] Moffitt, T. E., Arseneault, L., Belsky, D., Dickson, N., Hancox, R. J., Harrington, H., ... & Sears, M. R. (2011). A gradient of childhood self-control predicts health, wealth, and public safety. *Proceedings of the National Academy of Sciences*, *108*(7), 2693-2698.

[7] For a detailed overview of the research on the effects of punishments of both children and adults, see Kohn, A. (1999). *Punished by rewards: The trouble with gold stars, incentive plans, A's, praise, and other bribes*. Houghton Mifflin Harcourt.

[8] Deci, E. L., Koestner, R., & Ryan, R. M. (1999). A meta-analytic review of experiments examining the effects of extrinsic rewards on intrinsic motivation. *Psychological Bulletin*, *125*(6), 627-668.

CHAPTER 5

Regular Tantrums, Meltdowns, and Defiance

In this chapter we will look at the messages children may be trying to send us through regular tantrums, meltdowns and defiance. Common messages include a *Call for Boundaries*, a *Call for Affection*, a *Call for Consistency*, and a *Call to Slow Down.*

We consider a practical way to figure out which message(s) our children are sending, through implementing a *Pouring In the Love Campaign* and seeing how they respond. Then, more strategies for addressing each message are suggested.

When your personal life is out of balance, it strains your body's immune system. If you don't respond to your body's signals and get more sleep, work less, improve your nutrition or reduce the stress in your life in some other way, then you are quite likely to get sick.

When your relationship with your child is out of balance, then the *relationship's* immune system gets strained. A relationship's immune system can also get out of balance from stress, lack of sleep, over-commitment, lack of attention, or other factors. Our bodies "tell" us when we're at risk for getting sick by producing symptoms of excessive tiredness, aches and pains, or a low-grade fever. Children let us know when our relationship with them is out of balance by acting out—including regular tantrums, meltdowns over "nothing," or exhibiting defiance at even the most benign requests. This chapter will look at different ways relationships can get out of balance, how to figure out what might be going on, and what to do to effect positive change.

Sometimes, the stressors on a relationship with a child are obvious: a new sibling, a move to a new house, divorce, or even having a parent go out of town can shift the dynamics of a relationship. Other times, the stressors are less obvious, consisting of smaller factors that build up. Chaos, inconsistency on the part of beloved adults, or too many transitions over the course of the day or week can have an unseen strain on a relationship. Another sneak-attack on a relationship's immune system can come from small but persistent sleep deficits: in school-aged children, just an hour less sleep per night, for only three nights, caused a regression of two years worth of cognitive development.[1] Other studies show that the effects of sleep loss are cumulative, so that even a small deficit builds up over time.[2] This loss can be tricky to realize, because children who have a chronic sleep deficit tend to have a hard time falling asleep and a hard time staying asleep, leading parents to think that their children don't need as much sleep as they actually do.

Or, perhaps you can't pinpoint any one factor, but somehow things have gotten off-kilter and you find that you and your child have stopped enjoying one another. This sense of imbalance can often happen just before children go through developmental leaps, as they become either especially clingy or suddenly start pushing in new ways. Such developmental leaps are common at two and a half, and again at three and a half, but can happen at any time. Or, perhaps your child has always responded in challenging ways: some children just seem to push extra hard, experience their emotions extra deeply, and generally have a difficult time going with the flow.

Whatever the causes, one or both of you has stopped being responsive to the other. Remember, being responsive means responding quickly and positively, even—or especially—when you can't do what the other person has asked. When a relationship gets out of balance, a song or a game may lighten things up for a moment or two, but the mood quickly deteriorates again. Your relationship's immune system has taken a hit, and you need to take extra care to get back into balance. For example: Little Ava demands raisins, but then cries because you got her raisins—because *she* wanted to be the one to get them. So, you put them back and let her get some, but then the raisins are too small, or too sticky, or not the right number, and a meltdown ensues. Recognize then that *it's not really about the raisins.* Maybe she's telling you she's tired because of a missed nap or a molar coming in, but if incidents like these are the norm rather than the exception, quite likely Ava is trying to send you a larger message about your relationship.

Please don't worry about the quality of your relationship based on an occasional meltdown. Children are also learning to manage their emotions, a skill that most children struggle with, at one time or another. One study with 335 children, conducted by the University of Wisconsin, showed more than eighty percent of them starting to have tantrums between eighteen and twenty-four months; by thirty to thirty-six months, over ninety percent had them. However, most of those tantrums only lasted between thirty seconds and one minute, and seventy-five percent of them were less than five-minutes long. Nearly half of the children were done with tantrums altogether by age four.[3] If

> Richard, a dad in my online class, described the actions of his two-and-a-half-year-old, Annie, who was engaging in classic message-sending behavior:
>
> *She demands to be carried upstairs then shrieks "Don't hold me!" and bats at my hands, but clings on as if the air will propel her upstairs, not my hands. It is as if she wants to be right next to you, right on top of you sometimes, but doing things herself, and boy, if you interfere, let fury unfold.*

your child's tantrums last a long time, happen very frequently, or are not abating as he or she matures, then consider that he or she may be trying to send you a message.

Many parents think, "Well, this is just how two-year-olds are," and they try to tolerate and outlast such behaviors. A more effective strategy is to figure out how your relationship has fallen out of balance and put some repairs in place. That doesn't mean that meltdowns will never happen, but it can improve the quality of your relationship dramatically and develop positive relationship patterns that can last for many years.

When I say that your child is trying to send you a message, I'm not saying that he or she is consciously thinking about it. However, while children may not know what's wrong on a conscious level, they do know it intuitively, because when the imbalance is addressed, then the behavioral issues tend to melt away. I have found four common messages that children try to convey through regular tantrums and describe them as:

- A Call for Boundaries
- A Call for Affection
- A Call for Consistency
- A Call to Slow Down

We'll briefly look at the symptoms of each (although children can experience more than one at a time), and then I'll give step-by-step instructions of how to figure out what a child is asking for, along with some suggestions on how to address each one.

A CALL FOR BOUNDARIES

Children often send out a *Call for Boundaries* when their parents fall too far into the permissive side of parenting. This can happen when adults work hard at being responsive to a child, but do not expect and/or support their child to be responsive in return. When this occurs, we end up with a little dictator. Some children are quite happy to be little dictators, and are generally content as long as everything goes their way. More often though, these children seem like they're never satisfied, and even tiny things can set them off.

One mom described this situation with her three-year-old:

> *It sounds really odd as I'm describing it, but he gets bent out of shape and things have to be done over—I mean totally started again. If I try to help him put his shirt on, but he didn't want help, then all the parent germs have to be wiped off, hands washed, a new shirt found, etc. It's kind of funny, kind of nice to see his desire for competence, no wallflower here, but sometimes extremely tedious, like a skipping record: this is how our days begin.*
>
> —Elizabeth, mother of one

Elizabeth, like many parents, worried about stifling her son's process of individuation or crushing his spirit if she didn't go along with all his desires. In fact, she didn't realize that by having low "maturity demands" (the term used by early childhood researchers like Baumrind), she is actually holding him back from achieving his full potential at this time. As I have said again and again, children thrive when we have high warmth *and* high demandingness, and letting children run the show so that they don't become upset doesn't actually serve them.

Some parents say, "Well, I expect him to be responsive, but he refuses. I feel like I'm constantly yelling at him to do what I've asked! But he throws a fit and I'm at my wits' end." Many times, these parents are not giving that child the support he needs to be successfully responsive. As we discussed in Chapter 3, high expectations have two components: the child's ability to do the task, and the adult's ability to give as much support as needed for the child to be successful. Unrealistic expectations, being too busy or tired to help children follow through, or getting into a negative pattern of yelling instead of helping, can all prevent children from being responsive. When this occurs, parents may mistakenly think that their children need firmer boundaries, but this misbehavior is much more likely to be a Call for Affection.

A CALL FOR AFFECTION

A relationship can get out of balance if the adult is not being responsive enough. This can manifest in many forms:

- Forgetting (or being too busy) to take the time to connect
- Forgetting to enjoy your child for who she is
- Not taking time to appreciate beauty together
- Failing to be playful
- Not giving hugs and kisses that are filled with love, rather than just perfunctory

We may have understandable reasons for having lowered our levels of responsiveness: a new baby, or a health issue, increased responsibilities at work, or relationship troubles with a spouse or partner...all pull our energy and attention in different directions.

Whatever the reason, our patience diminishes, and normal child-like behaviors start to annoy us. Our children feel our lack of positive engagement and respond by acting out, either in protest, or because they're willing to take negative interactions over a lack of engagement. This acting out causes us to feel justified in our annoyance, and children continue with ever-more-drastic measures to get us to engage with them, until we don't enjoy spending time with them at all.

One mother who reached out to me for coaching had this to say about her five-year-old daughter, who was resorting to extreme behaviors in her efforts to get attention:

> *Since her brother was born one-and-a-half years ago, we have really been struggling with our daughter. I know some challenges are normal with a new sibling, but we are at our wits' end. Some of the behaviors that are common: being cruel to her brother and others, laughing at others' pain, ignoring parents' directions, only responding to rewards ("I'll only be nice to my brother today if you give me a present"), whining, nagging, yelling, screaming, being disrespectful. She is extremely verbal, very smart, and has not adjusted very well to having to share attention. We simply don't have as much to give her, so even though I know one answer is to love her up and spend more time with her, this is a big challenge with two demanding kiddos and work.*

We will go over how to break this cycle of negative attention-seeking behavior below. Let's first acknowledge that a *Call for Affection* can be especially challenging because the child's ways of asking for affection are so unpleasant, making it difficult for parents to say *yes* to their child's real need.

To complicate matters, relationships can get out of balance in both directions: perhaps *we* become too permissive, and our children act out in an attempt to point out the imbalance to *us.* Their acting out annoys us, so we stop being silly and affectionate with them. This makes them feel even less connected to us, and they respond with defiance. We react to their defiance with anger or inconsistency. Such a negative spiral can be hard to exit.

A Word about a Second Baby

Like for the mother above, a new baby in the family is a common trigger for an older toddler to get into a negative spiral. Mom and dad become less responsive because they're tired and their hands are full; the older child acts out; parents are tired and don't reconnect, and then wonder why the toddler has suddenly transformed from an enjoyable child into a little monster. I want to assure you that this cycle is not a given, and that even once it starts, the pattern can be broken at any time; we'll go over the practical steps below.

I also want to assure you that this negative spiral is not inevitable, and for many families, it never starts in the first place. Many moms I've worked with discover, upon a new baby's birth, that their third-trimester-dread of how their family would adjust was much worse than the reality. Sure, they're tired, but it feels better than pregnancy fatigue because of this amazing little being who has joined the family. They find that their capacity for love and connection has suddenly increased significantly and dramatically, and their older child's capacity for love and connection has increased as well. One friend of mine described her two-and-a-half-year-old interacting with his baby brother: "Even when he's having a really tough day and just lashing out at everyone, he will run by his baby brother and stop in his tracks, lean down and kiss him on the head, then continue on his way. I'm so grateful for the love he has." All manner of dynamics are possible when families grow.

If you currently have a new baby and your relationship with your older child is suffering, it doesn't mean that you're a bad parent, or that having another child was a mistake, or that your older child's horrible true nature is revealing itself; it simply means that your child is sending out a *Call for Affection*, in the only way that he knows how.

A CALL FOR CONSISTENCY

Most adults know that children like consistency, but few parents and caregivers realize just how important consistency is in order for children to function successfully. In order for a secure attachment to form, babies need two things from their parents: for them to respond lovingly, and for them to respond consistently. When parents respond *in*-consistently (either in whether or not they respond, or in how they respond), babies are more likely to form insecure attachments, which affect them over the course of their entire lives, as we discussed in Chapter 1. Being able to count on their adults is vitally important for babies and young children to feel secure in their relationships.

Children also thrive with consistency in their schedules. Part of this is biological: going to sleep at the same time each day prompts the body to release melatonin shortly before bedtime, and eating at the same time each day prompts the body to release the hunger-stimulating hormones leptin and ghrelin. Another reason why children crave consistent schedules is psychological: young children experience time differently than adults. For young children, time is sequential: first A happens, then B and then C. One mother I worked with was amazed when her husband went out of town for a week and their eleven-month-old daughter crawled to the linen closet each morning at 7:35 AM to tug on the ironing board where Daddy would iron his shirt each morning at that time when he was home. When children experience inconsistency in their schedules, either chronically or temporarily because of a vacation, for example, it takes them much more energy to simply get through the day. When children put so much energy into "holding it together," their stress is likely to leak out in some way: increased potty accidents, a regression to hitting or biting, or an inability to deal with even minor setbacks.

Additionally, young children thrive with consistency in *how* things are done. Young children learn through repetition. When we do things in the same way, every time we do them, then children know what comes first and what comes next. They can imitate the actions in their play, and then can do them on their own. This is how children become competent, one of the universal needs that each of us has.

Even children within the same family can be very different, and a child's temperament plays a significant role in how well he or she can handle inconsistency. However, even if your child can manage inconsistency, that doesn't mean it's optimal. Researchers have found that children who live in home conditions that are highly disorganized and unpredictable are less curious and less apt to explore the environment,[4] and advise that order and predictability in the environment support both cognitive development and children's abilities to control themselves (self-regulation).[5] All children do better with consistency, both in their environments and from us: secure routines, regular rituals around how we do certain tasks together, and consistently loving responses from us. Although it can seem counter-intuitive to some, consistency in the early years leads to flexibility in the later years. Children need consistency in order to thrive, and the more they have, the better they tend to do all around.

A CALL TO SLOW DOWN

Transitions are often the hardest parts of the day for any parent or caregiver. If many transitions involve full-fledged meltdowns over the course of the day, however, or if every transition turns into a power struggle where you're convincing, cajoling, or dragging your child every step of the way, your child may be sending out a *Call to Slow Down*.

The *Call to Slow Down* involves two different aspects: how *much* we do—the result of doing too many activities, having too many different caregivers, or involving too many transitions in a day—and the *way* we do things, because children cannot abide rushing. When we rush, this fills children with anxiety. They will do anything to get us to stop, including a full-on meltdown. They will hide if we're trying to get out the door. They will drag their feet if we're already late. Or, if they're playing happily by themselves in the living room and we try to quickly get something done before they notice, they will be at our sides in no time, pulling on our legs and whining. Children thrive when we can go at "kid speed." We'll talk more in Part III about how to do this and still accomplish what needs to be done.

WHAT'S THEIR CALL? DECODING THE MESSAGE

I've hinted at what behaviors tend to appear when children feel an imbalance in different areas of their relationship with you. In reality, it's often difficult to tell what's going on when you're in the thick of it. Having trouble with transitions might be a *Call to Slow Down*, but it can also be a sign of too much chaos (a *Call for Consistency*), or because we're being too demanding and not taking the time to connect (a *Call for Affection*). So, how can we tell what's going on, and then how can we fix it?

Over the course of my work with children and families, I've developed a technique to get relationships with our children back into balance so that the relationship can become mutually responsive again. Like many of the techniques in this book, it is simple in theory, but can be a challenge to implement. We'll go over it now, in detail, pitfalls and all.

The technique starts by doing a *Pouring In the Love Campaign* for one week, and watching to see how your child responds: if his behavior issues escalate, he's likely giving you a *Call for Boundaries*. If your child's behavior "magically" melts away, then he was likely giving you a *Call for Affection*. If your child's behavior improves just a bit, but then things go back to the way they've been despite the love you're still actively pouring in, then he's likely either sending out a *Call for Consistency* or a *Call to Slow Down*.

Step One: The Pouring In the Love Campaign

This is a one-week "campaign" where you put all of your reservations aside and do everything you can to connect with your child. You initiate games you know she loves. You cook her favorite foods. You invite her to be your special helper. You give her lots of eye contact, smiles, and hugs of appreciation. You laugh at her jokes. You happily go along when she initiates play. You look at pictures together from when she was a baby and *ooh* and *aah* at how cute she was. You pour love into her in every way you can think of, re-discovering how you used to enjoy this little person. You put your phone on Do Not Disturb and put it into a drawer, out of sight. You stop doing things by rote, and put attention and appreciation into your interactions.

When your daughter misbehaves during this week (even when you're sure she's done it "on purpose"), you don't get mad, you get sad. And then, you actively assume the best. For example, when you're at the grocery store and you've just asked little Anya three times to keep her hands on the cart and she looks directly at you and bats several boxes of cereal onto the floor, repeat after me: *Don't get mad; get sad.* "Oh no, these poor boxes of cereal. I hope they're okay." You pick up the boxes, expressing relief that they're undamaged. Next, you actively assume the best of your child: "It seems like you're trying to tell me that you're ready to go. You don't have to knock the cereal down to tell me that, you can just say, 'I'm ready to go, Mom.' Let me give you a little hug and I'll put you in the cart so we can go get in line. I know that you are kind and helpful inside, even when you're having a hard time."

Many parents really struggle with the idea of *Pouring In the Love* when their child is acting so unlovable. Give a child a hug when she knocks merchandise off the shelves? They worry that it's rewarding bad behavior. They worry that it's unsustainable. They are already exhausted by their child, and worry that they don't have the energy for affection. They worry that their child will expect this to be the "new normal." But above all, parents resist it because *they don't feel like* giving their child a hug when they've asked her to keep her hands on the cart and she knocks boxes of cereal onto the floor. They don't feel connected with their child and they want to punish negative behaviors and get her to "straighten up."

These feelings are completely normal, but I want to take a moment to reassure you that the worries are largely unfounded. When our bodies get sick we stay home from work, in bed or close to it, take vitamin C, do steam inhalations, eat things that are easy on our digestive systems, and generally baby ourselves. When we do this, we don't worry that we'll never go to work again, or that we'll have to eat toast and chicken noodle soup for the rest of our lives. We know that when we take the time to really take care of our bodies when they're sick, we'll be able to get back on our feet and back to normal that much more quickly.

The same is true for our relationships with our young children. The relationship's immune system is strained, and we need to take extra care now, so that it can get back to normal. Your child won't grow up to think that negative behaviors are okay if you do a *Pouring In the Love Campaign* for a week, and then do the work necessary to get your relationship back into balance. In fact, children are much more likely to drop their negative behaviors when you use this technique than if you simply got more and more punitive without addressing the imbalance in the relationship. Remember, *authoritarian* (rather than authoritative) relationships are high in demandingness but low in warmth. That parenting technique has been shown in study after study to have less than optimal results.[6]

Pouring In the Love is different from merely expressing approval. Do you remember the five-year-old girl who was acting so unlovable since her little brother came, a year-and-a-half earlier? When I suggested *Pouring In the Love*, her mother protested that she was already trying it, saying, "We try to 'catch her being good' and always point it out when she interacts nicely with her younger brother." I noted that approval is quite different from enjoyment. Hearing "You're doing a good job" isn't enough for your child to feel, "Finally! This is what I've been longing for!" which is what we want our child to experience during this week-long campaign. True interest, real enjoyment, and pouring in the love do that.

If you can see the value of such a campaign, but still feel a lot of resistance, then try this technique to get yourself going: for the next four days, I want you to pretend that you're not the parent of this child. Rather, I want you to pretend that you're a favorite aunt or uncle coming to visit the household for a quick trip. You love these kids and you think they're just super-cute, and funny, and really the best. You don't need to worry about the long-term consequences of their behavior. When they do something slightly naughty, you know they're just being silly and clever. Although you bet these kids' parents have their hands full, you can just enjoy your time together.

Don't say, *"But this isn't sustainable."* Of course it's not! That's the advantage of favorite aunts and uncles: they come and enjoy the children, and then they go home again. You are becoming the favorite aunt in order to hit the reset button with your child—in order to make him feel loveable and enjoyable again. Children long to be enjoyed by the ones they love. We think, "Well, if he would just act enjoyable, then I'd be able to enjoy him more." Unfortunately, we can't put the onus on the child—we must be the ones to change first. When we enjoy our kids more, this allows them to become more enjoyable.

Step Two: Note What Happens and Respond Accordingly

When you do the *Pouring In the Love Campaign*, one of three things is likely to happen: 1. Your child's negative behavior magically melts away; 2. Your child's behavior gets even worse; or 3. Things improve briefly but then go back to how they were. Each of these scenarios is telling you something different, and each will require you to respond in a different way in order to get your relationship back into balance.

1. If the Negative Behavior Magically Melts Away

Sometimes when you do a *Pouring In the Love Campaign*, your child just lights up. He basks in your positive attention, and his negative attention-seeking behaviors decline dramatically. It may seem impossible to you that this could happen, but I've seen it happen many times, and experienced such results myself. If this occurs for you, good job! Your child was giving you a *Call for Affection* and, by pouring in the love, you have responded and he feels satisfied.

When the one-week campaign is done, depending on how out-of-balance your relationship had become, you may need to extend your campaign for a second week. This extension allows you to more fully infuse your child with goodness, to remind her—so she truly believes again—that she is enjoyable and lovable. When you get to the end of your campaign, depending on how long you've extended it, ramp down gradually, until you settle in at a "new normal." The "new normal" is when you and your child remember that you enjoy one another, with each of you responding quickly and positively to the other, even—and especially—when you don't do what they want. As you are tapering off the full campaign, put extra effort into making sure to incorporate as many elements of SMILE into your day as possible. This additional energy will be offset by a reduction in power struggles.

> *One of our toughest transitions has been getting my little guy into his bath at night. I'd been unsuccessfully trying by using this little game I invented, with a plastic fish to talk with him and lead him into the bath. This never worked and I realized it didn't feel connecting enough for him. This week, I've tried scooping him into my arms, snuggling him and playfully singing the oldie song* "Splish Splash, I Was Taking a Bath"... *I dance with him in my arms up the stairs and into the bathroom, and he is giggling and smiling the whole time. There really hasn't been any struggle with this since I started this new practice, and the key is to really connect with him and make it genuinely fun for **both** of us.*
>
> —Rebekah, mother of one

If you did a *Pouring In the Love Campaign* that worked wonders but completely exhausted you, perhaps because you also have a new baby and were tired to begin with, or because you have chronic health issues, then I want to give you a kind, warm hug and let you know that "this too shall pass." You and your child *will* find a new balance in your relationship, and any efforts will *not* always feel this hard. Keep working on connecting. As your relationship gets back into balance, you can start calling on your child for ideas to do things in ways that work for everyone (for example, you staying on the couch and narrating, while he pretends to be a monster truck running over his toys).

More serious problems in dealing with a *Call for Affection* can come up if we truly have trouble enjoying our children. If you struggle with anxiety or depression, had negative or unhealthy relationships with your own parents, or have an especially intense child, it can be harder to connect for more than moments at a time. These can all undermine that "magical bond" with your own children that so many people dream of when they're pregnant.

If one (or more) of these scenarios describes your situation, trust the possibility that things can shift, and know that, despite all the happy photos of other families you see on Facebook, you are not alone. In their research on attachment, Mary Ainsworth and John Bowlby found that, in most of their studies, only about two-thirds of the children met the criteria for being "securely attached." In other words, one out of three children had ambivalent, anxious or avoidant relationships with their mothers.[7] That's a lot of children! The good news is that subsequent studies found that the quality of attachment really depends on the actions of the adult, rather than on the child.[8] Rather than inspiring you to feel even more guilt, let that knowledge reassure you that changing your actions can truly transform the quality of your relationship, the way your child responds, and the way you feel. You just may need some extra help to get there.

Get the support that you need, whether it's from a medical doctor, a mental health professional, a support group, a parenting coach, or something else. A valuable book for people who have trouble connecting because of an absent or unhealthy relationship with their own parents is *Mothering Without a Map: The Search for the Good Mother Within* by Kathryn Black.

Even if you're feeling challenged in connecting with your children, don't underestimate the power of the *Pouring In the Love Campaign*. I had one little girl in my toddler class who had been abandoned by her mother and suffered significant difficulties connecting with others. Although she exhibited many challenging behaviors, these would lessen and I would "magically" gain more patience when I did a *Pouring In the Love Campaign*. The effects of the campaign would linger for a month or so, and then start deteriorating again. Soon, I would find myself being annoyed more strongly by normal toddler behaviors when *she* did them, compared to any other child, and I would realize that it was time for another campaign. I would pour in the love for a week, and this little girl's face would light up again. These regular, periodic campaigns not only made it possible for her to stay in my class, they made it possible for me to love that little girl.

2. If the Negative Behavior Gets Even Worse

Perhaps you do the *Pouring In the Love Campaign* and, far from magically melting the negative behavior away, it seems like your child just "ups the ante" and becomes even more demanding and inflexible. You open the door, but she has a meltdown because *she* wanted to open the door. You give her what she has demanded, but she still throws a fit. If this happens, most likely your child is sending out a *Call for Boundaries*. The solution, unfortunately, is *not* to close the door again and let her open it, or to offer her more options until she's happy. Instead, what will serve your child is to teach her how to put her own desires "on hold" when appropriate, to recover from disappointment, and to respond to your requests even when she doesn't feel like it. These skills are vital components of a mutually responsive relationship, and while some children pick them up seemingly by osmosis, other children need to be taught explicitly by their loving adults, and still others need to practice these skills over and over before making them their own.

Perhaps the trickiest aspect of setting clear boundaries and dealing with the child's inevitable pushback and disappointment is learning how to do all this while still maintaining our warmth and connection. Remember, authoritative parents have high demandingness *and* high warmth. In Chapter 6, I will share some ways to manage your own anger and annoyance and maintain warmth in the moment, but if a pattern of permissive parenting has become strongly entrenched, you may need to change the way you think in order to support your children to learn to put their own desires on hold because you've asked them to. Parents who have fallen into the permissive end of the parenting spectrum can feel so connected to their children that they're pained to see their kids experiencing negative emotions. They might then explode with annoyance, or find they can be firm only if they withdraw their warmth, but this is not what the mutually responsive relationship is about. Children need us to be loving authorities, where we guide, correct, and help them with warmth and compassion. This is often easier to do with children we have some distance from, as we don't need to take their behaviors personally. Partly, this is why children often behave better for teachers: good teachers don't take children's behavior personally, and are able to maintain that calm, loving firmness. But, parents can develop that too! It can start with a clear picture of what's going on as children discover their individuality.

3. If Things Improve Briefly, Then Go Back to How They Were

Sometimes, when we *Pour In the Love,* things improve a little bit, but not much. Perhaps interactions occasionally go more smoothly, or perhaps they go better when we're just hanging out with our child but as soon as we actually ask her to do something, our interactions seem to go sour again no matter how much effort we put in. It may be that she is really putting out a *Call for Consistency* or a *Call to Slow Down*, as a result of too much chaos, uncertainty, or overwhelm/overscheduling in her life. This child is begging for life to be slower, more spacious, and more regular.

If you didn't grow up with consistency, it can be really difficult to do, and equally difficult to *want* to do. We tell ourselves that consistency feels so limiting, so constricting. If you had asked me, before I started working in early childhood education, how I would feel about doing the same things, at the same time, in the same way, five days per week, I would have had very negative things to say. But, when I actually started working with children, and when our toddler class gradually settled from chaos into rhythm, something amazing happened: I discovered that the solid structure of the day actually gave us freedom. When everyone knew exactly how things were going to go, I could stop focusing on getting the children to do what I wanted, and I could start focusing on the children themselves: if they could do something new; if they were being funny; or the quality of our love and affection for one another. Increasing my consistency allowed me to stop concentrating on the *what* and start focusing on the *how*. When the *how* was set as well, I could focus on the *who*—on our relationship.

Consistency and slowing down go hand in hand, but they're not the same. We will dive into the nitty gritty of how and why to slow down in the next Section, and look at the nuts and bolts of setting up a daily rhythm that's nurturing to children. A wonderful resource for learning to help limit the "load" that we place on children through inconsistency, overscheduling, too much adult information, and an overwhelming environment, is the book *Simplicity Parenting: Using the Extraordinary Power of Less to Raise Calmer, Happier, and More Secure Kids*, by Kim John Payne.

MELTDOWN PREVENTION AND RECOVERY SKILLS

All children will have tantrums, meltdowns, and exhibit defiance, at times. A big part of dealing with these is by prevention, helping them learn the skills they need to cope better initially when they don't get what they want. We will end this chapter by addressing three skills that are most effective at doing that.

Skill 1: Help Them Put Their Own Desires on Hold When Appropriate

The main key to accomplishing this task successfully is to let your children know that sometimes they get to make the choices, and sometimes they don't. When I say "sometimes," that can mean in some situations: "You will get to choose what to wear at bedtime. At nap, you wear your clothes." "Sometimes" can also mean at *certain times* within a situation. This is a subtle move that can make your life much easier if you employ it regularly. Perhaps you've told your daughter that it's time to go upstairs, but she ignores you completely. You offer, "Would you like me to carry you up the stairs, or will you walk?" The ignoring continues, and you say, "Okay, I'll choose for you. Carrying it is." Then, halfway up she throws a fit and wants to go on her own. Rather than letting her down, breathing a sigh of relief that she is going along, you say, kindly, "I'm sorry, the time for choosing is done. Next time, you can choose to walk."

Use this phrase a few times, and you will discover that children become much more responsive when it's time to move on from a fun activity. Interestingly, research on adults shows that having a "time for choosing" is useful for us, too: people tend to be much happier with the decisions that they make when the decisions are non-reversible.[9]

Perhaps you've traditionally given your child the power of making the decisions in a certain situation that no longer feels good to you. For example, your son Andre will only buckle into his car seat while you stand outside the door and look away from him with the car door open. You have tolerated this for quite awhile; but now it's winter and you'd like to stop this crazy-making ritual. Rather than simply refusing to do what you've always done until now, it can be helpful if you let him know that the rules are going to change. Do this slightly before the anticipated event, at a time when you're both calm. You may want to repeat his options several times in advance: "Up till now you got to buckle your car seat by yourself while I stood outside the door, but from now on things are going to be different. You can buckle in while I get into the front seat, or I will buckle you in. You can cry if you need to, although you certainly don't have to!"

When we shift our position from being too permissive to being mutually responsive, we are changing the unspoken rules of the relationship. If your child is sending out a *Call for Boundaries*, the game has probably been that you try to convince your child, but ultimately he makes most of the decisions. When we change the rules of a relationship, children will often struggle to maintain the status quo, even though things don't feel good the way they have been. Be prepared; he may act out even more at the beginning, to see if you're serious about changing who's in charge. The more consistent you can be, the more quickly he will accept the new order, settling into more enjoyable behavior as your relationship comes into balance again.

Skill 2: Help Them Learn to Recover from Disappointment

One of the prime ways to maintain warmth while having high levels of demandingness is by feeling compassion when children are disappointed. This doesn't mean that you change your mind. It doesn't mean that you do everything you can to help them avoid feeling disappointed. It simply means that you feel compassionate when they're disappointed. When you announce to your daughter that she doesn't get to wear pajamas at naptime, or whatever else she's been calling the shots on that drives you crazy, she will likely be quite disappointed. When this happens, you can be compassionate without changing your mind. "Wow, you wish you could be the one to choose, don't you?"

Since she's not used to you limiting her choices, she may well even throw a full-blown tantrum, or have a complete meltdown, when you say this. Stay with her (unless that's working her up even more), and stay compassionate. Let your children know through your calm, warm attitude that you're not scared of their big feelings. Actively think, "You're not used to the time for choices being done. You're just learning that sometimes you get to choose, and sometimes you don't. It's okay to be disappointed. I will protect you."

When we adults are able to stay calm, centered and sure of ourselves, most children will need to have only a few big tantrums—over not being able to choose—before they can start to relax into feeling safe. A surprising number of children don't have any tantrums at all. That is, as long as you stay consistent with your new rules. If you struggle with consistency, put systems and reminders in place, gather resources and people to help provide consistency for you and your children.

Once your child is done with big tantrums (if they occur), he will still need to learn to recover from disappointment. We will consider this process in depth in Chapter 7, but in short, people recover from disappointment by choosing to focus on something else instead. When children are very young and very new at it, we do most of the "heavy lifting"—by choosing something else and directing their focus to it (aka, "distracting" them). Soon, we should get on the path of helping them do this for themselves.

Since your child may be used to making decisions all the time right now, learning to recover from disappointment may be a struggle in the beginning. Changing habits is hard, both for children and for us! Just remember that underlying message that she's longing to hear: "You are the child, and your job is to explore, grow and help. I am the parent, and my job is to guide, protect and love. You will not be in charge of everything yourself. I will help you find your way."

In working with these recovery ideas in my online class, one mother opened up about her changing relationship with her four-year-old daughter:

It's funny—after telling her that no, she needed to do what I say and that she's not in charge, she said, "But I want *to be in charge!" But I must say, since I have been working on being more firm along with connected, the discipline is going better—meaning, I seem to be getting less resistance. And overall, things just feel more harmonious. Is she feeling safer? I bet. It could also be that identifying what I need and then sticking to it/sticking up for mommy that I am contributing to the harmony, too.*

—Hailey, mother of one

Skill 3: Help Them Learn to Respond to Our Requests

Helping children respond to our requests is what the entire first section of this book is about, with the elements of SMILE and the Habit of *Yes*. But, when a relationship has fallen out of balance, then the elements of SMILE don't work consistently, and the Habit of *Yes* may be nowhere in sight. In getting a relationship back into balance, there may need to be more "helping" that is not particularly fun or connecting in the moment. In this helping, then, we need to retain our compassion, and continue pouring in the love as much as we can during non-guiding moments. Whenever we increase our expectations, therefore, we must increase our affection at the same time. Our goal is to be a loving authority.

It is easy to think (either consciously or unconsciously) that young children could be responsive to us if they wanted to, but are choosing not to be. In reality, children long to have our approval. If they are not responsive to us, it could well be because:

- They have never learned how to do it
- They could respond with our support, but this support is inconsistent
- Our support has receded lately, perhaps because of a new sibling or other life change

Parents who feel uncomfortable setting boundaries, or who struggle with consistency, are often uncomfortable setting firm expectations and then doing what's needed to help their child *follow through*. Such follow through is exactly what their relationship needs, however, and what children are asking for with their outrageous behavior.

ENJOYING YOUR CHILD AGAIN

I mentioned before that our relationships can get out of balance in more than one way at a time. Ideally, children would love us to be affectionate *and* have high expectations *and* be super consistent *and* do everything in a slow, spacious manner without feeling rushed. But, only a rare parent can do all those things on a regular basis! Please be patient with yourself; it's okay to be human, and you need to be as kind with yourself as you are trying to be with your child. Certainly we work to improve ourselves, become better parents and better people. At the same time, we need to remember that growth is a process that takes time and effort, so the results are not likely to be linear.

Start with pouring in the love, and then address the first major issue that your child points out. That should give you enough breathing room to look at "tweaking" your habits to be increasingly supportive of your children's healthy development, and to start enjoying one another again. When we are responsive to our kids, *and* we expect and support them to be responsive to us in return, then the relationship is balanced, and, while not always easy, feels good.

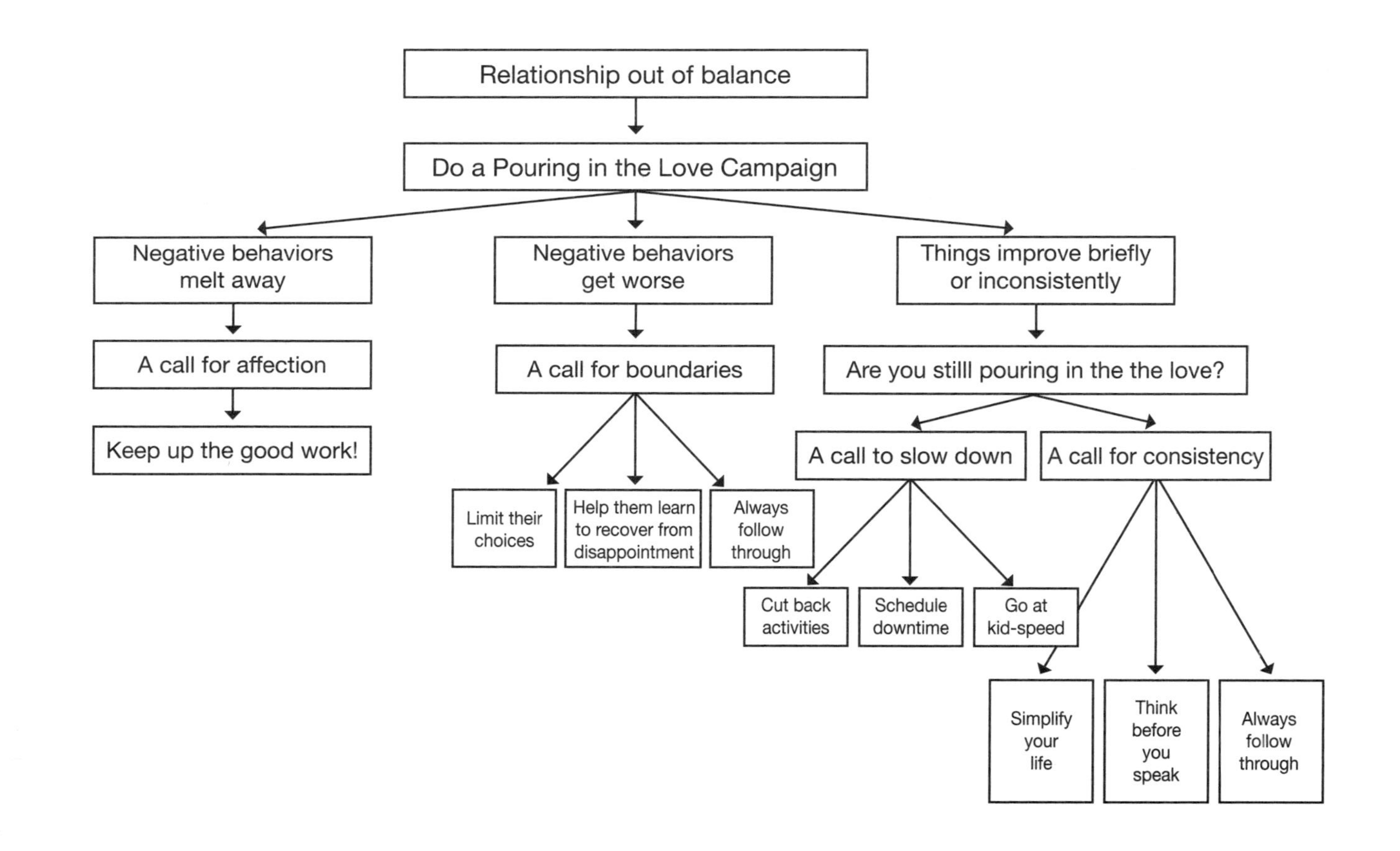
Relationship out of balance
Do a Pouring in the Love Campaign
Negative behaviors melt away
A call for affection
Keep up the good work!
Negative behaviors get worse
A call for boundaries
Limit their choices
Help them learn to recover from disappointment
Always follow through
Things improve briefly or inconsistently
Are you stilll pouring in the the love?
A call to slow down
Cut back activities
Schedule downtime
Go at kid-speed
A call for consistency
Simplify your life
Think before you speak
Always follow through

KEY POINTS

The Big Ideas in *Regular Tantrums, Meltdowns, and Defiance*

Regular tantrums and meltdowns are often a child trying to tell us that our relationship with them is **out of balance**.

Common Messages Our Children Try to Send, with Common Behaviors:*

1) A Call for Boundaries: often expressed through ridiculous demands and controlling behavior
2) A Call for Affection: often expressed through "attention-seeking" negative behavior, and sometimes through being mean if child feels unlovable
3) A Call for Consistency: often expressed by refusing to do things or trying to convince you to do something different.
4) A Call to Slow Down: often expressed through trouble with transitions

**Any of these behaviors can show up with any imbalance, especially trouble with transitions, and controlling behaviors. Also, children can send multiple* Calls *at the same time.*

How to Decode the Message:

Do a *Pouring In the Love Campaign* for one week, and see what happens.

Elements of a *Pouring In the Love Campaign*:

- Do everything you know your child will love
- Shower him with affection and loving gestures

- Be as fun and playful as possible
- Show him he's special to you in every way

If the behavior issues magically melt away: Your child was sending a Call for Affection. Keep up the good work, ramping down gradually to establish a "new normal" of mutual enjoyment. If you can't keep up the good work or have trouble expressing affection for your child, get help.

If the negative behavior gets even worse: Your child is sending a Call for Boundaries. Work on developing "high demandingness" while maintaining "high responsiveness." Help them learn prevention and recovery skills.

If things improve briefly, then go back to how they were: Your child is likely sending either a Call for Consistency or a Call to Slow Down. Work on setting up a life for your child that's slower, more spacious, and more regular.

Prevention and Recovery Skills

Help them to:

- Put their own desires on hold when appropriate
- Recover from disappointment
- Respond positively to your requests

Enjoying Your Children Again: Be patient with your child, and patient with yourself. Growth is a process that takes time and effort, and the results are never linear. But change is possible, and worth it.

ENDNOTES, CHAPTER 5

1 Sadeh, A., Gruber, R., & Raviv, A. (2003). The effects of sleep restriction and extension on school-age children: What a difference an hour makes. *Child Development*, *74*(2), 444-455.

2 Van Dongen, H. P., Maislin, G., Mullington, J. M., & Dinges, D. F. (2003). The cumulative cost of additional wakefulness: dose-response effects on neurobehavioral functions and sleep physiology from chronic sleep restriction and total sleep deprivation. *SLEEP*, *26*(2), 117-129.

3 Potegal, M., Kosorok, M. R., & Davidson, R. J. (2003). Temper tantrums in young children: 2. Tantrum duration and temporal organization. *Journal of Developmental & Behavioral Pediatrics*, *24*(3), 148-154.

4 Minuchin, P. (1971). Correlates of curiosity and exploratory behavior in preschool disadvantaged children. *Child Development*, 939-950.

5 Bronson, M. (2000). *Self-regulation in early childhood: Nature and nurture*. Guilford Press, p. 53.

6 For example, see Thompson, A., Hollis, C., & Richards, D. (2003). Authoritarian parenting attitudes as a risk for conduct problems. *European Child & Adolescent Psychiatry*, *12*(2), 84-91.

7 Ainsworth, M. D. S., & Bell, S. M. (1970). Attachment, exploration, and separation: Illustrated by the behavior of one-year-olds in a strange situation. *Child Development*, 49-67.

8 Goldsmith, H. H., & Alansky, J. A. (1987). Maternal and infant temperamental predictors of attachment: A meta-analytic review. *Journal of Consulting and Clinical Psychology*, *55*(6), 805-816.

9 Wilson, T. D., & Gilbert, D. T. (2005). Affective forecasting knowing what to want. *Current Directions in Psychological Science*, *14*(3), 131-134.

CHAPTER 6

Keeping Your Cool: Dealing with Frustration and Anger

This chapter looks at dealing with our own negative emotions in parenting. We start by examining how to manage annoyance and maintain high levels of warmth while enforcing expectations. The chapter goes on to look at deeper anger brought on by unresolved issues from our past, and fears about the future. Suggestions on how to side-step our emotional "baggage" are offered.

Every technique offered so far in this book has an enormous assumption built into it: that you're staying calm and composed as you respond to your children's actions. We know from research that children do best when adults act from a place of loving authority (high warmth, high demands), but frequently this is far more easily said than done. If staying calm is a challenge for you, rest assured that you're not alone in this struggle. Children bring out the best and the worst of all of us, and being a parent is difficult in ways people don't understand until they experience it.

Despite the fact that anger gets triggered so often in parenting, working to control our own behavior is vital if we want the best outcomes for our children. Yelling at children has real and lasting effects. In a study of middle-school students, parents shouting, cursing and using insults proved to have as lasting an impact as physical violence, and parental warmth at other times did not lessen the effects.[1] Even if we are not losing our temper to that extreme, anger tends to lead to inconsistency in our parenting responses, and we noted in the last chapter about how undermining our inconsistency can be.

Rahima Dancy, in *You Are Your Child's First Teacher,* offers an additional, very practical reason for learning to deal constructively with our negative feelings:

> *Because children are so imitative, we need to monitor our own emotions and actions when interacting with them, for our actions and emotions speak louder than our words.*[2]

Put another way, how we react when children do what we don't like teaches children how *they* should react when others do things *they* don't like. What we do when we get angry teaches children what *they* should do when *they* get angry. Seeing that young children learn through imitation, we must strive to be a person who is worth imitating.

Melinda, a mother in my coaching practice, had four rambunctious children, ages five and under. After working together for many months, she told me:

> *I had a terrible realization yesterday when my daughter wanted crackers and I said no. She threatened me! She said, "If you don't give me bunny crackers right now, I'll scream as loud as I can." I was so angry. I'm so sick of my kids fighting all the time, with me and with one another. They yell at each other, grab each other, and threaten one another all the time. For some reason, my daughter's threat about the crackers made me realize that the person they learned all of these from is me. How can I expect them to*

solve their differences kindly and politely if I'm constantly yelling, threatening, and dragging them around? I don't know how to change things, but I have to.

Once she realized how her own lack of control was affecting her entire home at all times (not just when she was actually yelling), this mother was able to make real changes in her parenting.

Responding kindly and consistently are key components in a mutually responsive relationship. If anger gets in the way of you providing those to your child, it's time to take a breath and develop some new skills. I will start this chapter by looking first at garden-variety annoyance, and go on to look at deeper anger.

MANAGING ANNOYANCE

When we ask a child to do something, and we've tried multiple ways to help them say *yes* without success, it is frustrating. When we move on to insisting they comply even though they don't want to, it can become downright unpleasant for all involved. We may *want* to have high demandingness and high warmth, but, it can be a serious challenge to stay warm when we're feeling annoyed (*This many tears over a jacket on a hook? Really?).* Conversely, when we keep our warmth and connection high, it can be a challenge to maintain our demandingness (*He's experiencing so much pain, and I could end it with a single word!*).

The key to keeping both warmth and demandingness high without letting one take over, is that we *must* keep a handle on our own emotions. This doesn't mean pretending they're not there, this means working on self-awareness to avoid setting traps for ourselves, recognizing and stepping back when we make mistakes, and repairing any damage done by angry or unkind words or actions.

1. Don't Wait Until You're Angry

Realizing that I can't wait until I'm at the end of my rope before setting firm boundaries has done wonders for my teaching and my parenting alike. If I wait until I've exhausted every effort and I have nothing left, then I end up angry, scaring the children or making them cry, and feeling bad about myself as well. Instead, I set that firm boundary as *soon* as that "I'm-starting-to-get-mad feeling" arises. I might say, "We can do this the fun way or the not-fun-way. Which will it be?" Then, if they can't manage to pull themselves together and choose the fun way, I can do whatever needs to be done firmly and compassionately, instead of firmly and angrily. This can make all the difference in the world! Having someone glare at you while you cry makes it much harder to get over being upset. On the other hand, having that person stand by compassionately makes it easier. If you know that your child is likely to be upset by something, don't avoid it as long as possible; set that boundary early so that you have a reservoir of patience.

Sometimes I'll *play* "getting mad." I'll pretend that I'm turning into a Big Mama Bear and I'll raise my arms and say, "I'm a Mama Bear and I'm angry! Come here, Baby Bear, or I'll *eat you up*!" The trick again is to do it right when you're starting to get annoyed, so that the anger is fun and not scary. I find that if I'm able to express my frustration in a way that's not overwhelming, it feels better than pretending that everything is fine when it's really not. Don't wait until you're actually angry.

2. Give Your Child a Bit of Space to Be Upset (without letting them get lost in their negative feelings)

Not being able to do as they wish is often *very* disappointing for children; this is part of why it's so important for me to move into the "helping" phase before I'm angry. I want to be as compassionate as possible about this obvious "bummer" for them—of having to do something they don't want to do. When we allow our feelings to become enmeshed with our children's feelings, so that we get unhappy when they're unhappy, or we get mad when they get mad, this puts the child in charge of maintaining emotional harmony in the relationship. When we can allow our children to have their own feelings without amplifying them with our own echoes, this allows children to recover from upset much more quickly.

I will often let children know that their big emotions won't rock the boat by giving them explicit permission to be upset. Shortly after my own daughter turned two, we took her in for a developmental assessment. She had started speaking, but then suddenly dropped all of her words except one. After a long morning of various tests, she was being examined by the pediatrician who needed to inspect the inside of her mouth. She refused, and the doctor asked if I would hold her while he forced the issue. I asked if I could have a moment to speak to her. I said, "Sophie, Dr. B needs to look in your mouth while you sit here on my lap. You can cry if you need to, but it's still going to happen. I will be here with you. Are you ready?" She looked up at me and tears welled up in her eyes, then she took a deep breath and opened her mouth for the doctor.

Unfortunately, giving permission for bad feelings doesn't always divert them. When we give a child permission to cry, then it must really be okay if that's the option they take. When this happens we can still help them do as we've asked, but we can do it from a place of warmth rather than steeling ourselves not to feel the child's distress.

3. Offer "Olive Branches" of Connection at Regular Intervals

When I'm compassionately-but-matter-of-factly helping children do what I've asked, I do my best not to disconnect and do things to them. In addition to keeping in touch with my warmth, I will send out an olive branch—a song, a game, a hug, a smile—every few moments. They can accept it, and we return to our fun, connecting way of doing things; or they can rebuff the olive branch and we continue on as before. I'm glad if they do the former, but I don't take it personally if they do the latter.

When children see that we are moving forward whether they throw a fit or not, they will often accept the olive branch and make the best of things more quickly.

If there was an interaction that went especially poorly, then the next time that situation arises I will put in some extra effort to make that activity fun or funny, or weave in appreciation. But, if that *no* is still there, I will remind them: "Even though you don't want to, it is time. Remember last time, when we had to do it the not-fun way? You can choose that again, but I'd rather sing a song!" Pretty soon the child realizes that when I say, "It's time," they will often move on to choose the fun way when I extend that olive branch; if not on the first offer, perhaps the second or third. Remember, don't wait until your patience is gone before moving into action, or you won't have the capacity to extend olive branches at all.

> *Also, to my surprise, just smiling helped (made me feel better too ;-)… on two occasions a smile got my three-year-old to soften her no, and give in. When it didn't work to get her to let go of her one-year-old brother's toys at the park, I became an airplane looking to deliver the toys to him (thinking of bunnies, airplanes and mice). It made no sense really, but I was so tired it was the only thing that came to mind. It worked!*
>
> —Hope, mother of two

4. Make Sure to Restore Your Connection If Your Help Is Not Well Received

Sometimes, no matter how many olive branches of connection you extend, that hard *no* remains. You may be helping your child hand-over-hand...or perhaps you're carrying her kicking and screaming...or, you're trying to maintain as much compassion as you can, making your actions as matter-of-fact as possible, but the reality is that you've just stuffed your daughter into her pajamas, and it was quite unpleasant for everyone involved. What now?

When we've gotten into a full-on power struggle with our children, especially if we were not as good at maintaining our composure as we might have wished, it is important to take a moment to restore our connection. If things were only somewhat bad, you might start with a little E (Exaggeration). "Whew! I'm *so* glad *that's* done. Oh my gosh." You collapse into a chair and look for a giggle. If the connection is not quite there yet, you think of SMILE and grab a teddy bear. "You know who else hates getting jammies on? Teddy." You make Teddy dance around, saying in a falsetto voice, "I hate putting jammies on! No, no, no!" You look at your daughter and ask conspiratorially, "Should we make Teddy get his jammies on?" She nods gleefully, or she shakes her head and grabs Teddy to give him a reassuring hug. You play along either way. Connection is soon restored, and you can go on with your bedtime rituals.

Other times, the connection is damaged a little more. If you've just forced your daughter into her pajamas and now she's having a complete meltdown, she is likely to need L (Love) with rocking and snuggles until she calms down. If she's in a full tantrum, she may need a few moments before she can even accept an overture from you. Despite this seeming rejection, know that she still needs your love, affection and support, now more than ever.

After connection is restored, I might lightly bring up, "Wow, you sure cried a lot when it was time to get jammies on. I wonder how we could make it more fun next time." Children are often better at coming up with solutions than we give them credit for. However, making a child promise not to react a certain way is developmentally inappropriate and unlikely to work. This is a time for brainstorming, not exacting promises. This is also a time when I might offer her some tools: "If you feel like you need a break when you're getting jammies on, you can say, 'Let's take a break,' and I'll give you a snuggle or a hug." I also brainstorm on my own for ways to make the activity more connecting the following time; I might consider doing the activity at another time of day (jammies right after dinner), doing things in a different order (a small snack after jammies are put on), or abandoning it altogether for a while (let her sleep in her clothes for a week). I don't want a negative interaction to turn into a negative ritual.

5. Don't Let a Negative Interaction Turn into a Negative Ritual

Each additional time that we insist a child do a specific action and it goes poorly, it becomes increasingly difficult to maintain any sort of warmth. *Negative rituals* can easily result, where everyone knows exactly how things go, but those actions divide rather than connect us. Even when negative rituals have become deeply entrenched, though, putting in some of the elements of SMILE can shift things dramatically. Here's what one mom with three rambunctious kids did:

> *We were struggling with a really difficult transition in the evening, after bath, to wash teeth and get dressed to go to bed. That would become a big mess, where my children would jump up and down naked on their beds, screaming out in joy, while I am trying helplessly to get them to put on their pajamas. It usually ended up in me yelling at them, and sometimes even having to take one of them out to the other room to cool things down a bit. A really awful transition.*
>
> *I then decided to make some changes: I brought all their pajamas into the bathroom. Then, they have become seals who are swimming in the sea, and there is a dragon in the water (my older girl is really into dragons), so we just have to put on our magic power suits (the pajamas), and then we have to brush our teeth with a magic paste; we have to do it really, really quickly to be able to chase the dragon*

away... That just worked like a charm. We were all dressed up and ready for bed after ten minutes. When we got to their room, they immediately snuggled up in their beds and I started to read them a story. There was no jumping up and down naked anymore. No me shouting and yelling.

No anger.

They now ask to play this game a few times a day, but I tell them it's a game we play in the evening when we go to the bathroom. So, this was a huge relief.

—Natalia, mother of three

MANAGING OUR ANGER AND FEAR

If the suggestions above feel like putting a Band-Aid on a gushing wound, you are not alone. Many of us were on the receiving end of anger from our own parents, and even if we vowed "never to do that," when under stress we tend to revert to what we grew up with. Poor role models have lasting effects.

Another reason that children can spark big reactions in us is because we use the present to predict the future—inaccurately. When our children misbehave, we tend to take what's happening in the moment and expand it into an imaginary future where that problem is never solved. If little Antoine hits another child, we think, *Oh no, he's going to grow up to be a bully.* If Avery tells her friend, "If you don't give me that toy you're using, then I won't invite you to my birthday party," we think, *Oh no, she's going to grow up to be manipulative and domineering!"* When we see misbehavior as a prediction of our children's future selves, this generates fear, anxiety, and the conviction that we need to solve this *right now*, or else dire things will occur. This fear causes us to react in a big way to behaviors that, while needing to be corrected, are often completely age appropriate, and if someone else's child exhibited this behavior, we might hardly notice.

Such fear is based not on reality, but on a negative fantasy that we have made up, perhaps without even realizing it. We can't stop our brains from rolling out these imaginary futures. But just like the bogeymen from the closets of our childhoods, when we stop believing in them they lose power over us.

Perhaps the biggest reason children trigger anger, however, is because they will find any unresolved issues you have from your past, and they will point them out to you, again and again. Whether you rebelled against authority, had trouble speaking up for yourself, or were abandoned through no fault of your own, your children will discover your issues and they will activate them. They do not do this consciously, and they do not do it maliciously. Rather, it is the day-in, day-out nature of parent–child interactions that makes us likely to have *every type of interaction* with our children. When our children misbehave and we calmly and consistently correct them, they can drop the behavior and move on (they are just trying to learn how the world works). But, if they do something and they get a flash of emotion from us, then they are drawn to repeat that action, even if our response was negative. It's like accidentally scratching a mosquito bite, and suddenly it itches like crazy; you know that scratching will just make the itching worse, but you can't help it, you are drawn to it. Perhaps you even try to distract yourself, only to look down and find yourself scratching away. In a similar way, children can find themselves drawn to do actions that get flashes of emotions from us, even if they know that they will be punished.

If you're striving for a mutually responsive relationship, but anger keeps getting in your way of responding kindly and consistently, then it's time to develop some new tools for self-calming. I will briefly offer some tools that I've discovered in my years of working with children and parents, but please know that trying these is only a start. If your struggles with anger go beyond what these techniques can reach, I encourage you to seek help from a professional who specializes in this area. Your family is worth it, and so are you.

When You Start Getting Angry

Start Over

When you're interacting with your child and you slip beyond annoyance into anger, this is the crucial moment when things are still salvageable. If you suddenly notice yourself yelling, an easy way to change directions is simply to stop mid-sentence, take a deep breath and say, "Let's start over again." This can feel awkward the first few times you do it, but it can be surprisingly effective. When you find yourself yelling and your child is in tears or yelling back or running away, if you stop and say, "I don't want to yell. Let's start over again," then it's possible to turn on a dime and go from confrontation to connection in a moment. Perhaps your child will need a hug, a snuggle, or imagination to reconnect, and then you can go forward again on the same team. If your child rejects your offer of affection or imagination/humor, try getting them into movement instead. Running a "race," spinning around, even doing jumping jacks can completely change the energy and make children (and you) ready to start fresh. Do not underestimate the power of movement to connect with your child.

Model Anger Management

If you need a little more than just taking a deep a breath to calm down, one technique that appeals to me as a teacher is to model "what to do when you get upset" to your children. We know that children live what they see, so why not show them techniques for getting negative feelings under control? When I feel myself getting angry, I might say, out loud, "I'm feeling really frustrated. I'm going to get a drink of water to help calm me down." Then, I do it. The children have heard me announce my plan, and seen me do it. I come back a little more calm, and we can continue our interaction on a better note. Other things you could announce and do include:

- Going into another room
- Stepping outside
- Washing your face
- Taking several deep "yoga breaths"
- Stretching as high as you can
- Counting to ten
- Petting a dog or cat
- Asking for a hug
- Giving yourself a hug

Generally, anything works that involves getting more oxygen to our brains and/or creating a little space from our trigger. Verbalizing what we're doing to help ourselves regulate our own emotions is a powerful tool because when children see us using these tools, they can begin to use them as well. The problem is being transformed into a positive teaching moment.

Step Back into Spiritual Support

Another powerful tool for getting a handle on anger and overwhelm is to remember that we are not alone. I personally use the idea/image of a Goddess who supports me in my teaching and parenting. For you, another image may feel right: a Guardian Angel? The Mother Mary? Cosmic Energy? Group Consciousness? Something else?

Whatever supportive energy you choose, imagine it behind you, as something larger than you. I imagine an ancient Goddess about eight feet tall, who stands behind me with her arms down and palms toward me. When losing my patience and getting angry, I take a deep breath and then take a literal *step backward* into my "Goddess Space," into the arms of this loving image. She envelops me in her arms, and all of my anxiety can pour out and be absorbed by her loving presence. I know that am not alone, I am supported in my caregiving by the spiritual world. When I breathe in again, I am filled with clear vision. With this clear vision, I can look at the child in front of me and see more accurately what he or she needs in order to grow into his or her best self. Even if the newly-envisioned action is exactly what I was going to do before, when I come from this place of clear vision and support, I find that the children can settle into my loving authority in a different way.

The most challenging part of using this imagery is remembering to do it. I coached one childcare provider who searched for "ancient goddesses" on the Internet, and printed out half a dozen pictures to tape up around her classroom. One way I remind myself to do this in my teaching is by doing a brief mediation each morning, along with reciting a verse. I especially love this one by Herbert Hahn for remembering to step back into my Goddess Space:

Remember daily that we are continuing the work
of the spiritual world with the children.
We are the preparers of the path for these young souls
who wish to form their lives in these difficult times.
Remember that the spiritual world will always stand by us in this task.
This is the wellspring of strength which we so need.[3]

Recovering from Anger

When we lose control and act on our anger in ways that we're not proud of, we might be tempted to ignore what happened and continue on as if the breakdown never occurred. The better option is to acknowledge the incident and take the time to repair the hole our actions have created in our connection with our child. However, it's vital that we do these "repairs" in age-appropriate ways that feel reassuring to our children, rather than further indulging our own emotions by pouring out our feelings of guilt and remorse. Children need to know that they can depend on us—now more than ever.

The first step is to acknowledge what happened, and let them know that our angry outburst is over. This is best done very simply: "Wow, I was really mad, wasn't I? I'm learning to keep my temper just like you. I'm done being mad now."

Next, take the time to reconnect. Remember that children feel connected in different ways than adults do, and tailor your efforts to be the most connecting for your child. Reread Chapter 2 to refresh yourself on the elements of SMILE if you need some ideas.

Once your child is feeling connected again, then you can talk about what happened if it seems appropriate, with a focus on what could be done differently the next time. Make sure that this is an age-appropriate discussion. For example, in the case of a child running toward the road and not listening, you might say, "It's really important that you come away from the road when I call you." Then, switch from explaining into movement with a game that helps you and your child practice doing the type of thing that sparked the blow-up. You might propose: "Let's play shooting stars. When you shoot through the sky, you run as fast as you can. When I say 'Shooting Star!' then you stop and make a star shape with your body (*legs spread and arms raised up*). Come on!"

If your child was quite scared when you got angry, or brings it up again without prompting, you can provide some helpful imagery for him to make sense of what happened and feel safe. Suppose your three-year-old says, "You were mean." Instead of apologizing again, you might say, "Yes, I lost my temper, didn't I? I was like a mama bear who saw her bear cub running toward a beehive. I didn't want my baby bear to get hurt."

Figuring Out a Different Way

Once your child has a sense of completion and seems able to move on, your personal work is not yet finished. Talk with a spouse or a friend about what happened, why you got triggered, and what you could do differently the next time. Sometimes we lose our cool because we're not taking enough time for ourselves in some way: we need more sleep, more space for our own interests.

If self-care is not what's at play, then a common reason to get triggered is that we assign some sort of meaning to a child's action, and this meaning is usually attached to a fear about the future. Of course taking a break from parenting to deal with our issues in therapy would be nice, but children can't wait for us to become perfect. Luckily, there is a technique that I use with parents all the time that can help us side-step these reactions and change your patterns if you find yourself responding with anger to behaviors that should be merely annoying:

Side-Step Technique

Step one: When you have some time for reflection, start with the question, "What am I afraid of when he does that?" If you are enraged by your little boy using a disrespectful tone, you might respond, *I'm afraid that he'll grow up to be demeaning to his wife and kids, like my father was.*

Step two: Politely thank yourself for bringing up that fear, and decide to put it aside for now. Realize that this fear is a combination of issues from your past, and projecting them into an imaginary future.

Step three: Ask yourself, "What's another possibility?" *Well, I know that my kid is often kind and generous. And I think it's pretty normal for four-year-olds to "try out" different ways of interacting, right? It's certainly true that he* always *gets a response when he uses that tone, even if it's a negative one. Maybe he's doing it to get attention.* Okay, your new interpretation is that it's age appropriate and he's doing it to get attention. Remember, none of this means that it's appropriate to do nothing—you're still trying to guide your child and live from a mutually responsive relationship. Also, you don't have to be sure this new interpretation is correct, it just has be plausible, and useful as a new way of viewing his actions. You might even think of several plausible interpretations.

Step four: Ask yourself, "What could *I* do differently that would shift the energy of our interactions?" *Well, I guess I could respond differently when he uses that voice. Faith says that if he's trying to get attention it's probably because he needs attention, so I don't want to ignore him. But I don't want to pretend that it's fine for him to talk that way, either. Maybe I could try to respond with humor by being fake-horrified. Let's see...how would this work exactly? I could pretend that a bad imp is making him talk this way. I'll check behind his ears to see if the imp is hiding there. That would definitely change the energy around.*

Great—you have a plan!

You know from past interactions that it won't take long for your little boy to use "that tone" again, and sure enough, the next day you ask him to take his plate to the counter and he yells, "No. You do it!" you feel the familiar surge of anger. This time, however, you put the anger aside and you implement your new "Side Step" response (see the box). You say, "What?!? Where did that yucky voice come from? It can't be Aidan. Is there an imp hiding behind your ear and talking for you?" You go up and look behind his ear, tickling his neck while you do so. Aidan is shocked, surprised, and delighted. He dissolves into giggles. You say, "Oh, I got that little imp. Now why don't you try asking me again?" Aidan looks a little confused, so you prompt him: "You can say, 'Will you help take my plate today?'" Aidan repeats your words, with your exact intonation. You respond, "Sure, honey-bun. I'd be happy to help you today." Or perhaps you respond, "Well, I bet now that imp is gone, you're strong enough to carry it to the counter. Why don't you give it a try?" Just like that, the cycle has been broken.

Does this mean that Aidan will never use that tone again? Of course not. But now that you've seen that the "meaning" you've given to his disrespectful tone is really a fear/fantasy, you can more easily respond in different ways—if not with humor and affection, at least with equanimity. If you can be consistent with your loving authority, then he will be able to drop the behavior and move on. Realizing that much of our anger may stem from our own unresolved issues, and from fear of an imaginary future, makes it more feasible to respond differently and break negative patterns of behavior. We don't need to solve all of our issues (although that would be nice), we just need to side-step them.

Anger May Get Short-Term Results; Loving Authority Gets Lasting Results

Research shows that when parents get angry during a child's tantrums, the problems are more likely to continue over time. But, if parents are supportive and set clear limits, fewer behavioral problems occur.[4] Besides staying calm, staying positive is also important for parents. Emotions, especially negative ones, are contagious.[5] Remaining in contact with our own warmth makes our criticism or correction easier for others to take in. This isn't true just for toddlers, but for adults as well. In her book *Raising Happiness: 10 Simple Steps to More Joyful Kids and Happier Parents,* Christine Carter shares: "In one study, employees whose managers gave them negative feedback while still exhibiting warm feelings—their voices and expressions were compassionate and positive—came away feeling positive about the conversation."[6] Remember, having parents and caregivers who keep calm and stay friendly while still being firm makes a real and lasting difference for children.

SOME CLOSING THOUGHTS

When we don't parent like we imagined we would before we had children, we can easily fall into feelings of guilt. As a motivation for positive change, guilt might be useful, but usually it does little more than weigh us down—or whisper in our ear that perhaps we should be more permissive to make up for our shortcomings. I love this quote from *You Are Your Child's First Teacher:*

> *If we can see parenting as part of our own inner growth and development and see our children as unique individuals with their own personalities and lives to live, we will be less likely to fall into feelings of guilt. The problem with guilt, aside from being bad for your health, is that it takes you out of the present moment, which is where your child lives and where you need to see and act clearly right now.*[7]

Rudolf Steiner, Austrian philosopher and founder of Waldorf education, suggests that children and parents *choose* one another in the spiritual world before they are born. Sometimes, he claims, we choose people who challenge us because we have areas in which we need to grow. Once we appear on this earth, however, we forget those spiritual agreements. We can choose to grow in facing our challenges and developing ourselves, or we can choose to ignore or resist these invitations. This is the nature of free will.

Although I have no idea whether this might be a literal reality, I find this viewpoint a useful way to view parent–child relationships. The idea that our children have chosen us is a powerful one. The idea that *we need one another* to grow into our best possible selves is powerful as well. Change and growth are always possible, regardless of what has occurred up to this point.

KEY POINTS

The Big Ideas in *Keeping Your Cool*

If your anger gets in the way of responding kindly and consistently, it's time to develop some new tools for self-calming.

Controlling Annoyance

1) Set firm boundaries the moment you feel that flash of annoyance; don't wait until your patience is gone.
2) Let your child be upset if he needs to be, and stay calm/compassionate. Don't let your child's emotions control your emotions.
3) Offer "Olive Branches" of Connection at Regular Intervals.
4) Make Sure to Restore Your Connection if Your Help Is Not Well Received.
5) Don't let negative interactions turn into negative rituals.

Managing Our Anger and Fear

When children feel a flash of emotion from us, they feel compelled to return to that behavior even if they will be punished.

When you notice you're starting to get angry: announce that you'd like to start over. Show your children how to deal with negative emotions. "I'm getting angry. I think I'll get a drink of water/step outside/pet the dog/do some stretches/ask for a hug/give myself a hug."

Recovering from anger: let your child know that you're done being mad. Take some time to reconnect. Practice ways to do things differently, through play.

Side-Stepping anger: Many times our anger stems from baggage from the past, and fear of an imaginary future where these behavior issues are never resolved. To deal with these:

1) Ask, "What am I afraid of when s/he does that?"
2) Thank yourself for that answer and set it aside
3) "What's another possible explanation?"
4) "What could *I* do differently that would shift the energy of our interactions?"

ENDNOTES, CHAPTER 6

[1] Wang, M. T., & Kenny, S. (2014). Longitudinal links between fathers' and mothers' harsh verbal discipline and adolescents' conduct problems and depressive symptoms. *Child Development, 85*(3), 908-923.

[2] Dancy, R. B. (2014). *You are your child's first teacher: What parents can do with and for their children from birth to age six.* Ten Speed Press (3rd ed.), p. 139.

[3] Adapted from quote attributed to Herbert Hahn: http://www.waldorflibrary.org/journals/15-gateways/63-autumn-1995-issue-29-birth-to-the-age-of-three-our-responsibility

[4] Denham, S. A., Workman, E., Cole, P. M., Weissbrod, C., Kendziora, K. T., & Zahn–Waxler, C. (2000). Prediction of externalizing behavior problems from early to middle childhood: The role of parental socialization and emotion expression. *Development and Psychopathology, 12*(01), 23-45.

[5] Waters, S. F., West, T. V., & Mendes, W. B. (2014). Stress contagion: Physiological covariation between mothers and infants. *Psychological Science, 25*(4), 934-942.

[6] Carter, C. (2010). *Raising happiness: 10 simple steps for more joyful kids and happier parents.* Ballantine Books, p. 24.

[7] Dancy, R. B. (2014), p. 22.

PART III

Raising Children You Enjoy Being Around

The Competence of Self-Regulation

CHAPTER 7

Your Polite and Patient Child

The very same skills that make children enjoyable to be around (manners, patience, not whining, and dealing with frustration) are also the skills that promote future successes in their schooling, relationships, and careers. By a wonderful coincidence, these skills increase children's levels of happiness almost immediately. This chapter looks at how we can support the development of those skills to increase our enjoyment of one another.

The second half of the chapter looks at how to support children who are especially intense or "too much" in some way. It introduces the idea of promoting a *Balancing Virtue* that will help your child's challenge become an asset. Suggested virtues include being kind, respectful, helpful and caring. Extra time is spent examining respectfulness.

Once we've addressed any major imbalances in our relationships with our children, it's time to increase our pleasure and enjoyment of one another so that we can truly begin creating a life that both we and our children love. After thirty-seven years of research in parent–child interactions from birth to age three, however, Burton L. White, Ph.D. wrote,

> *I have now concluded that helping a child acquire a high level of intelligence and language is surprisingly easy to*

> *do in most instances. On the other hand, helping a child to become socially effective and a pleasure to live with has turned out to be considerably more difficult.*[1]

Fortunately for us, Dr. White's long-term observations of thousands of families allowed him to see patterns of parenting behaviors that did lead to happy, well-adjusted children, and he wrote a book about it.

We all want our children to be happy, and we probably *wish* that they were enjoyable as well. But, it often feels like we have to choose between "happy" and "enjoyable," and that happiness almost always wins out. "As long as she's happy, I can put up with some amount of sassy/bossy/whiny/needy behavior," we think. "It's my job to take care of her, and I just want her to be happy." This thinking, while common, goes against what the research tells us.

Dr. White discovered that the children who were the happiest were those who spent the least amount of time being unhappy. Makes sense, right? While you might assume that children just come into this world happy...or not very happy...that's only partially true: current research shows that "happiness is better thought of as a collection of habits rather than a genetically endowed trait."[2]

Interestingly, the children who spent the least amount of time being unhappy in White's studies were *not* those whose parents did their best to make sure they were happy. Rather, the children who spent the least amount of time being unhappy were those who learned early *how to recover from disappointment.* And the children who learned early how to recover from disappointment were those whose parents held firm and consistent boundaries.

Throughout the previous chapters, I've promoted the idea of consistency, paired with high warmth and high demandingness (another word for firm boundaries), in order to improve our own enjoyment of our children. This "formula" improves our children's happiness as well, as Dr. White shares:

> *In these homes [of parents with enjoyable children], telling a child not to do something was ordinarily not repeated more than once, and the command was almost always followed up if the child resumed the forbidden behavior. Despite the real effort needed to follow through on such occasions, all of the successful parents we studied did so. In return, as the weeks went by, such parents had an easier time than most, and their children became happier than most.*[3]

When children learn early that "No means no," they spend less time whining, demanding, convincing, cajoling, and generally being unhappy. When these children hear a parent's decision on something, they can accept it and move on. White's observations—that parents' efforts to protect children from unhappiness can have the opposite effect—are backed up by studies on older children as well.[4]

This ability to move on from disappointment is a specific type of self-control that is referred to as *emotional regulation*. This type of competence is important not just for a child's (or anyone's) ability to move out of their own unhappiness in a specific situation, but promotes a host of other benefits as well. Children who master emotional regulation:

- Develop better friendships[5]
- Have fewer behavioral problems[6]
- Do better academically and have higher reading and math scores.[7/8]

Conversely, poor emotional regulation is related to:

- Lower social competence
- Lower peer acceptance
- Lower peer liking.[9]

And, the effects are lasting: when children with high levels of emotional regulation grow up, they are more likely to have effective work/life balance, good skills for stress management, and be less likely to deal with depression, anxiety, or aggression issues. Overall, they are likely to be happier and more satisfied in life.[10]

According to White's research, the optimal time to begin teaching children to recover from disappointment by setting firm boundaries is much, much earlier than most parents might think. His long-term observations with families showed that the way we interact with children when they first become mobile (between seven and twelve months) sets patterns that are likely to endure. During this time, he says, parents should let children know that they are part of a larger family unit, and that everyone's needs in the family are important. "During this time a child should be taught that although she is indeed special, she is no more so than anyone else, especially you."[11] At this early age, children can easily turn their attention to something else to recover from disappointment, which then becomes a skill that is used easily and naturally. The later they wait to learn that skill, the harder it becomes.

If you, like most other parents, didn't know about this "magic window" for setting positive patterns, don't lose hope. The process of learning to self-control or self-regulate is a gradual one that children learn over time.[12] In fact, learning to control one's level of arousal and express negative emotions in socially acceptable ways are skills that can be learned at any age, although it does get harder. Much better that we work on these skills with our children *now*, rather than leaving them to our children's future therapists!

SELF-REGULATION

Emotional regulation is one of three branches of the skill and study of self-regulation; the other two are *behavioral regulation* (impulse control; the ability to follow rules), and *attentional regulation*, which is the ability to stay focused and not get distracted by other interesting things. Abundant research exists on children's abilities to regulate themselves, because of its enormous and lasting consequences in almost every area of their lives: their friendships; their romantic relationships; their academic success; their career success; their physical health, and their levels of happiness and wellbeing.[13] Although I stated earlier that self-regulation can be learned at any age with enough desire, effort and support, research has shown that "the child's early human and physical environment has a major impact on the strength and direction of self-regulatory functions,"[14] and that a child's ability to regulate himself or herself at age four is generally indicative of how it's likely to be for the rest of his or her life.[15]

Babies start out with few tools to regulate themselves, and depend on their environment, their routines, and their loving adults to regulate almost every aspect for them. We, as caregivers, are responsible for monitoring and adjusting their body temperature, physical position, hunger, level of stimulation, and emotions. Newborns even have irregular heartbeats and breathing, which become more regular if held in skin-to-skin contact with an adult.[16] That's not to say that infants are totally helpless. Ainsworth and Bell, in 1972, talked about a "competent mother–infant pair" where the infant is competent with respect to securing what he or she needs by influencing the behavior of a responsive mother.[17] Babies are great at getting us to love and care for them!

As children grow, they gradually take over the ability to control more aspects of their physical bodies, their emotions, and their attention. However, toddlers in particular still depend on their relationships, their environment and their routines to help them regulate themselves. Gradually, when these interactions are regular and predictable, these neural pathways are strengthened and that regulation becomes internalized. From ages three to five, children are working hard on internalizing this ability to control themselves. While not fully developed yet, and still inconsistent—depending on whether they're tired, or hungry, or exposed to lots of new things going on—self-control is happening.

A child's regulation goes from being external to being internalized a bit at a time. Learning this, I was struck that, as parents and caregivers, *we are the external manifestation of a child's self-control.* That is why children need our help to follow through on tasks, to control their impulses to hit or grab, and to calm down when they're upset. As both a maturational and a learned skill, their ability to control themselves depends on our support. Gradually, through practice and repetition, they become more able to manage for themselves, and control shifts from external to internal.

Understanding that children depend on us for control is vital, but difficult to put into practice. Certain cultural beliefs tend to undermine their development of control—the belief that children should be encouraged to express themselves at all times, that they need their feelings validated, and that letting them be "in charge" when they are young will lead to strong, self-directed adults. These are cultural beliefs, but they tend to be misrepresentations of the research. Add to the mix that parents desire to avoid causing unhappiness in their children, and it's easy for loving, well-intentioned parents to slip into a *permissive* style of parenting.

About Katie

Katie is a vivacious, curious, active three-year-old girl, and her parents are kind and loving.

Nonetheless, they are not helping her learn to control her behavior, her attention, or her emotions. Their "be careful" and "don't do that" drone in the background as she drifts from activity to activity. Their desire to avoid unhappiness for her has resulted in an extremely permissive style of parenting. Katie shows up with regular tantrums, unreasonable demands, and an inability to move on from disappointment.

An Observation

Katie and Dad are sitting at a table in a breakfast nook, where Katie is eating a sandwich and Dad is drinking some juice. Katie takes a bite and then stands up on her chair.

Dad: Katie, sit down while you're eating, please.

Katie ignores him. She reaches out and pulls on the blinds, putting her hand through the slats and placing her palm flat on the window.

Mom: Kate, don't pull on those blinds.

Katie *(ignoring the command)*: It's cold!

Dad: Yes, the window is cold, isn't it?

Katie reaches out with the other hand and grabs a bite of sandwich (still standing). Nobody says anything. She loses her balance a little bit and pulls on the blinds.

Dad and Mom *at the same time*: Careful! Careful of the blinds!

Katie jumps down from her chair and runs around the living room for a minute, then goes back to the table and takes a bite from her sandwich, standing next to the table.

Mom: Katie, sit down if you want to eat.

Katie *(ignoring the command)*: I want strawberries.

Mom: You have to eat all of your sandwich first.

Katie: I want strawberries!

Dad: Well, you've eaten almost all of it. I think you can have some.

Dad goes to the fridge and gets her some strawberries.

Katie: I want three of them!

Deteriorating Impulse Control

Katie's parents are far from alone in letting their desire for her immediate happiness undermine her ability to control herself. Children today tend to have significantly lower levels of self-control than children in the past. In 2001, a group of researchers reproduced a study from the 1940s on impulse control, looking at children's abilities to stand still when asked to do so (I described this study way back in Chapter 2). In the 1940s, three-year-olds were not able to stand still very long, five-year-olds could stand still for a few minutes, and seven-year-olds could stand still as long as they were asked to. In the 2001 study, the seven-year-olds were barely able to stand still as long as the five-year-olds had been in the earlier studies, and the five-year-olds of 2001 performed like the three-year-olds of the past.[18]

In discussing these changes in children's impulse control over the decades, Christine Carter shares in her book *Raising Happiness: 10 Simple Steps for More Joyful Kids:*

> *These research findings are no small deal: the ability to self-regulate is an important key to success and happiness. Remember, preschoolers' ability to delay gratification... predicts intelligence, school success, and social skills in adolescence... In addition self-disciplined kids cope better with frustration and stress.*
>
> *...On the other hand, kids with poor ability to regulate themselves have more problems with things such as substance abuse, aggression and violence and are more likely to engage in risky sex.*[19]

The biggest factor in supporting children's development of self-control is being firm in our decisions as parents, and not letting children's upsets change our minds very often. We can also support them in being enjoyable to be around in numerous ways that also promote the internalization of self-control. We will examine some of these factors in the remainder of this chapter.

YOUR POLITE CHILD

Manners and Whining

I never knew how important manners were to me until I had a table full of one- and two-year-olds all yelling, "More! More!" as I went to get milk from the fridge. This behavior didn't sit well with me, so we practiced our *please*'s, *thank you*'s, and *you're welcome*'s for the next four months. When my mentor came to observe my classroom, she was charmed by my two-year-olds' "thanking" and "you're welcome-ing" one another left and right.

Manners are the lubricant of social interactions, and make a positive difference in our enjoyment of one another. We promote manners through modeling and repetition of these with our children. Do you say "please" and "thank you" *every time* you ask your child to do something, or ask someone else in your child's presence? I worked with one mother who said, slightly aghast, "But that would mean saying please probably a hundred times a day!" Yes, indeed.

Modeling is not quite enough, however; you must also expect *please*'s and *thank you*'s to come back to you from the child, cueing if necessary ("You can say, 'Thank you,'") and pausing to make space for him to respond. I don't demand that children say "Thank You," I just expect it and support it. If they can't or won't say it, I might say, "I can tell you're saying it in your head," or "I bet you'll be able to say it next time," or even, "I'll say it for you this time. 'Thank you, Miss Faith.'" (Or, in the case of my daughter, "Thank you, Mama.") Be aware of your manners in other areas, as well: say, "Excuse me," rather than "Watch out," for example. Work with the end in mind: what would you like your children to say? Are you modeling this and expecting/supporting it in return? One of the few times I was grateful for my daughter's speech issues was when a business colleague was over at my house and the two of them were petting the kitty together. My daughter looked up and said sweetly, "Her name is Damn Cat." My colleague smiled and nodded, not being able to hear her clearly. You can believe that my husband and I had a bit of a conversation about being worthy of imitation that evening!

Whining is sometimes a request for connection, but can also be a request for boundaries or consistency, or the fact that your child is tired. With so many possible reasons, whining can be a challenge to nip in the bud. When I encounter whining, the first thing I will try is repeating what the child has said in the way I *wish* they had said it. If little Annie is whining, "I want juice...I want juice..." I will stop, look right at her and say in an interested voice, "May I have some juice, please?" More often than not, Annie will respond by saying, "May I have some juice, please?" in the exact same tone of voice I used. I can then respond to her request and we can go on our merry way.

Sometimes, however, the whining returns almost immediately, and doesn't go away. Rule out physical reasons first—hunger, fatigue—and then think about the quality of your interactions. Children don't need our direct attention all the time, but they need direct, positive interactions from time to time in order to be able to drift away from us. We'll explore this more deeply in Part IV, but if you've only been giving just enough attention to get by, they may be asking for that direct attention (a request for connection). Play a game or be silly together, and see if that whininess disappears. If it works while you're providing full attention, but your child never seems satiated and able to go off on his or her own, the whining may actually be a request for boundaries or consistency: Burton White found that children whose parents did not provide firm, consistent boundaries often became very whiny toddlers.

If you get worn down by whining and "give in," or set limits but change your mind if your child gets upset enough, remember that "intermittent rewards" are what train your child to keep wearing away at you. Start working to make *No* mean *No*, then move on to helping your children learn to recover from disappointment, as I will describe below.

YOUR PATIENT CHILD

The Ability to Wait, Delayed Gratification, and Impulse Control

Perhaps the most famous study on self-regulation is referred to as "The Marshmallow Study."[20] In it, four-year-olds were told that they could have a marshmallow now, or if they could wait for fifteen minutes they could have two marshmallows. Then the children were left alone in a room with the marshmallow in plain sight on a table. The children who were able to wait the fifteen minutes went on to do better in school, have better relationships, and do better in their careers. Being able to delay gratification is an incredibly important skill.

Start small and help this "waiting muscle" grow in your child. It can be very helpful to give children some sort of cue to know when the wait will be over: for example, they come to know that you sing a song and when the song is over they'll get what they're waiting for. Or, if you're talking to another adult and your child wants your attention, hold your finger up while you're asking them to wait, then take it down when you're ready for them. Start small and help them build the capacity.

For activities or objects that require a longer wait, such as waiting for a toy to be free, or for dinner to be ready, help your child learn to do what the successful marshmallow-waiters did: find something else to do or focus on until the time is done. "Dinner's not quite ready yet. What should we do while we wait?" Make suggestions that include the elements of SMILE if they have trouble coming up with something on their own, or just begin a song, story, nursery rhyme, or activity. Once children learn the skill of consciously finding something else to do, their capacity for patience will skyrocket. If they've been waiting for a toy and found something else to do in the meantime, when I notice that the toy is available I will always point it out, even if they're playing happily with something else. I want them to know that waiting pays off. "Look, you waited and now it's your turn!"

Starting to do activities that have waiting built in is also useful: cooking and baking, gardening, or multi-stage arts and crafts projects can help children build patience.

In terms of impulse control, remember to talk in pictures: say how the object *can* be touched (Gently? With one finger? Or perhaps it's for eyes only?). How a child *can* go in the street (holding hands or being carried). Or perhaps redirect the child's curiosity to a different place. Burton White says, "Distraction redirects curiosity. Saying no discourages it."[21]

If you find that you are giving your child constant admonitions, then take a closer look at what's going on. Do you need to make changes to your environment so your child can explore more fully? Or, are you admonishing constantly because your child is ignoring you, like Katie at the beginning of this chapter? If that's the case, try talking less so your words count when you do speak.

YOUR RESILIENT CHILD

Recovering from Disappointment

The best ways we can help our children learn to recover from disappointment is to improve our consistency in boundary setting, so they know that getting more upset will not help their cause. When your answer always stands, then children can feel that stab of disappointment and move on.

Next, remember that it's okay for children to be unhappy sometimes. Indeed, how are they expected to learn to handle being upset if they are not even allowed to get upset? Allow the feelings, be empathetic, and then help them learn to move on.

If a child is distraught, she will need to lower her level of arousal before she can move on to something different. This can be challenging for a child who is just learning to manage her emotions, but we can help her learn to do it by giving her something different to focus on. Here are some ways that I help children accomplish this:

Get Moving

Anything that gets the blood flowing can help a child lower their level of arousal and find something else to focus on. Going into another room or stepping outside can help, or getting a special "something" that comes out only for upsets: a small doll or animal, a healing crystal, sniffing a bottle of rosemary oil (in through the nose and out through the mouth), all can become rituals that help children learn to calm themselves. My personal favorite, which I use with children all the time, is getting a drink of water. The act of getting a cup together, pouring the water, then regulating their breathing enough to take sips all help children stop focusing so much on their negative feelings. Then it is easier to go on to the next step.

Play Transference

A game that I use to help children recover from disappointment is to find a doll or stuffed animal and transfer the upset feelings to it. "You're crying because you wish you could go outside right now? You know who else is sad? Bunny. Here he is. 'Boo-hoo-hoo, boo-hoo-hoo, I want to go outside.'" I make the bunny cry against my leg. I speak to the toy in a pretend-lecturing voice, "Now Bunny, you know that it's almost dinner time and we can't go outside now." Bunny replies, "I don't care! Boo-hoo-hoo! I want to go outside *right now.*" I pick Bunny up to my shoulder. "Oh, poor Bunny! Let me give you a hug! Come here, sweet Bunny." I snuggle the Bunny and then watch to see what the upset child needs. Often tears have stopped by now and he is watching in fascination. Sometimes, I will send Bunny to him for more hugs, while other times I'll continue addressing Bunny's feelings, perhaps taking him to the window to look out, or suggesting that he find a book to look at. Sometimes Bunny becomes happy and silly, moving on quickly and jumping all around.

Say Yes to Their Desire

Finally, if a child is upset because they can't have or do something, I can say "yes" to the desire without saying yes in reality. I can do this by imagining out loud how great that thing would be, making the desire even bigger and more incredible (Exaggeration). I might say: "Yes, I wish we could go outside, too! I wish we could stay outside all day right now! Maybe we could even eat dinner outside! And sleep outside, on the deck! We could stay out there all day and all night. Wouldn't that be fun?" I'll continue with the imagination, inviting the child to contribute if he is verbal enough. A candy denied turns into hundreds of candies granted in imagination (rolling around in them, giving them to friends). A toy fire truck not bought at the store turns into a giant toy fire truck that we could ride around on, to all of his friends' houses, with a siren and real hoses that work. What else could that fire truck do? I want a fire truck that can fly! I'd ride it through the air with sirens blaring, and everyone would look up and wonder who was there. By saying *yes* to the desire and transforming it into an imaginary adventure, we can help children move on from their disappointment.

Once the level of emotional arousal is under control, then it's time to move on. When a child is young, or just learning to recover from disappointment, then I'll provide guidance, often making it a physical "moving on" rather than just an emotional one. "Come on, let's go set the table so we'll be ready when the timer goes off." As the child gains more capacity, I'll invite him or her to figure out what to do next.

YOUR PERSISTENT CHILD

Dealing with Frustration, Finishing Tasks, and Following Through

It can be hard to watch our children become frustrated, but the first thing we can do to help them develop the capacity to handle frustration is to keep our mouths shut. Let them work and struggle a bit on their own. If their emotional arousal is getting too high, then rather than jumping in to rescue them or even suggesting a solution, try encouraging them to ask for help: "If you'd like some help, you can say, 'Help, please.'" If they choose to say, "Help, please," then perhaps start by suggesting a smaller step that will help them move forward, rather than jumping in. Give as little help as needed so they can continue, while being generous with your attention. This is known as "scaffolding" in the early-childhood academic world: where you give small amounts of help to allow a child to do a bit more than they could do without you.

At times, children ask for "help" from an adult when what they really want is attention. When a child asks for help, give attention first and see if help is actually needed. Empower them to keep doing whatever it is, as you pay attention. Other times, however, especially if I'm in a time of being busy-but-available, I might simply say, "I'm working on dinner/sitting on the couch/eating my breakfast right now. I can help you when I'm done if you still need help." If this is disappointing, I might prompt, "What will you do while you wait?"

We normally want to "rescue" our kids from feeling bad, but children tend to interpret this differently than we intend, at almost all ages. Kids don't say, "Oh, my parent loves me and wants me to be happy"; instead, they think, "My parents don't think I can handle this." They tend to conclude either that there would be terrible consequences if they fail, or that they're not good enough to handle things.

Self-confidence and self-image become increasingly important in the preschool and kindergarten years. If a child believes, "I can't do that," or "I'm not like that," then likely they simply won't try. We can influence children's self-image by attributing positive traits as inherent, while explaining negative actions as circumstantial. For example, when Katara offers a toy to her little brother, you say, "He likes it! You're such a kind sister." A couple of hours later, however, she sees him approaching and screams, "No, go away!" and pushes him over. This time, you say, "Oh no! It's important to be gentle every time. You must be getting hungry / tired / need a little space)." You attribute her kind actions to her inherently kind nature, while attributing her unkind actions to the circumstances of being hungry or tired or overcrowded. Another phrase I'll use when a child just has problem after problem is, "You're having a hard time, aren't you?" This is usually followed fairly quickly by an offer for snuggles, herbal tea, or another way for me to support them so that they're better able to be the wonderful child that I know is in there...somewhere.

It's also important for us to let children of every age take on more age-appropriate "responsibilities" themselves, so they start to see themselves as competent. Be extremely careful of exaggerated or false praise, as children can sense it just like we can. Also, remember that even when children are capable of something, that doesn't mean that they will be able to do it consistently upon command. Sometimes they are able to, but other times they need our help to follow through. Be as consistent as possible, and give them as much or as little help as they need, each time. Children's abilities to follow through stem directly from our own ability to help them keep on task and on track.

Occasionally we want children to stick with tasks that are either frustrating or perhaps not enjoyable. In those cases, I'll sometimes wonder aloud, "How could we make this more fun?" I'll wait for a bit to see if any suggestions are forthcoming, and then I'll incorporate an element of SMILE: perhaps I'll use E (Exaggeration) and pretend like the task is even more arduous and boring than it really is. Or perhaps I'll pretend to do it wrong and that I need the child's guidance. Be wary of offering rewards: if you do so, remember that getting a reward lowers the intrinsic value of the action the reward is for.

The development of speech is unexpectedly critical for the development of children's self-control. The spoken word helps children remember how to do things, and can serve to encourage right behavior. Slowly, children become able to initiate or inhibit actions based purely on a caregiver's words, and eventually those words become "internal speech," which children use to talk themselves through situations and help them regulate their own behavior. Encourage this by using the same words and the same phrases each time you ask a child to do a similar action of self-control. Little is sweeter than seeing a child do something, begin to get frustrated, then take a breath and whisper to herself, "Try just a little harder."

BALANCING VIRTUES: WHEN YOUR CHILD IS "TOO MUCH"

All children come into this world with their own inherent temperament. The book *How Toddlers Thrive: What Parents Can Do Today to Plant the Seeds of Lifelong Success* describes temperament as "how a child reacts emotionally, how sensitive they are to noise or other distractions, how active they tend to be, how focused they can be, and how they approach new people or things."[22] What a child comes in with, however, is only half the story. And when I say half, I mean that literally: the studies on nature versus nurture (temperament versus life experiences), done with identical twins separated at birth, for example, show that genetics determine about half of what we become, while life experiences—including how a person is parented—account for about half as well.[23]

Many parents today want their children to be able to express themselves fully and be "true to themselves." If we encourage this too much as toddlers and preschoolers, however, we are giving undue weight to their temperament, since their life experiences are yet so limited. Instead of strengthening the parts of themselves that are already strong, think about what your child needs in order to become his or her "best self." Consider this quote of Goethe's, which I love:

> Treat people as if they were what they ought to be and you help them to become what they are capable of being.
>
> —Goethe

We all notice that sometimes we're more of our "highest selves" than at others. When we get enough sleep, when we're getting support and fun from our friends and spouses, and when we get enough time for ourselves, we are able to be much closer to our "best selves" with our children. Then, we roll with the punches, use humor and compassion to help our children through hard times, and enjoy ourselves and them.

Likewise, we've probably all noticed that children are sometimes much closer to *their* "best selves" than at other times. One of our tasks, as parents and caregivers, is to help children be their "best selves" as

My Insight into Balancing

This "balanced in strengths" idea struck me like a thunderbolt through an offhand comment by a friend. We were at an early childhood conference together, and between workshops we were eating lunch and talking about the sessions we had attended. She had a son who was six years old, very intelligent, very intense and somewhat overwhelming. Interested in everything, he always wanted to be the center of attention, and often dominated conversations. She said: "My workshop leader made an interesting comment. She works with a group called The Virtues Project,[24] *and she said that it sounds like my son has an excess of enthusiasm, which is a virtue. Instead of trying to dampen down his enthusiasm, I could work to strengthen other virtues that would balance him out. In this case, she suggested that I strengthen his sense of respectfulness."*

Knowing her son as I did, I was astounded. Yes! That was exactly what was needed! What an incredible way of viewing the situation. This idea has never left me, and I work with this view of balancing virtues all the time. A couple of years later I mentioned to that friend how instrumental that conversation had been, and she did not even remember having it.

often as possible. Naturally, we would be wise to set them up for success by making sure they get enough sleep, providing a strong daily rhythm, following through with support when they need help doing things, and being our own "best selves" as often as possible. But, another significant piece in helping children grow into their "best selves" involves helping them become more balanced in their strengths.

You can look at any behavior that is "too much" as a virtue that is calling out for a "balancing virtue." For example:

- A whiny child might need to strengthen her patience; with patience, a child who knows what she wants or needs can be a joy.
- A child who doesn't take direction might need to learn self-control, or respect; with respect, being strong-willed is a great strength.
- A child who cries a lot might need to learn resilience, or bravery; a resilient child who experiences things deeply is a blessing.

What virtue you should choose depends not only on the strength that a child already possesses, but on the child's temperament and personality as well. To help a child who is bossy, for example, you might encourage him to develop empathy, or respectfulness, or helpfulness, or even fairness. Think of which characteristic might really catch your child's imagination. For four-year-old Kieran, you might decide that helpfulness is what needs to be strengthened, and you decide that the image of being a knight who helps those who are weaker than he is would really excite him. With this as your focus, you work to develop that virtue of helpfulness in all areas of his life. The two of you might bake cookies to take to a nursing home; you might let him help his little brother dress to go outside; encourage him to assist you carrying in the groceries; and think ahead to what might help dad when he gets home, or his teacher at school. You can also tell stories about other people who go out of their way to be helpful, notice by speaking aloud when you see people being helpful, and generally work to make "knightly virtue" (or any other one) a value in your family. Your bossy son can grow into this image, putting his strong organizational skills to work helping those around him and becoming someone that everyone wants to have around.

What values do you want to promote in your family, and in your child? Why not write them out and put them where you can see them. Here are the ones that I live with in my work with young children:

> It's important to be kind to others.
> It's important to be respectful.
> It's important to be helpful.
> It's important to care for our space and our things.
> It's important to show love to those you love.

The best way to instill these values is to state them, to live them, to expect them from those around you, to enforce them and reinforce them. You are the parent, and it's important for you to help your child learn these and internalize them.

Toddlers copy words and behaviors, but preschoolers are beginning to form judgments and make decisions based on what they observe. They are developing a sense of right and wrong and of how things "ought" to be, and they're doing it largely based on the actions and attitudes of the adults in their lives. Therefore, we model the type of behaviors and values we wish to see, and use the words we wish to hear. It's also helpful to give expression to caring behaviors that we're strongly committed to, for example, "We always help people who are in trouble," or "It's important to give everyone a turn that wants one."

BEING RESPECTFUL

Respectfulness is a quality that many of the families I work with wish to promote but don't quite know how. Creating a home in which respect manifests involves working in two directions: with you and your partner showing respect with one another and with the children; and working with your child or children. I suggest starting with the basic mechanics of promoting manners: expect kind words, cue your children if necessary, and provide the space for your children to repeat these words. The tone of your voice is important too; children will imitate tone just as they imitate words.

In addition to simply learning the mechanics of respectfulness, we want to fire up our preschoolers' imaginations with the idea. Tell stories about respectful and non-respectful behavior; some of my favorites are carefully selected stories from the Brothers Grimm, "Mother Holle" and "Sweet Porridge." [§]

With a preschool or kindergarten-aged child, you could also engage imaginatively in the ideas of respectfulness through play. "Let's play that it's time to clean up your room and I'm the Mean Mom." Then pretend to yell: "You clean up this room right now! *Right now*!" Your son (or daughter) will probably start cracking up with laughter. Then you say, "Wait. That's not very respectful, is it? How about this?" Then take on a really whiny voice, "Come on… please?...please?...come on, clean your room. Okay?" You look at him. "Was *that* a kind and respectful way to ask? No?" Then stand up straight and say in a clear, kind voice: "Okay, I'm ready to say it kindly and respectfully. 'Jace, it's time to clean up your room. Shall we do it together, or would you like to do it all by yourself?'"

[§] I have changed the story of "Sweet Porridge" very slightly so that the correct phrase to make the magic pot stop cooking the porridge is "Please stop little pot, please stop." The mother forgets the "please" and makes increasingly ridiculous demands, eventually yelling at the pot, "Stop right now! Stop, stop, stop!" The children in my care *love* this part of the story.

If you would describe your child's behavior as "too much," look more deeply at the quality of "too much" that your child exhibits. Is he too loud? Too bossy? Too self-absorbed? Can you see how each of these qualities could be a strength if it were balanced with empathy, respect, keen powers of observation, or some other quality? This considered exploration will help you to more fully understand your child, and we know that people are more open to change when they feel that we truly understand them.

One way to work at balancing with respect is to point out when he uses his "too much" quality for good: "You used your voice to help everyone gather for dessert. Thank you!" "You were helping the children play in ways that everyone enjoyed." You can also let your child know, in gentle, slightly-playful ways, how negative manifestations of those qualities actually make you feel. "When you speak to me like that it makes me want to cross my arms and shut my eyes so I can't hear you." Then scrunch your eyes shut and hum a silly tune to pretend like you can't hear him. Crack an eye and then say, "Would you like to try asking again in a more respectful way?" Then give him the words and the tone if he needs some prompting. We don't need to be mean in order to be firm; we can use all of the elements of connection to make it easier for our child to develop a habit of respectful voice and actions.

The Moment I "Got It"

In observing families for my dissertation, I visited two families who on first glance were similar. Both had a two-and-a half-year-old boy, and both moms did many of the actions I had observed that set parents up for success: each mother successfully flowed together and apart with her son, letting him come in and out of her tasks, which she made inviting and fun. Both would take breaks for cuddles, snacks and play, then go back to their own activity or task.

At the end of the day, however, I left one visit feeling inspired, while after the other I felt exhausted and wrung out. The reason, of course, was the children themselves: one child was "enjoyable," and the other was not. Was it their temperaments? Perhaps to some extent. But both said no, both threw little fits, and both wanted to do things their own way. They were both typical almost-three-year-olds.

The more I thought about it, the more I realized how the mothers themselves where shaping their children. The mother of the "enjoyable" little boy would correct him when his tone turned rude. She would ask him to try again, and give guidance if needed. She reminded him to say "please" and "thank you," and waited for him to do it. The other mom did none of those things. Although she was kind and respectful in the ways that she *talked, she never seemed to expect him to be kind and respectful in return. He yelled and demanded and whined and she responded calmly and kindly as if it were perfectly normal, never correcting him or asking him to treat her differently. I realized that being kind and respectful is not enough: we must expect and teach our children to be kind and respectful in return. For us to create a life that we and our children can both love, in order to truly enjoy our time with our children, we need to have a mutually responsive relationship—something truly possible to create, no matter when you start.*

KEY POINTS

The Big Ideas in *Your Polite and Patient Child*

- The happiest children are those who have learned to recover from disappointment.
- Children can learn how to recover much younger than many people think (seven–twelve months of age) by parents setting consistent boundaries.
- Babies depend on their environment, their routines, and their caregivers to regulate them.
- As babies grow into children, their regulation gradually goes from being external to being internal.

Children depend on us:
We are the external manifestation of their self-control

Manners: Expect, practice, repeat.

Whining: Repeat what you wish they were saying, in the tone you wish they were using. Stop and really look and listen. Offer affection.

Waiting: Start small and grow the "waiting muscle." Give them ways of seeing when the wait will be done. Teach them to find things to do while they wait.

Delayed Gratification: Talk in pictures. Use positive language. Help them redirect their attention.

Recovering from Disappointment: Be more consistent. Don't be scared of their unhappiness. Help them lower their level of arousal: deep breaths, change of scenery, getting a drink of water, transferring upset feelings to a doll or stuffed animal, offering "yes" in an imagination game.

Dealing with Frustration: Don't jump in and rescue. Watch…then encourage them to ask for help. Start with encouragement. Then suggestions. Then give as little help as needed to tip the balance. Know that rescuing children too often lowers their self-esteem.

Staying On Task: "What can we do to make this more fun?" Incorporate elements of SMILE. Be consistent in helping them follow through with what you've asked. Use he same words and phrases each time you do a task.

When Your Child Is Too Much: If your child is too intense in some way, look for a balancing virtue: kindness, helpfulness, respectfulness, etc.

ENDNOTES, CHAPTER 7

1. White, B. L. (1995). *New first three years of life: Completely revised and updated.* Simon & Schuster, p 2.
2. Carter, C. (2010). *Raising happiness: 10 simple steps for more joyful kids and happier parents.* Ballantine Books, p. 7.
3. White, B. L. (1995), p. 267.
4. Seligman, M. E., Reivich, K., Jaycox, L., Gillham, J., & Kidman, A. D. (1995). *The optimistic child.* New York: Houghton Mifflin.
5. Contreras, J. M., Kerns, K. A., Weimer, B. L., Gentzler, A. L., & Tomich, P. L. (2000). Emotion regulation as a mediator of associations between mother–child attachment and peer relationships in middle childhood. *Journal of Family Psychology, 14*(1), 111.
6. Eisenberg, N., Valiente, C., Morris, A. S., Fabes, R. A., Cumberland, A., Reiser, M., ... & Losoya, S. (2003). Longitudinal relations among parental emotional expressivity, children's regulation, and quality of socioemotional functioning. *Developmental Psychology, 39*(1), 3.
7. Graziano, P. A., Reavis, R. D., Keane, S. P., & Calkins, S. D. (2007). The role of emotion regulation in children's early academic success. *Journal of School Psychology, 45*(1), 3-19.
8. Izard, C., Fine, S., Schultz, D., Mostow, A., Ackerman, B., & Youngstrom, E. (2001). Emotion knowledge as a predictor of social behavior and academic competence in children at risk. *Psychological Science, 12*(1), 18-23.
9. Eisenberg, N., Fabes, R. A., Bernzweig, J., Karbon, M., Poulin, R., & Hanish, L. (1993). The relations of emotionality and regulation to preschoolers' social skills and sociometric status. *Child Development, 64*(5), 1418-1438.
10. Liliana, B., & Nicoleta, T. M. (2014). Personality, family correlates and emotion regulation as wellbeing predictors. *Procedia-Social and Behavioral Sciences, 159*, 142-146.

[11] White, B. L. (1995), p. 263.

[12] Zimmerman, B. J., Boekarts, M., Pintrich, P. R., & Zeidner, M. (2000). A social cognitive perspective. *Handbook of self-regulation, 13.*

[13] For a good overview of the research, see Bronson, M. (2000). *Self-regulation in early childhood: Nature and nurture.* Guilford Press.

[14] Bronson, M. (2000), p. 168.

[15] Casey, B. J., Somerville, L. H., Gotlib, I. H., Ayduk, O., Franklin, N. T., Askren, M. K., ... & Glover, G. (2011). Behavioral and neural correlates of delay of gratification 40 years later. *Proceedings of the National Academy of Sciences, 108*(36), 14998-15003.

[16] For a review of many benefits babies receive from skin-to-skin contact, see: Moore, E. R., Anderson, G. C., & Bergman, N. (2007). Early skin-to-skin contact for mothers and their healthy newborn infants (Review). *Cochrane Database of Systematic Reviews, 3,* 1-63.

[17] Ainsworth, M. D. S., & Bell, S. M. (1972). Mother–infant interaction and the development of competence. *Grant Foundation, New York, N.Y.; Office of Child Development, (DHEW).*

[18] Carter C. (2010), pp. 119-120.

[19] Carter, C. (2010), p. 120.

[20] Mischel, W., & Gilligan, C. (1964). Delay of gratification, motivation for the prohibited gratification, and responses to temptation. *The Journal of Abnormal and Social Psychology, 69*(4), 411.

[21] White, B. L. (1995), p. 269.

[22] Klein, T. P. (2014). *How toddlers thrive: What parents can do today for children ages 2-5 to plant the seeds of lifelong success.* Simon & Schuster, p. 11.

[23] Polderman, T. J., Benyamin, B., De Leeuw, C. A., Sullivan, P. F., Van Bochoven, A., Visscher, P. M., & Posthuma, D. (2015). Meta-analysis of the heritability of human traits based on fifty years of twin studies. *Nature Genetics, 47*(7), 702-709.

[24] https://www.virtuesproject.com/

PART IV

Creating a Life That Meets Everyone's Needs

CHAPTER 8

Your Helpful, Confident Child

This chapter starts by looking at research showing some of the many benefits that people gain through helping others, and suggests that part of why helping may be so powerful is that it allows people to meet their needs for *contributing*, *competence* and *connection* all at once.

It goes on to suggest that a way to let children know that their help makes a real difference is to allow them to contribute to real tasks necessary for running the household (aka "housework"). We can create the time needed to do these at *kid-speed* by transforming them into enrichment activities and simplifying our schedules.

In the final section, we consider practical ways to set ourselves up for success as we invite children into our tasks: how to keep children engaged, and how to reconcile the results-oriented nature of housework and the process-oriented nature of young children.

Up to this point in the book, we've examined ways to help specific interactions go smoothly. We've explored how to head off big negative feelings from our children and in ourselves, and we've looked at how to promote strengths in our children. This chapter goes back to the universal needs outlined in Chapter 1, *connecting, competence,* and *contributing*. It covers ways to set up a life where opportunities to engage with each of these three needs are provided for us and for our children every day. When we can structure our days with these needs in mind, we can start to enjoy our time with children on a whole new level.

THE BENEFITS OF HELPING

A large body of research shows that people are healthier, happier and feel more fulfilled when they are able to contribute to the well-being of others: helping others reduces chances of dropping out of high-school,[1] contributes to job satisfaction,[2] can be effective treatment for depression,[3] reduces symptoms of post-traumatic stress disorder,[4] and increases longevity,[5,6] among other things. While people who are happier and healthier are more likely to help, the research is clear that helping actually *causes* people to become happier and healthier as well.[7]

Research on toddlers between fourteen and twenty months old shows that, given the opportunity, this age group overwhelmingly wants to help others.[8] By the time they enter kindergarten, however, some children have lost the desire to help, and from this time a child's level of helpfulness is likely to remain the same all the way through school.[9] This suggests that these toddler and preschool years are vitally important if we want our children to garner all of the benefits of helpfulness later in life.

HOW CAN TODDLERS ACTUALLY CONTRIBUTE?

Part of why helping is so powerful is that, in its best form, helping involves all three of the universal needs that this book focuses on: in helping someone we are using our *competence* in the service of others, and we are inviting *connection* through our generosity. In receiving a helping action, the recipient is able to respond with an especially deep type of connection: *appreciation*. When we appreciate someone for the difference they've made in our lives, and the person soaks in that appreciation, a level of connection is achieved that is much deeper than simple enjoyment. Humans are social beings, and to truly feel like we are contributing, we want to see how our actions make someone else's life better or easier.

We can provide opportunities for toddlers and preschool-aged children to help in tangible ways that use their skills and competence, nurture their generosity of spirit, and assure them that they're making a real difference. The sure path is right at our fingertips: by successfully involving them in the visible tasks of helping a household run smoothly and be beautiful (aka, housework or homemaking).

I understand why many parents are not especially interested in having their toddlers involved in actual housework: it takes twice as long (at least!), and tends to be done only half as well (at most). In an interesting study by Harriet Rheingold with eighteen-to-thirty month olds, despite the fact that *every single* child in the study spontaneously jumped in to help "with alacrity" when he or she saw an adult doing housework, the parents of these same children talked about how they tried only to do housework while their children were asleep, to avoid their children's "interference."[10]

We will go over, in detail, how to involve young children successfully without wanting to strangle yourself, but first I want to convince you that it's worth the effort. Don't just take my word for it...there's research here, too.

A wonderful husband/wife pair, Whiting and Whiting, did a long-term, cross-cultural study of young children in six different countries, of which the U.S. was one. They discovered that young children who were expected to do chores *that benefited others* at ages two and three (rather than chores that promoted independence, such as making their own beds) tended to show significantly more "pro-social" behaviors later, at age seven.[11] Pro-social behaviors include kindness, helpfulness, sharing, and cooperation, all qualities we hope our children will exhibit as they grow older.

Another study, done entirely in the United States, showed that children who were expected to help their parents at age two were less likely to have behavior issues at age five,[12] and a third study found preschoolers' levels of helpfulness towards friends correlated with the amount of household tasks in which they were involved.[13] Studies on children's involvement in housework at later ages have shown more mixed results: children who got paid for chores, or felt that their parents made up work for them, expressed low value for the tasks. However, in situations where children could clearly see the difference they were making in their parents' lives, such as farm families and urban single-parent homes, older children reported much higher satisfaction with their involvement.[14]

Taking part in household tasks is so beneficial because, first, it allows even very young children to gain real competence. Visitors to my childcare programs have often expressed amazement when they see one- and two-year-olds setting the table, clearing their dishes and scraping their bowls, wiping the table and sweeping the floors with me. Very young children are often capable of much more than we give them credit for; one of my favorite books on this subject is *The Cultural Nature of Human Development* by Barbara Rogoff. She has done a great deal of research (with photos!) on what different cultures believe is "normal" development for young children, and some of the cultures she studied have significantly higher expectations at younger ages than we are used to: e.g., when children can be expected to use sharp knives responsibly (by eighteen months in some places), light and handle fires (as young as age two), go on errands by themselves (by two and a half), or care for younger children (by age four in many cultures). She has a wonderful photo of an eleven-month-old child handling a machete as large as he is, under the supervision of his mother.

Second, allowing children to help enables us to interact with them in positive ways, over and above simply playing with them. Children benefit from not being the center of attention at every moment, but it's also difficult for them if they feel like they're being ignored. Working together toward a common goal permits us to be side by side and interacting positively in a different way.

Finally, even though it's more work to let children help, such shared effort is an important piece in establishing a *mutually responsive relationship*. In Part I we noted that responding to their need for connection helps them say *yes* to our requests. As we recognize children's desire to help (and make space for that to happen) we are being responsive to their needs, fostering their sense of "being a helpful person," and thereby encouraging their ability to be responsive to us when we ask for this in other areas of life, like when we re trying to get out the door in the morning.

HOUSEWORK: THE ULTIMATE ENRICHMENT ACTIVITY

Hopefully I've convinced you that it's worth the effort to involve your toddlers and pre-schoolers in your household tasks! The next steps involve the practical aspects of making this happen. How can we possibly find the time to do housework at *kid-speed*, when perhaps we already struggle just to keep up? And how can we make such work into an enjoyable, successful experience for children and adults alike?

The good news is that I have lots of experience with this, having gotten feedback from hundreds of parents in my classes who have tried these same techniques. The quotes sprinkled throughout this chapter are from those parents as they reported on their experiences. These parents discovered that when they changed their attitudes toward their goals for housework and the way they went about it, they were able to do housework at times during the day that had never been available for housework before. This allowed them to get more done around the house *and* have more time for other things they wanted to do. Let's look at how that can happen.

Many parents today work extremely hard to provide "enrichment activities" for their children. Enrichment activities can be valuable, serving two purposes. They provide opportunities, first, for children to practice skills necessary for healthy development (gaining competence); and second, for parent and child to spend "quality time" together, time where there is nothing on the agenda other than enjoying one another's company (connection). The problem with enrichment activities is that they are completely child-oriented, and they are huge time-suckers. We may end up feeling like we spend all day catering to our children, and when they finally go to sleep, then we have *everything* left to do to make our lives run. With no time for ourselves, no time for self-renewal, it's easy to get burnt-out.

The solution is to transform our household tasks *into* enrichment activities. Instead of setting up a "water table" where our children can play, they can help us wash the dishes. Instead of putting the square blocks into the square holes and the triangles into the triangular holes, children could gain similar sorting skills helping us unload the dishwasher, or match and fold the socks. Instead of setting up a "sensory experience" with Play-Doh, children could help us bake real bread or muffins. When we work successfully together, children can get the developmental support and the sense of connection that they need from us, and we can get our housework done at the same time. In fact, when we do necessary household tasks as enrichment activities, they are even *better* than many activities engendered by children's toys, because children know that they are truly contributing to the necessary work of the household.

> *I'm thrilled that I feel so much more relaxed throughout the day than I ever did before. And that, basically, I was able to get the same amount of work done even though I've slowed way down. I can't believe that I never thought of slowing down to enjoy my time with Sammi before. It seems like such good common sense.*
>
> —Diana, mother of one

With one necessary task, children are able to meet all three needs—connection, competence, contribution—at the same time! Even better, when we do housework *as* enrichment activities, then even if it takes us all day, the tasks are done. Once our children go to sleep, we don't have piles of laundry and dishes to do, because we did them with our children. Suddenly, we'll have some time for self-renewal, or to reconnect with our partner and friends. Suddenly, we've created time in our days where none existed before.

This great idea begs the question: why aren't more people doing it? The biggest reason is that enrichment activities are designed to be process-oriented, while housework is by nature results-oriented. Most of us try to get household tasks done as quickly as possible, and those of us who do like to linger over a certain task generally do so because we have a specific idea of how we like to do it, and exactly what the results should be. All this necessarily changes when we invite toddlers and preschoolers to participate. Instead of trying to reconcile the results-oriented nature of housework and the process-oriented nature of enrichment activities, most parents choose to separate them and only do housework when their children are asleep or otherwise occupied.

When we realize this inherent push-pull of process vs. results, we can work to reconcile the two in ways that recognize and honor both. If the two ever get out of balance, we can go back and see what needs to be tweaked: do we need to slow down and smell the roses a little more, or do we need to step up our expectations and really make sure that tasks are finished and done well? Truly, we can do both, even with children in the mix. When we balance process and results successfully, we strengthen our relationships and create more possibility to have time to ourselves.

One mom made me want to hug her and laugh at the same time when she shared: "It feels so nice to be with my children now, which I don't know that I could have said that a few weeks ago. I was so overwhelmed. And my kitchen is now always tidy, which is such a surprise!"

Imagine putting your child to bed and putting your feet up, because all of your housework is done.

HOW TO SET YOURSELF UP FOR SUCCESS

The suggestions I'm about to share on how to incorporate children successfully into our housework are drawn from three sources: my own experience involving children in household tasks; feedback from the parents in my online classes; and doing my dissertation on the subject of two- and three-year-olds' involvement in household tasks. My dissertation, called "Pitching In: Toddlers Helping with Household Tasks," was a combination of reviewing the research and observing in the homes of ten families. From all these sources I have learned a lot about what helps or hinders children's successful involvement in household chores.

> *I have found that my house has never been cleaner or less stressful. Maybe it's still me and this new mindset, but purposefully including my kids in everything, if they want to, is very freeing. I am no longer figuring out ways to keep them excluded from tasks. We are more of a team and I know they feel it as well.*
>
> —Marcella, mother of two

Cultivate a Sense of Spaciousness

This is *the* most important aspect of successfully incorporating your children into real household tasks. What I mean by "spaciousness" is the attitude or feeling that you have enough attention for your task *and* to interact with your children at the same time. You know that you have more than enough time to get things done, and to do them well. There's no rush. With a sense of spaciousness, you can be both process-oriented *and* results-oriented.

> *Honestly, the very idea of spaciousness has taken a lot of pressure off me. I actually did quite a bit in the house today without feeling like I was somehow failing in that department (which I always do). It's funny how much time I have spent meditating over the years, but haven't really applied the mindfulness principles to housekeeping, either alone or with my kids. But, this is going to be very good for us. Very Thich Nhat Hanh.* ☺
>
> —Shayna, mother of two

Most of the time, having a sense of spaciousness involves slowing down, but you don't necessarily have to be slow. You can be quick and spacious at the same time if you're still connecting with your child. Perhaps you and your three-year-old are "racing" to get the table set as quickly as you can. But, rather than just focusing on the task, you're hamming it up, making zooming sound-effects, with lots of eye contact and smiles, and a high-five followed by a hug when all done. You have enough attention for the task *and* your child. Even though you're rushing, it doesn't feel rushed, it feels fun! You have done the job with a sense of spaciousness.

> *So far, laundry and unloading the dishwasher in the morning have become our main tasks together. I know that Daniel is loving the fact that he is getting to contribute—he is so excited to do these things with me, and he does them really well! But I think that I am actually the one benefitting the most! Slowing down, really experiencing what we are doing, inviting my child to be with me in the experience of life are all tremendous values of mine that I've held for years. So, this is all bringing me into much greater alignment with how I'm wanting to live my life anyway!*
>
> —Monique, mother of one

1. Minimize the Wait

In the families I observed, the most common way for a parent to lose a child's involvement was to ask the child to wait while the parent rushed around, paying attention to other things. This happened most frequently while parents gathered supplies, ingredients, or tools needed for the task. For example, one mother invited her three-year-old daughter Natalie to help make zucchini muffins. Natalie was eager to help and pulled a chair up to the counter, pulling the squash out of a bag, while her mother gathered ingredients. Mom got upset to see Natalie reaching for a sharp knife, but then had no child-friendly knife to offer her instead. She asked her to wait. They finally found one and started chopping, but then the mother stopped everything again to have Natalie wash her hands. Then, they had to stop again for Mom to search for an apron when the daughter got flour on her shirt. Finally, Mom was ready to mix the batter, but her daughter had wandered off to do something more enjoyable and could not be enticed back.

When parents *set themselves up for success* by gathering everything they needed before inviting the children to join them in a task, things tended to go much more smoothly. Then, children can be in motion from beginning to end, without sudden starts and stops. Children almost always do better when they're in motion, able to go with the flow.

> *I thought about what you said about "setting yourself up for success" and I decided to wash the children's chairs after nap. I got a bowl full of warm, wet cloths and went to work wiping them down, humming a soft song as I did. One by one, the children came up and asked me if they could help, and I was able to hand them a cloth and continue with my work without stopping. The children enjoyed it so much that when we were done with the chairs they wiped the entire floor with their cloths. What a quiet and enjoyable afternoon!*
>
> —Anna, after-care teacher

Gathering your supplies doesn't mean you need to do it without your child being present, or without your children seeing you do it. In fact, gathering your supplies is a legitimate part of the activity itself, not just something that needs to happen before a child gets involved. You might gather everything you'll need spaciously while your child plays nearby, or, if your child is excited to get started, then you can involve him or her in the process. "Ah, we're making zucchini muffins. First, let's gather our supplies. What will we need? I can see the squash on the counter. Do you think we'll need some knives? A bowl? Some aprons? Let's collect everything we'll want." Other times your child will show no interest in participating, but be sure to think ahead about how you might incorporate him easily without having to go search for supplies, should your activity draw him over.

2. Lead with Actions Instead of Words

In my research, almost every single time an adult said, "Would you like to help me ______?" before they started their task, the child would say, "No." However, once the adult started doing the task in a spacious and inviting way, then the child would often want to participate. The biggest problem with parents asking and children saying *no* was that after hearing their children's refusal, parents tended either to abandon the project or to do their tasks as quickly as possible (either driving children away or causing them to whine and pull for attention).

Remember, young children live in the moment, and they either enjoy or don't enjoy what they are experiencing *right now*. If you would like to make a household task into an enrichment activity, then gather your supplies and let them get curious about what you're doing. Begin your task with a sense of spaciousness, and children will be right there.

> *I am finding that slowing down and approaching every single thing that I do as something that [my kids] are welcome to do with me has brought an enormous sense of inner calm and relaxation to me. It is like we are part of a team and it feels like the day is a lot more seamless.*
>
> —David, father of two

3. Make the Activity Fun and Inviting

Once you are ready to have children involved, you don't need to try to convince them to join you. Instead, make it so inviting that they just can't resist. SMILE: sing a little song, talk about what you're doing, use silly voices or funny movements. Pretend to be a robot. Imagine that you're Snow White in the Disney movie, singing happily while the woodland creatures come in to help you do the chores.

In my research, I observed that when adults used imagination, sang silly songs, and gave their children love during the tasks, then children stayed engaged and were able to take direction on how to do the task.

When we make the activity fun and inviting, then we may discover that we have a new problem on our hands: children throwing a fit when the task is finished—no more dishes to wash or clothes to fold or things to put away! If this happens, remember that what they're asking for is not really the task itself, but the connection and the fun. You can say *yes* to that desire by doing a new task, playing a new game, or singing a new song. You don't need to explain and convince, you can lead with actions and use the elements of SMILE to help them move on to the next thing.

> *I brought a pile of clean laundry and three baskets into the living room. My sixteen-month-old remained absorbed in another activity, but when I began singing, my four-year-old was drawn to me like a fly to butter. He helped me to sort into the kid's basket, Mommy's, and Daddy's. By the end, he wanted me to back off and let him match up the socks all by himself!*
>
> —Jubilee, mother of two

4. Use Imagery to Form and Correct Children's Behavior

While young children learn through imitation, they are almost completely process-oriented and not results-oriented. They easily get caught up in the fun of the movements they're doing, often to the detriment of your end goal. When they are splashing the dishwater, tossing laundry up in the air, or spreading flour all over the table, we can start to regret having invited children into our task to begin with.

We can honor the process-oriented nature of the young child while not losing sight of our end goals by using imagery to shape their behavior. Instead of "Stop splashing," you could try, "This little fishy [the sponge] needs to stay underwater in his home! He's looking for some yummy food to eat. Can he find any on these dishes?" Or, if you're giving your toddler an egg to crack into the bowl, and you're nervous about how it will go, you could create an image for her: "You can tap that egg so gently on the side of the bowl, like a baby bird that's tapping his way out of the shell. Like this: tap-tap-tap. Now you try, baby bird!" Make an image of what you want, rather than talking about what you don't want.

Of course, sometimes it's too late. In those cases, use imagery to create a picture for next time. "Oh no! That milk went everywhere! Next time you can pour slowly and carefully, just a drip-drop at a time." Then, on to the new task at hand: "Now, we'd better get our rags and wipe it up. Come on! We can polish the floor till it shines like the floor at Buckingham Palace." "What's Buckingham Palace?" "Oh, that's where the queen lives. Do you think if she came here, she would want to..." and on you go, handing your child a cloth.

> *The other day I was trying to pull my older daughter into folding the laundry with me. Of course, at first she didn't want to help, but then the clothes became all kinds of sea creatures, and each and every one of them had to get back to its special underwater home. I showed here where the sea cat (the towels) live, and where the little fish (underpants) live etc. That was the first time ever she helped me with the laundry! A big success. Thank you so much, Faith!*
>
> —Erica, mother of two

> *At first, he very carefully and purposefully crumpled the cloth napkin into a ball. But then I started singing: "Fold the corners, lay them flat, press them flat," and he loved it and was so focused. He folded about ten napkins and was so skilled and proud at the end. The singing was key for us. At first I started talking the instructions about folding. I could see him feel pressured and frustrated. But, putting the folding tips in a song made it fun and light for both of us.*
>
> —Shonda, mother of one

If coming up with imagery is a challenge for you, try using one of the other four elements of SMILE to shape your child's behavior.

5. Keep It Small

To avoid small hands unraveling large amounts of effort, do your work in small batches. For example, an adult working by herself would likely fold an entire basketful of laundry, and then put it all away. An adult folding a load of laundry with a toddler helping would be wise to fold a little bit with her child, then put the little bit away. Fold a little more, and then put it away. This way a rambunctious movement only causes a few moments of extra work, rather than forcing you to start over. Children love making "deliveries" and may soon be able to put things away for you as you stay and fold.

Similarly, when sweeping the floor, don't sweep the whole floor and then go get the dustpan. Instead, sweep a little and throw that little pile away. Sweep a little more, and throw that little pile away. Even very young children love holding the dustpan, and you can help them hold it steady as they walk to the trashcan, until they gain the skill to do it themselves. At the same time, this keeps it to only a small annoyance rather than a large one when your child grabs the broom and sweeps for himself, right through the middle of your pile.

Keeping things small also enables you to step away if another child needs you, or the doorbell rings, etc. When I wash dishes with a child and am suddenly needed somewhere else, I'll have my helper child sit down on their stool ("...just like you're glued tight to the seat") to await my return, or I'll have them come with me. I won't leave a child alone with a sink full of soapy water unless I feel confident in that child's ability to refrain from the joy of large splashes without my support.

Even very young children want to help, and often can do so if we give them a way. Elise, a home daycare provider, tried letting twelve-month-old Heather get involved with folding laundry, while the other children were napping. She reported surprise at how well things went.

> *Heather wanted to be near me and touch the clothes and towels. We quickly got into a game of me holding out both my hands towards her, looking at her in an expectant way and her handing me an item. I said, "Thank you," quickly folded it, set it aside and held my hands out again. She did this with me over and over again till the whole load was folded! This blew my mind! At twelve months old Heather wanted to participate and be contributing, a part of what I was doing!*
>
> —Elise, home-daycare provider

6. Let Your Children Come In and Out of the Task

I did almost one-hundred hours of observation for my dissertation, watching children and parents in their everyday lives. I watched for things that helped or hindered "helping interactions" from going smoothly. From the parent's end, three major conditions could trip things up. The first was to ask their child if he or she wanted to do a task, and then believe them when they said *no*. The second was to be unprepared for the child to join, asking the child to stop and wait while the adult rushed around. The third was to think that when a child left the task, that he or she no longer wanted to participate. In the families I observed, when a child wandered off some parents would suddenly speed up to finish more quickly. This would either cause the child to try to get away from the parent, or the child would come back and try to get the parent to stop their task and play instead. Tasks were then often left unfinished. On the other hand, if a child wandered away and the parent continued doing the task in a slow, child-friendly way, then the child would often play for a bit and come back and join in again. The task could be completed and done well.

7. Avoid the "Good Job" Trap

One of the reasons that we are involving young children in our household tasks is to allow them to feel connected and like they're making a real difference to the family; I talked briefly about the value of generosity and appreciation at the beginning of this chapter. However, appreciation can become a little trickier than one might expect. A lot of research correlates the importance of children's self-esteem on their later success. As a result, many parenting experts began to suggest searching for more and more reasons to praise children, in an effort to boost their self-esteem. Unfortunately, it soon became clear that praise alone does not necessarily boost self-esteem and, in many instances, can actually undermine or damage it. The research is quite clear that when children are praised for every little thing they do, they either become praise junkies, or you lose your credibility and they come to

> *I chose to have Noah (age three and a half) help me with dinner prep. I'm usually rushing around trying to get dinner together while the boys play all around me. I end up feeling guilty because I'm not giving him attention after I've barely seen him all day. Noah used to be a bit more interested in helping me in the kitchen, but I think I turned him off by being too results-oriented. He's been saying no every time I ask him to help me make dinner.*
>
> —Kala, mother of two

distrust praise coming from you, even when it is sincere.[15] (For an engaging article about the effects of different types of praise, search online for Po Bronson's article "How Not to Talk to Your Kids" in *The New York Times Magazine.*) Offering rewards for being helpful can be even worse: while rewards can induce cooperation in the immediate term, they can diminish pro-social behaviors overall, and these effects can be seen in children as young as twenty months of age.[16]

> *Tonight I approached it differently. I got all of my ingredients and materials out first, then invited him in by incorporating it into his play. He was a helicopter and I was the chef who prepared food for the helicopters. I said that I needed to teach someone new how to cook so that I could do another job.*
>
> —Mark, father of one

How then do we show our appreciation, if not with praise or rewards? Sincere praise can make a difference when a child feels that he has earned it, and true appreciation can be communicated with a simple "Thank you for your help," or even just eye contact with a

> *James was eager to join in this time (yay!) and I made sure to maintain an air of spaciousness during each task. First, we separated the beetroots from the leaves and stems, then we washed each part in cold water, wrapped the beets up to roast, chopped the leaves and stems, etc., etc. This all went well—he was losing interest while washing beet leaves so I said we were washing the leaves like people wash their clothes in a river and sang, "This is how we wash our clothes, wash our clothes, wash our clothes; this is how we wash our clothes, in the river cold." He seemed to enjoy it. He went back to his play for a while, then came back to help me with new tasks as I called him in. All in all, this went very smoothly and I felt so happy to spend lovely time with him while preparing dinner.*
>
> —Amy, mother of one

smile and a nod. But, rather than having judgment dispensed "from on high" (which is what praise is, if you think about it), the surest method that I've found to have a child puff out his or her chest with pride is to stand back and admire the work that we've done together, and done well. This lets the child know that his efforts truly contributed to something greater than himself, and that the two of us are a team. "Look at those gleaming countertops, and that stack of clean dishes! We had a lot to do, but we kept at it and every single dish is done."

OLIVER'S STORY

What follows is the transcript of one of the observations that I did for my dissertation. This particular family lived in London. Father worked full time and mother (I'll call her "Mum") worked outside the home four days each week. Friday was her day for cleaning, which she did with her little boy Oliver (not his real name), age two years, five months. And did they clean! They vacuumed, scrubbed, took the food out of the fridge and wiped down the shelves, and wiped the outsides of every cabinet, until the kitchen, the living room, and the bathroom were all spotless, the beds made and everything tidy. Oliver knew exactly how things went, and from the way he and Mum flowed through the day, clearly they did this every Friday.

Oliver, at just shy of two-and-a-half, was not a particularly easy or compliant child. He was a pretty average two-year-old, with his fair share of "No!" and "Me do that!" and a couple of meltdowns. Mum was spectacular. She worked with him when he wanted to be involved, she worked around him when he took breaks to play, and she redirected when he wanted to take over. When they all needed a break, they went out for a walk, then came home and cleaned some more. Here is a sample of just one of the interactions they had. Notice all of the elements of SMILE that she incorporates.

Setting the Scene

Lunch has ended and I duck out briefly. Upon returning, I pass Mum in the kitchen and find Oliver (twenty-nine months old) and his high chair outside on the wooden patio. It has been raining and the patio is wet, although it is not raining at the moment. Oliver is spraying the high chair with a spray bottle and swiping at it with a scrub brush; the spray is clearly much more interesting to him than the brush, however. A bowl of soapy water and a few scrub brushes sit on the patio next to him.

The Exchange

Mum (to Oliver): We'd better get your apron on!
(She steps inside to get a plastic apron and brings it out to him. He holds out his arms and she puts it over his head. He immediately goes back to his task of cleaning his chair; he sprays and swipes at it with the brush, then sprays again. Mum joins him and they clean together, Oliver mostly spraying and mum scrubbing.)

Mum: Look, I see some noodles! What a mess we have to clean up! *(Then)*

Mum: Who sits in this chair? Who made this mess?

Oliver (*proudly*): Me!

Mum (*pretending shock*): You? This is your chair?

Oliver: *(grins widely and continues to spray)*

(A little later)

Mum: Okay, one last spray and then it's time to do some scrubbing.
(He sprays again and Mum starts scrubbing in an exaggerated fashion.)

Mum: Get down to the real cleaning now. Use your muscles. Put your back into it, that's what they say! Scrub-a-dub. Scrub-a-dub. Scrub-a-dub-dub.
(She starts hamming it up, scrubbing really hard. He grabs a sponge and starts doing the same, scrubbing really hard.)

Mum: Oh, I think I see a noodle! And there's a bit of orange! Scrub-a-dub.
(They scrub together for a while.)

Mum: Oh, she's looking better. She's starting to sparkle! *Singing:* Scrub, scrub, scrub-a-dub!
(Later)

Mum: What about her ears? (*They scrub the top of the chair.*) What about her feet?

Oliver: Yeah. (*They scrub the chair's legs.*)

Oliver (*Quietly, to himself*): I'm washing her.
(He continues to scrub as Mum goes inside and puts on the radio to a classical music station. She comes back out, and he is still scrubbing.)

Mum: Is the sun trying to come out? I think it may be!
(She picks up a scrubber and starts singing a song about the sun as she joins him. They continue to wash together. After a while):

Mum: Is she ready for a rinse now?

Oliver: No.

Mum: Let's do our last scrubbing.
(They scrub for just a moment, then Mum begins to rinse. Oliver participates and does not complain. Mum picks up the chair brings it back inside. Goes back out.)

Mum: OK? It's been cleaned? Oliver nods.

Mum: Good news!
(Oliver falls over onto his bum.)

Oliver: I'm wet now.

Notice how almost every time Mum was ready to move on to the next thing (from spraying to scrubbing, from scrubbing to rinsing), Oliver didn't want to. But, she'd move on and make the next task enjoyable, and he'd move right along with her. Did you notice that she used all of the elements of SMILE? Singing (twice); Movement (scrubbing really hard); Imagination ("what about her ears?"); Love and appreciation ("she's starting to sparkle!"); Exaggeration and humor (the scrubbing again, and also, "Who made this mess? You?!?"). Impressive! She used all the elements to keep him on-task, and to keep things moving.

I can assure you that things didn't *always* go this smoothly for the two of them; for example, at another point in the day they were trying to vacuum (or "hoover" as they say in London), and Oliver kept coming in and trying to take over, grabbing at the wand and then waving it around and trying to bang it on the coffee table. Mum tried to redirect him, but he was having none of it. She ended up putting the vacuum away because "it was time for a snack." After the snack they cleaned in the kitchen, and later she pulled the vacuum out and hoovered while he played happily nearby.

THE POWER OF ROUTINES

The more regular we can make our schedules, and our household tasks within those schedules, the more accepted and expected those tasks become to children. If you always make your beds together after breakfast, and you always unload the dishwasher while preparing for lunch, and you always fold laundry when the children wake up from a nap or get up from rest-time, then this does two things:

- First, it allows children to gain competence. What is competence except knowing exactly when to do something, exactly how it goes? The more we do things the same way at the same time, the easier it is for children to gain that competence.
- Second, it lets children *know* they are contributing. They know without doubt that this task needs to be done; they've seen you do it many times before.

This regularity, of doing things in the same order each day, comes easily and naturally to some people, while it feels binding or constricting to others. Some people desperately *want* to incorporate routine, but didn't grow up this way and report feeling completely mystified in that domain. If establishing regularity doesn't come naturally to you, then start small.

To "start small," engage your child in a task that he has seen you do many times before. This allows him to know what's expected (even if he's never participated before), and to know that he is truly contributing.

If you've been saving the housework for when the children are asleep up till now, you might need to do the chore yourself several times before your child is interested in helping. Whatever task you choose, try to do the same task together at least three times over the course of the week, if you can. Three times will normally be enough to let you work out the kinks, and for the activity to feel like "something you do together." Then, choose another task to invite your children into.

IF A CHILD DOESN'T WANT TO HELP

Sometimes, no matter how spaciously you do things, or how inviting you are, your child just doesn't want to join in. That is fine! Doing our household tasks in a spacious, expansive way can also serve another purpose, allowing us to become "invisible" so our children can dive into their own deep, imaginative play. This type of play leads them to explore their own world and gain competence; in fact, play has been called "the work of early childhood." Everyone benefits when we encourage the development of independent play in our children.

We'll look more in depth in the next chapter about how to foster independent play, but I introduce the idea now because I want you to know you're not failing if you do your housework in a wonderfully spacious way and your children don't seem interested in being involved at all, or if they drift in and out of your tasks.

We've all experienced the times when we see our children playing happily, and we think to ourselves, "I'll just try to get such-and-such done while they play." We know that, as soon as a child senses us doing work, they are likely to come and interrupt us. So, we do our task as quickly as we can, to get as much done as possible before they notice and come back to pull at our attention. Right? What we may not realize in this type of attempt is that children are not pulling at us because we're doing work, they are pulling at us because we're rushing! I mentioned this in a previous chapter, but it's worth noting again: *Children cannot abide rushing, and they will do whatever it takes to get us to stop, even if that means leaving their play, or pitching a fit.*

When we are rushing, when we have lost that sense of spaciousness (that we have enough attention for our task and for children), then they feel the need to come and remind us that they're still there. On the other hand, when we can do our tasks in that spacious manner, when children know they can join in or not, as they choose, then they will be able to get on with their play. They might come and join us for a few minutes, getting a dose of connection as we incorporate them into our task in a connecting way, and then they'll wander off again, back into their play. You can do your tasks spaciously, and trust your children to know what they need: more space or more connection. As long as they're not pulling on you and pestering you to leave your task, you're not "doing it wrong."

If your child *is* pulling at you to leave your task, he's likely telling you that he needs a dose of connection. But rather than going off to join him in his play, you can weave that connection into your task and accomplish the same thing. If you're washing dishes, tell a story about a mama raccoon teaching her baby raccoon to wash its food. If you're sweeping the floor, tell a story about a squirrel trying to collect nuts on a windy day, and he can be the squirrel getting the "nuts" into his dustpan and depositing them safely into his winter hiding spot of the trash can. If your toddler is quite young, add sound effects and movement/touch, perhaps giving a gentle "boop" on her nose after each article is folded. When you bring humor and imagination into your task, children will be happy to do it with you, and feel connected with you.

If you try these techniques and they make a real difference in your life and you want to go deeper, I encourage you to take one of the online courses from LifeWays North America or consider taking their full LifeWays Early Childhood Certification Program. I took this training in 2006 and it literally changed my life, leading me to settle into my career in early childhood. The training is designed for parents and caregivers, and provides a model for parenting and mixed-age childcare based on the teachings of Rudolf Steiner, the creator of Waldorf education. LifeWays values using "real life" as the curriculum, and involving even very young children in household tasks is valued and encouraged. You can learn more about Lifeways North America and their classes at http://lifewaysnorthamerica.org/.

KEY POINTS

The Big Ideas in *Your Helpful, Confident Child*

Helping others has long-lasting benefits for both health and happiness.

The toddler and preschool years are a key time for establishing a child s level of helpfulness.

Involving children in **household tasks** lets them contribute in ways where they can see the differences they make. We can transform housework into enrichment activities that are inviting to children if we do them more slowly, allowing them to become both process-oriented and results-oriented at the same time.

Ways to Involve Children Successfully:

- Cultivate a *Sense of Spaciousness*: you have enough attention for your task *and* your child!
- Set yourself up for success before you start: gather everything you'll need to incorporate children successfully. Children can see you do this, just do it spaciously and let them help in the gathering if they wish.
- Lead with action instead of words: get started and *then* invite children in.

- Make the activity fun and inviting: use make-believe, songs, funny voices, and other elements of SMILE.
- Use imagery to form and correct children's behavior: paint a picture of how they can interact with what you're doing.
- Keep it small: don't have more out than you'd be upset if it got undone.
- Let your children come in and out of your task: keep doing it spaciously. Invite them in and make your task more interesting/connecting if they try to pull you away. Don't worry if they're not interested in being involved.
- Harness the power of routines: do certain tasks in the same way and/or at the same time of day to help your children become competent and settle into them.
- Enjoy yourself, the tasks, and your child or children!

ENDNOTES, CHAPTER 8

1 Moore, C.W., and Allan, J.P. (1996). The effects of volunteering on the young volunteer. *Journal of Primary Prevention, 17(2)*, 231-258.

2 Smith, T. W. (2007). Job Satisfaction in the United States (University of Chicago National Opinion Research Center). Retrieved 1st January, 2013 from http://www-news.uchicago.edu/releases/07/pdf/070417.jobs.pdf

3 Musick, M. A., and Wilson, J. (2002). Volunteering and depression: The role of psychological and social resources in different age groups. *Social Science and Medicine, 56*, 259-269.

4 Heirholzer, R. W. (2004). Improvements in PTSD patients who care for their grandchildren. *American Journal of Psychiatry, 161*, 176.

5 Brown, W. M., Consedine, N. S., & Magai, C. (2005). Altruism relates to health in an ethnically diverse sample of older adults. *Journal of Gerontology: PSYCHOLOGICAL SCIENCES, 60B (3)*, 143-152.

6 Luoh, M. C., & Herzog, A. R. (2002). Individual consequences of volunteer and paid work in old age: Health and mortality. *Health and Social Behavior, 43*, 490–509.

7 Post, S. G. (2005). Altruism, happiness, and health: It is good to be good. *International Journal of Behavioral Medicine, 12(2)*, 66-77.

[8] For examples of this, see:
Warneken, F. (2013). Young children proactively remedy unnoticed accidents. *Cognition, 126.* 101-108.
Dunfield, K., Kuhlmeier, V. A., O'Connell, L., & Kelley, E. (2011). Examining the diversity of prosocial behavior: Helping, sharing, and comforting in infancy. *Infancy, 16*(3), 227-247.
Svetlova, M., Nichol, S., & Brownell, C. A. (2010). Toddlers' prosocial behavior: From instrumental to empathic to altrusitic helping. *Child Development, 81(6),* 1814-1827.
Warneken, F., & Tomasello, M. (2007). Helping and cooperation at 14 months of age. *Infancy, 11(3),* 271-294. Rheingold, H. L. (1982). Little children's participation in the work of adults, a nascent prosocial behavior. *Child Development*, 114-125.

[9] Côté, S., Tremblay, R. E., Nagin, D., Zoccolillo, M., & Vitaro, F. (2002). The development of impulsivity, fearfulness, and helpfulness during childhood: Patterns of consistency and change in the trajectories of boys and girls. *Journal of Child Psychology and Psychiatry*, *43*(5), 609-618.

[10] Rheingold, H. L. (1982). Little children's participation in the work of adults, a nascent prosocial behavior. *Child Development*, 114-125.

[11] Whiting, B. B., & Whiting, J. W. (1975). *Children of six cultures: A psycho-cultural analysis.* Oxford, England: Harvard University Press.

[12] Kuczynski, L., & Kochanska, G. (1995). Function and content of maternal demands: Developmental significance of early demands for competent action. *Child Development*, *66*(3), 616-628.

[13] Rehberg, H. R., and Richman, C. L. (1989). Prosocial behaviour in preschool children: A look at the interaction of race, gender and family composition. *International Journal of Behavioral Development,* 12, 385-401.

[14] For a survey of studies on children and chores, see Goodnow, J. J. (1988). Children's household work: Its nature and functions. *Psychological Bulletin*, *103*(1), 5.

[15] Cited in: Bronson, P., & Merryman, A. (2011). *NurtureShock.* Random House, p. 20.

[16] Eisenberg, N., Fabes, R. A., & Spinrad, T. L. (2006). Prosocial development. In W. Damon & R. Lerner (Eds.) *Handbook of child psychology, vol. 3, social, emotional, and personality development,* 6th ed. (pp. 647-702). Hoboken, NJ: John Wiley & Sons.

CHAPTER 9
Promoting Independent Play

This chapter discusses the benefits to children of exploring the world without us, and entering a state of flow through self-directed play. It then explores ways to be present but "invisible" to allow children to develop the capacity for independent play. One of the easiest and most effective ways is to do the same household activities we've already discussed—but in a different way.

Other means to promote independent play—through the creation of welcoming play spaces, by turning off screens, by more time outdoors, and by letting children take age-appropriate risks—are suggested.

THE IMPORTANCE OF TIME ALONE

Like the last chapter, this chapter is also about letting children gain competence, but of a different kind—not the competence that comes from interacting with others or working as a team; rather, the competence that comes from children being comfortable with themselves, exploring the world and solving problems on their own. Such competence includes exploring what their bodies can do, a capacity that is changing monthly—or even weekly—for children at this age. It involves creating and sustaining their own play, using imagination and movement. Noticing and trying things they might not have noticed or tried had they been paying attention to someone else. This new exploration involves butting up against frustrations, and either coming up with a solution or deciding to do something else instead. This is competence and confidence that emerges from a child spending time acting only from motivations that come from within.

Most of us don't think about our very young children benefiting from having time alone. In fact, many parents I work with feel guilty for doing their own activities while their children are playing; they believe they should be actively promoting their children's development at all times, and worry whether ignoring them might be some form of mild neglect.

Far from being neglectful, I think it's important that we *not* be high-octane entertainment for our children all the time. Not only because we may wear ourselves out, and become desperate for breaks from our children, but also because children need time to explore the world without our constant commentary, even at very young ages. When we can successfully promote children's ability and desire for independent play, this also creates time and space in the day for us to re-charge and renew our energy, without having to be away from our children to do so.

In Denmark, time alone for children is valued highly; many homes and even daycare centers have a room or a space where they will post a sign saying "No Grown-Ups Allowed." These rooms are available not just for kindergarten-aged children, but for toddlers, too. In daycare centers!

Our attitudes toward children's explorations when they are very young are important for setting the tone for later exploration, play, and competence: studies show the importance of the caregiver's role in supporting autonomy and competence in young children,[1] and parents' and caregivers' responses to children's explorations at age one affected their levels of competence, and their willingness to explore, as preschoolers.[2]

Let's consider in more detail why independent play is so valuable for children.

Independent Play Increases Children's Ability to Focus Deeply and Have Longer Attention Spans

The capacity for sustained, focused attention is an ability that is extremely important for later academic success, but is also important for our children right now. A great deal has been written in the field of psychology on the value of *flow*, which is described as: *"a mental state of operation in which a person performing an activity is fully immersed in a feeling of energized focus, full involvement, and enjoyment in the process of the activity."*[3] While a state of flow is something that adults have to work hard to achieve, many young children are able to enter this state of *flow* quite easily—it is their birthright. However, they are often jolted out of flow by questions, praise or other interruptions from the outside ("Whatcha doin'?"), or because we adults are ready to move on to the next activity, meal, diaper change, or outing. By the time children enter kindergarten, many have lost this natural ability to enjoy themselves on their own, and instead expect to be entertained by outside sources. They have not outgrown their ability to experience *flow*, which can be achieved at all ages; rather, the capacity has not been valued and promoted, so it goes dormant.

We adults want children to be focused and not get sidetracked when we want them to do what we ask. But, how can we expect them to develop this ability if we also want them to drop whatever they're doing whenever *we're* ready for them to be done, or simply because we want to interact with them socially? Our culture doesn't expect young children to have long attention spans, and we tend not to value or cultivate this capacity...until we suddenly want them to do so on demand, when they start academic learning.

If we'd like children to be able to focus deeply on subjects that we choose, we would be wise to promote uninterrupted engagement in areas of the child's own choosing, as well. When we give children chunks of time in which we back off, and don't interrupt, this provides the space for them to enter *flow* more often and more deeply, not only laying a foundation for an academic future, but also enriching their lives now.

As nice as this concept is, we often *do* have to interrupt children: it's time to go to school, or dinner is ready, or you smell a poopy diaper. Despite these necessities, we can support flow in a few simple ways. First, pause and sense what your child is experiencing energetically before making a big announcement. If she is deep in her play, ask yourself if you could wait a moment to see if a natural break in concentration comes along. Often, children "come up for air," which can be a good time to step in and redirect. If that natural break doesn't come, and you can't wait, then think about how to bring her gently out of her play. Many parenting books suggest giving children warnings that their activity is coming to an end, but I have found that warnings are often counterproductive, leading to protests, frantic behavior, or children ignoring us completely.

Instead, step in and physically join your child "where she's at"—in her flow—and lead her back to the everyday world in a gentle way. Sit down next to her, and look at what she's looking at. Have a moment of conversation about her play before bringing up what you're doing or about to do. If you can, use imagination to continue the thread into the activity that you want her to move into: "It's time to trot those ponies back into their stables, because they need to eat their lunches, just like you do!" One study showed that parents who were able to coordinate their requests with a child's ongoing activity received less resistance and had greater levels of compliance.[4] This is hardly a surprise to many who spend their time with young children, but it can be easy to forget in the everyday life of parenting. Remember—if we want to promote deep play, we must value it and help children emerge gently when we do interrupt.

Independent Play Gives Children a Chance to Experience the World Without the Interpretive Filter of Our Commentary

We may not even realize that we're interpreting a child's experiences in life, but every time we talk about what a child is doing, or describe what's going on, we shape the child's perspective about what's important and how the world works. In fact, this is an important aspect of raising children, but it is done best if we can do it consciously, and judiciously. So much parenting advice encourages us to talk to children all the time. Not only is this exhausting, it also doesn't give children space to have their own experiences. Many times I've seen a child playing contentedly in a play-kitchen, or elsewhere, and watched an adult come up and say, "Oh, are you cooking some *soup*?" The child looks down, looks up at the adult, and nods. He may not have been cooking soup before, but he surely is now! That adult has directly and immediately changed this little boy's experience through her innocent comment. The new experience is not necessarily worse, but it is certainly different. There are times when engaging in our children's play is completely appropriate, but if we value independent play and want to promote it, then we should be aware of the effects our interpretive comments can have.

Our idea of what constitutes "play" is often different from a child's. Perhaps a child is sitting in the grass alone, quietly. His mom or caregiver sees him and wonders if he's lonely. She comes over to check in: "Hey, whatcha doin'?" She looks in the direction the little boy is looking, and says, "Oh, are you looking at that purple flower? How pretty!" This mom or caregiver may think that she's merely connecting with the child over the flower (or she may go on to take advantage of "a teaching moment" by telling him the name of the flower), but in fact, she may well have jerked that little boy's attention away from something else entirely. He might have been looking at an ant crawling through the grass, or the way the sunlight and shadows were playing on the ground; he might have been feeling the breeze on his cheek, the sun on his back, or listening to birds. When we adults make such comments to children, we cut off other possible experiences and shape what the children pay attention to instead, both now and in the future. This is fine sometimes, but a child also needs the time and space to experience the world without us pointing out what's worthy of his attention.

Restricting our commentary about what our children are experiencing is challenging—we love these little beings so deeply, and we want to check in with them, to let them know that we're thinking of them, that we're there and available for them. While popular parenting books, experts and websites tell us that continual chatter promotes speech development, studies show that speech development is not promoted through the number of words we use. Rather, how responsive we are to our children's own efforts to communicate is what makes the difference.[5] Let them decide more frequently when and how often to check in with us.

For people who are chatty (like me), to stop talking so much can feel like a challenge; for parents who are naturally quieter, this information may come as a relief. I find that the easiest or best way to stop myself from talking all the time is to hum a tune. While singing out loud generally attracts kids and pulls them to me, humming seems to allow me to fade into the background. As an added bonus, I find that the children tend to play much more peacefully when I hum: my tune sets the tone for the entire room, and the littler children don't have to keep pulling themselves out of their play to check on where I am; they can feel my soothing presence without looking up.

Independent Play Lets Children Solve Problems on Their Own

When I first started teaching, I remember reading a book about the RIE method (Resources for Infant Educarers), from the work of Magda Gerber and Emmi Pikler. The introduction addressed how we often project our own feelings onto children, giving examples such as making a child put on a sweater because *you* are cold, or wanting to jump in and help a child who is frustrated because *you* don't like being frustrated yourself. The first example made some sense to me, but the second one felt totally baffling: why would you let a child stay frustrated, if you could easily help him or her? Isn't part of our job in caring for children (whether our own or someone else's) to help them when they need help? Only after several years of working with young children did I start to see the value of not "rescuing" children at the first sign of frustration, but instead: 1) watching and waiting, 2) giving encouragement, 3) suggesting new ideas, and 4) prompting a child to ask nicely for help, all before finally, and 5) coming in to give just enough help to tip the scales.

When children know that we are present to smooth the way all the time, they react differently to challenges. Who among us hasn't seen a child fall down, look around to see if we're nearby, and either burst into tears if we are, or brush himself off and keep going if he doesn't notice us? When children encounter obstacles with no one around to solve the problem, they either figure out how to solve it themselves, or they make the decision to do something else instead.

Overcoming obstacles, making adjustments (not because they're told to, but because they've made the decision for themselves), and recovering from disappointment are all important skills for developing resilience. Resilience, or the ability to bounce back from hardship, is a key factor in determining both success and happiness in later life. If we allow our very young children age-appropriate struggles, where we don't step in and smooth things out for them, they can develop that can-do attitude that is the foundation for resilience. Some children find it much more challenging to deal with frustration than others, but wherever your child may be on this "resilience scale," you can start moving toward resilience now. As you do, notice how much of the difficulty comes from your child, and how much actually comes from your own discomfort in seeing your child struggle.

Independent Play Allows Children to Process Emotions and Experiences

It has been well documented that young children process experiences and emotions through their play.[6] As a childcare provider, I've seen many examples of this: A little girl who shockingly falls into the potty goes on to play "falling off of things," each time yelling "Oops!" and laughing hilariously. A little boy whose father recently started working from home digs aggressively in the sandbox for over a week, yelling, "Go away, I'm working!" whenever anyone approaches. A child with a new (colicky) sibling at home spends the entire playtime pacing the floor with a baby doll, patting it on the back and shushing. A little boy picks up a doll and yells harshly, "Never do that again. Never again!"

When we back off and give children space to create and sustain their own play, they can process what they experience and see. Adults like to talk things over, while children act them out. One play therapist explains:

> *Play is children's main way of communicating. To stop a child from playing is like stopping an adult from talking and thinking. To control every minute of their play is like controlling every word someone says.*[7]

To promote true independent play and exploration, it is also important that we not simply turn our children's time over to a screen (TV, iPad, electronic game, etc). Lawrence Cohen, author of *Playful Parenting*, puts it this way: "[This] doesn't empower children, it leaves them at the mercy of the best marketing money can buy—marketing that doesn't just tell children what toys to purchase, but also how to play with them." Marketing is not the only negative element; the nature of "screen time" turns children into observers instead of creators, even with so-called "educational" games or apps that have children push buttons or drag images across a screen.

Independent play comes from movement and imagination that is sustained by the child himself. If your child is used to having a screen whenever you are busy, then the transition may be a bit more difficult for both of you, but lessening this dependency is worth the benefits that come from true independent play. See the section *Creating Welcoming Play Spaces* later in this chapter for ideas on how to wean from the screen.

BE BUSY BUT AVAILABLE

Unless you live in Denmark (where time alone for children is the cultural norm), you likely are not encouraged in the view that toddlers should be *truly* alone for any length of time. In our milieu, many children are used to having their parents and caregivers as their attentive, interactive playmates. For children not used to playing alone, how do we encourage them to start spending time on their own while we're still right there?

Children love the excitement of having the direct attention of the adults they love most, whether it's telling a story, snuggling with them, or even yelling at them (so be careful of that!). But, having our direct attention all the time is like eating nothing but gravy: it's too rich. What we need to do is to make sure children have a balanced diet of our attention. This doesn't mean ignoring or leaving them; that's simply less gravy. Instead, we want to give our children emotional fruits and veggies by alternating times of direct attention with times when we're "busy but available" so they can play and explore without the lens of our constant interpretation coming between them and the world.

When we push children away from us, they inevitably clamor to be closer. When we are physically present but energetically unavailable (on the phone or checking email, for example), children will immediately become needy and clingy. So, if we want children to be able to ignore us, diving into their own experiences while we are still there, the "trick" is to be *emotionally* available but *physically* busy. And, we have a way to do this right at our fingertips: by doing household tasks! Yes, the very same tasks that we talked about doing with our children in Chapter 8. The difference comes in how we perform them.

If we want to invite a child into our task so they can be helpful, competent and connecting, we can:

- Talk out loud about what we're doing
- Sing a cheerful song
- Use funny sound effects or imagination that draw the child in.

On the other hand, when we want to use the task to "disappear," we can:

- Slow our movements down even more
- Hum quietly and contentedly to ourselves
- Use our activity as an active awareness meditation.

One thing I do when I'm trying to be invisible is to pretend that what I'm doing is very important and I'm secretly being filmed—like I've been asked to demonstrate a task in an instructional video about how to do whatever I'm doing gracefully and with quiet focus. This imaginary camera crew encourages me to be spacious and mindful. Imagination is not just for kids!

Even when children are playing deeply, they will send out periodic "feelers" to make sure that we're still there and still available to them. If we are available but not too interesting, then they can go quickly back to their play. They might do this three or four times, and then they will be ready to take a break and be with us more fully. At that point, we might switch gears and incorporate some of the elements of SMILE into our task to connect with them. On the other hand, if they check in and find that we're not energetically available, then they will leave their play to pull us back, even if they would have benefitted from more play.

Some Ways to Be "Busy"

- Make something that is beautiful or useful for your home: write handmade labels for your spices; sand, stain and attach hooks to a board for hanging keys near the door; make an "outing bag" to hold a water bottle, snack, and small sundries for your child when you go places, or a "nature bag" to bring back treasures from your walks together.
- Some sort of handwork project: knitting or crochet; embroidery; woodworking or whittling. Painting can be difficult because you'll likely not want children to touch your paints, and it's difficult to leave your piece unguarded if you need to step away.
- Do seasonal or holiday projects: Make strings of fresh cranberries for the Christmas tree or to use as garlands around the house (you can also hang them outdoors for the birds). Work on a Halloween costume. Make a birdhouse or a tissue-paper butterfly on a stick. Get some wool to wash and card, then make felted balls in soapy water; or learn to make a simple doll.
- Make gifts for grandparents or neighbors: bake treats, draw pictures or make cards, plant bulbs in a pot to bloom early inside, etc.
- Chop vegetables for today's or tomorrow's supper. Bring your cutting board and a bowl to the kitchen table, along with a second cutting board and age-appropriate knife so your child can chop, too, when she comes to check in.
- Work in the garden while your child is playing outside.
- Sit and drink your coffee or iced tea.

The way we let children know that we're available energetically, without distracting them from their play, is to do things with that same sense of spaciousness we talked about in the last chapter, where we have enough attention for our task *and* our child. But, rather than having this energy be expansive, we keep it smaller, gradually fading into the background until we are virtually invisible. We are still physically active, and we can bang dishes around or make other household sounds, but children are able to ignore us. One really useful tool, which I mentioned earlier, is humming. When we hum, our children don't need to send their "feelers" as far to know that we're present and available; they can hear it and feel it without looking.

Household tasks are ideal for being busy but available, but if you really hate housework—or your house is so sparkling clean from doing tasks both with and without children that you need something new to do—there many other options. The best ones are those in which your hands are busy but your mind is relatively free, where children can see your progress and imitate you in their play, or join in when they need connection.

Being busy but available, you may find you're doing a lot of tasks that you never used to do. Perhaps now you set the table for lunch with folded napkins and a small centerpiece of flowers from the garden, when before you would have been playing with your child. Perhaps you bake an apple pie from scratch, when you've never made one before. Other tasks will be regular ones, but you used to do them when your child was asleep, and now you do them (and with much more spaciousness) while he's playing nearby.

You don't need to be on your feet all the time, either. You don't actually need to be busy, just occupied. (Did you notice that drinking coffee or tea was on the list of things to do?) The main point to remember is…be physically occupied, but available energetically. As your child gains the ability and interest in deep, independent play, you will find that you're able to wander farther away, or get more deeply involved in your own projects and interests.

Unfortunately, computer work is one thing that doesn't work for being busy but available; we are almost always energetically *un*-available if we are staring at a screen (this includes smartphones, too). I think my own two-year-old can tell if I'm on the computer from three rooms away, and will leave whatever she's doing to come and whine at me. Likewise, academic reading is out. Reading a novel works for some people, while others get annoyed when they're interrupted. Reading the newspaper is generally fine, as are things like crossword puzzles, Sudoku, or coloring.

GETTING STARTED

When you first begin actively promoting independent play, children will need to check in pretty frequently, and will still need you for direct interaction fairly often. However, as their capacity to create and sustain their own play develops, they will be able to stay engaged longer. At this point, you'll be able to do tasks that require more intense concentration, but even then you'll need to be able to leave your task as needed. When we tell children, "Hang on," or "Just a minute," or "I'm almost done," it sets off little alarm bells in their minds—perhaps we're unavailable—and they feel impelled to leave what they are doing to pull us back. To avoid this, try one or more of the following five suggestions.

1. Be Prepared to Invite Children Into Your Task

Children will want and need to check in with us while we're busy but available, but that doesn't mean that we leave our tasks as soon as they call. Think in advance how you could incorporate your child *when* she checks in, and be prepared. Then, when your daughter Rosie invites you to come play, you can say, "I'm washing the dishes right now. You can come and wash dishes with me, or you can play." You are inviting her in. You are verbally and emotionally available, but not at her beck and call. You are no longer her "main playmate" during these times. Make your energy sweetly inviting. Remember, children will often "help" for a moment or two, then go back to their play. If you invite Rosie to join you and she jumps in and doesn't go back to her play again, then she's ready for more direct attention, and that's completely fine. Trust her knowing. She will develop the ability to be "alone" for longer and longer times if she's given the opportunity regularly.

If you're doing something that Rosie can't really join, like knitting or reading or nursing the baby, let her know that you're still available by inviting her for snuggles if she wants to come sit with you.

2. Help Them Energetically (with Your Voice) Rather Than Physically

If your son Evan is really accustomed to you being his main playmate, letting go of having you constantly engaged may be a bit tough at first for him. During this transition time (and whenever he needs it after that), you can "be with him with your voice." That is, you're physically washing the dishes, but you can see him across the counter in the living room. Go ahead and "play" with him, with your voice. What would you say if you were over there playing with him? Go ahead and say those same things: "What will you find to play with? Oh, some play food? Will you bake me a pie? I'm feeling *very* hungry. Where's a pie-pan to put our fruit in? Oh! There it is, you found it! Now, which fruit will you put in the pie? Ah, you chose bananas. I love banana cream pie."

However you normally talk with Evan while you're his "main playmate," go ahead and do it with your voice and your attention. I find that if I'm with a child with my voice and my attention, they often feel as if I'm actually playing with them. Your child may feel the same.

You won't need to be this involved with Evan's play forever; rather, using your voice is a bridge between being right there with him, and his having the capacity to create and sustain his own play. As he gets used to not having you physically close, you can start to quiet down a little, and let him have his own experiences more and more.

I use this technique in my childcare program all the time when multiple children need my attention at once: I can give one child my touch, while I give another child my voice. I have enough attention for both at once. If a third child needs me too, I might invite her to come sit close by my side while she waits, or encourage another child to help instead. I have enough attention for all of the children, and my tasks. I have an attitude of spaciousness. If your child is just learning to play alone, you can go over and find something for him to play with, get him settled into his play, and then move elsewhere to start doing something else, staying with him with your voice until his play is well established. Then you can change to humming a quiet tune so he knows you're still there without having to look up.

3. Give Children a Way to See for Themselves When You'll Be Available

For children who are used to having you at their beck and call, it can be helpful to do activities in which they can *see what you've done* and *how far you have to go*. That's why drinking tea, coffee or another drink is useful for relaxing. If your daughter Evie asks if you're done yet, you can tell her, "You'll know that I'm done relaxing when my tea cup is empty." Then, each subsequent time she comes up to ask if you're done yet, you can lower your tea cup and say, "Is it empty yet?" and Evie can answer for herself whether you're done or not. Likewise, it can be useful to create clues for your child to watch for with other activities as well: if you're reading the paper, tell her you'll be done when you're on the last page. If you're going to do three rows of knitting, get three little balls (or other toys) and say, "I'll put one ball in this bowl every time I finish a row. When all the balls are in the bowl, then I'll be done." That way, she can check for herself whether you're done or not. As time goes by and she gets used to your being "busy," you won't need to go to such lengths. But, for the transition time, such demonstrations can be helpful.

4. Be Drawn Back to Your Task by an Invisible Rubber Band

Sometimes, children need us to leave our task and help them: to settle disputes between siblings, help them change activities, or get them settled into their play. Go do these things, but imagine that you're attached to your busy but available task by an invisible rubber band. You go and help them for a moment or two, but you are gently and inevitably drawn back to your task. If they protest, invite them to join you.

5. Recognize When Children Are Done Being Alone for Now, and Do an Adult-Led Activity

Children will often play alone, check in, play again, and check in again. But, soon enough, they will need more than just a check-in. They will be ready for some direct attention. You'll be able to tell when a child is ready for more direct attention because the quality of the play deteriorates: siblings have trouble with each other repeatedly; single children get mopey or whiney. When this happens, respect their (unspoken) request, put your task aside, and give them your full attention.

OTHER WAYS TO PROMOTE INDEPENDENT PLAY

Being busy but available isn't the only thing we can do to promote our children's independent play. The physical space in which children spend their time is an unexpectedly important factor in whether children can wander away from us and go deeply into their play. Is the space welcoming and engaging? Are children able to explore freely without lots of admonitions and warnings from us to be careful? Or, is it over stimulating: too bright, to jangly, too loud, too many hard surfaces or things that might break?

Create Welcoming Play Spaces

Have you ever visited a Waldorf kindergarten or LifeWays childcare room? They are warm, beautiful and welcoming, filled with many little areas just calling children to come and play. You certainly don't need to paint your walls peach-blossom-pink, and festoon your space with naturally dyed silks, if that's not your style. Still, many lessons can to be learned from these early childhood rooms that can apply to any decorating style.

Let each toy be special. Parents, grandparents, aunts, uncles and friends all love to give children toys. However, children can easily become overwhelmed by having too many options to play with. Think of graphic design: if the designer wants us to notice something in particular, then she will make sure that item has space around it, so it captures our attention. In the case of a child's space, items in a bin or toy chest filled with stuffed animals, toy food, trains, cars, and all kinds of things, are less likely to be engaged, and more likely to be dumped out into a jumbled pile. If a child has only two or three stuffed animals, just a few special play-food items, or a few cars—all neatly arranged—then each one is likely to be special and noticed.

Take the dive and try getting rid of *most* of your child's toys, and you will likely find that your child plays more deeply with the ones that remain. Read the book *Simplicity Parenting* by Kim John Payne for step-by-step instructions and valuable tips if this feels overwhelming to you. Don't feel bad about passing on toys that are filling up your space; even a toy that was given by a beloved family member. Marie Kondo, author of *The Life-Changing Magic of Tidying Up: The Japanese Art of Decluttering and Organizing*, shares the idea that the purpose of a gift is to bring the giver happiness as he or she chooses the gift, and then the experience of giving and receiving. Once that purpose has been fulfilled, then the object itself should only stay in your house if it brings you joy.

Create inviting scenes. Rather than having toys hidden away, arrange your child's toys in ways that lure him in: when everything is "put away," leave the play table set with the play plates, cups and silverware with a piece of play food in each one. Young children's memories are associative rather than recall-based. This means that, before around age five, they don't decide what to play and then go play it; rather, they look around and play with whatever attracts them. If we make their toys inviting and attractive, they will be able to play independently much more easily, and for longer periods of time, than they would if toys were either out of sight or strewn everywhere.

Turn Off the Screens

Many parents who work with me complain that the only time they get a moment free of their children is when they put a children's show on the TV, or hand them an iPad. But, giving children a screen to watch when we want them to play is counterproductive, as it merely hands over the responsibility for creating fun from parent to device; children remain consumers rather than creators.

Many parents who are used to having the television on in the background insist that their children "don't notice" it, but studies indicate that having programming on does in fact affect both the content and the quality of children's play.[8] This might happen in ways that we don't even notice: for example, a child playing more simplistically because it's difficult to sustain imagination or a storyline with noise and flashing images in the background.

One way to wean from the screen is to spend more time outdoors (more on that below). The outdoors is stimulating in all the right ways. The natural world is full of curiosities, and children don't expect a screen as much outdoors.

For time indoors, if you'd like to get rid of the iPad or TV as a main source of entertainment, try rearranging your space to pull children's attention away from the screen. Put a cloth over the television or get an entertainment center with doors that close. Get rid of other toys at the same time (so the screen isn't the only thing to go) and create one of those warm and welcoming spaces that we just talked about, with toys set out to invite children in. If your child is used to having a tablet on demand, try putting it out of sight and reach, and creating new rules about when and how long it will come out for. As long as you are consistent with the new rules, it will likely not take more than a few days before requests begin to drop off. When a request will not be granted, remember that you can say yes to the desire: "You love playing those games, don't you. They ARE fun, huh? Which one is your favorite? Yeah, I like that one too."

Spend More Time Playing Outdoors

I understand how challenging it can be to get outside for playtime with toddlers and preschoolers. Between the interminable amounts of gear, the challenges with pottying, and then the fact that most of us haven't really set up an outdoor space that *we* enjoy hanging out in, outdoor play time can seem like a good idea in theory, but not really worth it in the moment.

Despite these challenges, getting your children outdoors for a significant chunk of time as a regular part of your daily routine is well worth the effort. Research has shown that children who regularly play outdoors tend to be happier, healthier, and stronger than children who spend most of their time inside.[9] Studies looking at children ages two to five years old found that those who regularly spent time outdoors:[10]

- Become fitter and leaner
- Develop stronger immune systems
- Have more active imaginations
- Have lower stress levels
- Play more creatively
- Have greater respect for themselves and others.

These are all things we want for our own children! I have witnessed the magic of time outdoors for children of all temperaments: rowdy, aggressive children are able to run and yell without overwhelming others; children with sensory integration issues discover new textures, and many learn to love the feeling of bare feet in grass or sand; thoughtful children can often find a time or space to be alone in nature. Even in the depths of snowy Colorado winters, when I make the effort to get out and spend half an hour outdoors, the entire rest of our morning is calm and connected. I am always glad we did.

If you live in an apartment or an urban setting with no outdoor space, then you will need to prioritize outings to parks, woods, or playgrounds, make friends with a family with a great back yard, or go to a play group that's largely outdoors. Even going for walks in your urban neighborhood can be beneficial. If you live in a more suburban area and have a boring square of grass with a few bushes in your back yard, I encourage you to create an engaging space that you and your children can both enjoy. You don't need to spend a lot of money to do this, unless you want to.

In order to create outdoor spaces that draw children in, here are a few elements you might want to consider, along with low-cost suggestions for how to create them. To see many of these ideas in action, visit my Joyful Toddlers Pinterest board, www.pinterest.com/joyfultoddlers/.

Enticing Outdoor Spaces

- **Children love kid-sized spaces:** Get a plastic trellis from any home improvement store and put it in an arch at the intersection of two fences. Trim the lower branches of a bush so that it makes a space where children can crawl and sit.
- **Children love climbing, jumping and spinning:** Get a log or a bunch of stumps that can be set in a row, circle, or moved around. Set some large stones or boulders in a group. Twizzlers are great for spinning if you have a branch to hang one from.
- **Children love different textures:** Have a tree where no grass will grow? Turn the soil over with a shovel and let your child have their own dirt-pit. Or, put down a piece of landscaping cloth and surround it with boards or logs; fill with sand.
- **Children love growing things** and will eat food from the garden that they'd never eat on a plate. Even a couple of half-barrel planters or a few five-gallon buckets with holes drilled in the bottom will grow peppers, broccoli, chard, herbs, and a tomato plant.
- **Children love transforming their environment.** Be sure to have "loose parts" that children can haul around, use to build things, or play with imaginatively. These can include a pile of bricks, a crate of smooth river-rocks, a basket filled with pine cones, shells, a bunch of small pumpkins...small wheelbarrows, baskets, and Tonka trucks to move things around with can also be useful.
- **Children love to be close to their adults:** Set up a space where *you* are comfortable and enjoy hanging out. Bring your iced tea, your knitting, your vegetable chopping, or anything else you're working on outside with you.

Eliminate the Phrase "Be Careful" from Your Vocabulary

Not long ago I went on a coaching visit with a mom of a three-and-a-half-year-old, and within the first fifteen minutes of the visit the mom had told her daughter to "be careful" at least half a dozen times. The daughter didn't seem to be particularly reckless, so I brought it up. Turns out the mom didn't even realize she was saying this! Children learn how to interact with the world from us; they learn how to treat things, other people, and their own bodies, from us. Sensitive children who hear the message "be careful, be careful, be careful," can start holding themselves back in an effort to please us, and never find out what they're actually capable of doing.

If you discover that you say "Be careful" a lot, start biting your tongue…a little more. Let your child jump off of that slightly-too-high platform. Let your child try to carry something that's a little too big, or too unwieldy, or too delicate. And then if things go wrong, be sympathetic, help them clean up the mess if they need help (just help; they should be the primary "do-er"), and encourage them to try again, along with their new knowledge.

If you have a child who is more timid, try replacing your cautions with verbal encouragement. "You can do it!" "Try a little harder!" "I'll watch from here." "You're doing it!" Try to restrain yourself from jumping in to do the task for them; milk can be wiped up, and paper can be taped. Better for children to learn how to remedy things and know their own limits than to be too scared to try.

Of course, I'm not recommending that you let your children do things that are truly dangerous. In those cases, however, tell them exactly what you would like them to do rather than the generic "be careful." You might say, "If you need to take a rest you can put that down gently on the floor." Or, you can set a clear limit: "You may only climb as high as that big limb that goes off to the right. Do you see it?" Or, "You may run ahead as far as that yellow bush, and then turn around and wait for me." It's also good to have children practice running to you when you call out a specific phrase. With my daughter I whistle a little birdcall when I want her to come running. We play games where I "hide" and do my whistle, she searches me out, and we have a joyous reunion. This way you can gather one or many children quickly in case of a problem, or when it is time to leave.

COMINGS AND GOINGS: THE RHYTHM OF THE DAY

As children practice going more deeply into their individual play, they can drift away from us for longer and longer periods. However, young children are attached to us by energetic tethers, and they can't stay away for too long. When days with children go smoothly, we drift together and apart again, like waves on the beach. When we are together, we do a "must-do" task and make it as enjoyable as possible: a meal, something to care for our home, or a task of bodily care. Then ideally, our children drift away from us, becoming engaged in their own play. This gives us some time to renew our energy, or do something we enjoy, or do a task that must be done so that we'll have time to ourselves once they go to sleep. Our children come to check in once, twice, perhaps even three times and go back to their play, but eventually they will be ready for more direct attention from us.

We will know that children are ready for direct interaction because they are suddenly unable to be alone. They will give us small hints, and if we don't respond to these, they will increase the intensity: siblings will get into tiff after tiff; single children will get whiny or perhaps deliberately do something they know we don't like (while watching us to make sure we see). All surefire ways to get interaction from us.

When these hints for a change of course arise, we might easily get annoyed, and choose to engage in a negative way. Rather than falling into the annoyance trap, I suggest that you roll with the wave...take a deep breath, and redirect the energy, letting them know they can ask in a different way, for instance. You might say: "Are you ready for something new? You don't have to hit the dog, you can just come and sit on my lap." For this intervention to be effective, however, you must respond to attempts at lap sitting *just as consistently* as you do to dog hitting. "Oh, you're coming to sit on my lap! I'm ready for something new, too. Shall I tell you a story while I finish my breakfast?"

Once your child is ready for something new, you can certainly invite him into your task, if you're doing something he can join. But that's not the only option. I recommend engagement in the Living Arts as developed by LifeWays North America.

About LifeWays North America

Many of the ideas in this book started as seeds planted by the LifeWays Early Childhood Training. The teachings of LifeWays are inspired by the insights of Rudolf Steiner and the work of Waldorf education, and are supported by contemporary early childhood research, as well as by the common sense wisdom of many generations of parents.

Most LifeWays trainings take place in four week-long segments over the course of a year, with assignments and regular mentoring help between sessions. If you are interested in learning more about the trainings, visit their website, www.lifewaysnorthamerica.org. They also offer online courses such as "The Living Arts" and "Life as the Curriculum—Home as the Model."

The Living Arts

A core tenet of LifeWays is the recognition that young children flourish through meaningful, ongoing relationships. Another is that we can best support children's development through a curriculum based on an elevated view of "daily life" as expressed through what Cynthia Aldinger described as "The Living Arts: Nurturing, Practical, Social and Creative."[11]

Many of the activities described below will be those that you/we already do regularly. What makes the activity an "Art" is *how* we do it: when we take a chore and elevate it into an Art, we strive to infuse it with beauty, creativity and connection. This infusion transforms the experience, both for us and for the young child. For example: when we take a task like changing a poopy diaper or brushing tangled hair and "elevate it," we are no longer just doing an unpleasant job. What that means is that we don't try to get it over with as quickly as possible; rather, we turn the diaper change or the hair brushing into a special experience that we share with our children.

When your children let you know they're done playing independently, you can choose an activity inspired by the Living Arts listed below, and do it *artfully*. Once children feel satiated, they will then be able to play on their own again.

- **The Nurturing Arts** include all aspects of "taking care" of someone: dressing/undressing, pottying or diapering, cooking or feeding, seeing to a person's comfort.
- **The Practical Arts** include caring for your physical space, food preparation, laundry, gardening, and so forth.
- **The Social Arts** *include all aspects of social interaction and relationship-building.*
- **The Creative Arts** *encompass making things that are beautiful and doing things that foster the imagination.*

Which of the Living Arts you choose at any given moment depends partly on the time of day (if it's lunchtime, then have lunch!). Partly, your own interests will guide you. And finally, your child's temperament and age will determine your choice as well.

Comings and Goings in Daily Life: An Example

Let's say that you have three children: Amelie, age four; Jonah, age two and a half; and baby Georgie, ten months. It's 9:00 AM, and the children are dressed and fed. You're reading the newspaper and drinking your coffee while Georgie plays with a bowl and spoon at your feet, and Jonah and Amelie are in the living room. Everything feels good. At one point, Amelie runs up to show you the beads she's strung, and at another point Jonah comes over, sticks his thumb in his mouth and leans against your leg to show you that he wants a snuggle. You bring him onto your lap and he sits for a moment before wiggling down and running off again.

After a while, however, the play starts to deteriorate. Jonah grabs Amelie's beads and they spill everywhere. You get up and help the children pick them up, but they are beginning to squabble. You offer Jonah a toy truck and everything is peaceful for a moment, but just as you've found your spot in the newspaper again, Amelie pushes Jonah over and he begins to wail.

Time now for some direct attention. You feel the urge to give negative attention (four years old is too big to be pushing a little kid!), but you think of the Living Arts instead. Which one will you choose? You've recently eaten and the children are dressed, so maybe some singing or a movement game would be fun (Creative Arts). You go over to where the children are and put a few toys away to clear a space. The children stop bickering and watch you. "What are you doing?" asks Amelie. "Ah, why don't you put your beads up in the craft cupboard and you'll soon find out," you say. Jonah watches with interest, tears forgotten.

In a moment the rug is clear. You stand and hold out your hands, humming the opening bars of *Ring Around the Rosie*. While the baby sits and watches, the three of you play *Ring Around the Rosie* and when you all fall down, you have a little verse to get everyone up again: "Cows are in the meadow, eating buttercups. Thunder, lightning, we all jump up!" You notice the baby crawling toward your little group. "Look, Georgie wants to be with us too," you say, picking him up and setting him in the center where he can feel like he's part of the action.

You do the game three more times. The first time you sing in a Giant Voice and move with Giant Steps around the circle. The second time you're like silly bunny rabbits, hopping around. The third time you sing in a soft Fairy Voice and take teeny-tiny Fairy Steps on tiptoes. This last time, when everyone falls down you pretend to fall into a deep sleep, snoring gently. Jonah laughs and jumps on top of you, and you roll him into a big hug.

"What fun!" You say. Then, "I'm ready to collect the dirty clothes and start a load of laundry." You climb to your feet, pick up the baby, and start toward the laundry room. Jonah is right behind. "Would anyone like to come with me?"

"Yeah!" says Jonah.

"No thanks," says Amelie. You look over at her.

"I wonder if you'll do some coloring," you suggest in a thoughtful voice. She jumps up and goes to the craft cupboard for crayons and paper while you and Jonah collect the dirty clothes. You make admiring comments about what a hardworking helper you have as he struggles to hold all the clothes on the way to the washer. You pick him up so he can put them in himself, then you add detergent and let Jonah push the button to start the washer. You pull clean clothes out of the dryer and put them in a clothesbasket, which you and Jonah carry together to the living room where Amelie is coloring contentedly. Georgie crawls after you.

You begin to fold and Jonah wanders off, so you slow your movements even more and start humming a soft tune, becoming "invisible" as you fold. Amelie comes over to show you her picture, then starts another. Jonah is pushing a doll carriage around. Baby Georgie crawls up and pulls on you, letting you know that he wants to nurse. You look at the clock and it's almost time for his nap. You put the folded and unfolded laundry up on the table where it won't get destroyed, and settle down on the couch to nurse, then take him to his crib. When you come back, things have deteriorated again: Jonah is ramming the doll carriage into Amelie's chair, and she's whining, "Stop it. Stop!"

"Jonah, I hear your sister asking you to stop," you say. "Besides, this clean laundry needs someone to take it to its place." He ignores you; his sister's protests are obviously much more interesting. You put a small stack of laundry into a basket with a handle and sing as you head over to them.

"A tisket, a tasket, a brown and purple basket. I folded some laundry for my love, but on my way I lost it." As you say "lost," you put the basket down.

"Who will find that basket?" you wonder aloud.

Amelie jumps up. "I will!" She picks it up and you resume your song.

"A tisket, a tasket, a brown and purple basket, I carried my shirts over to the dresser, but on my way I lost it." Amelie runs to her room and you can hear the dresser drawer open and close.

Now Amelie and Jonah both want the basket, so you find another basket and fold laundry briskly to keep up as they ferry small amounts of folded laundry back to the bedrooms as you sing the song over and over, changing the articles of clothing you name. You ask Amelie if she will help make sure Jonah's clothes make it into his dresser, and she does. When the laundry is almost all put away, the two children fail to come back; they are playing together in their room and giggling. You bring the last bit and put it away, then stand back and say, "All of that laundry, folded and put into the right drawers. Thanks, kiddos!" You leave them lying on the floor with their heads under the bed, and you go to the kitchen to start some lunch prep, or finish reading the paper, or something else of your choosing.

If you're thinking, "That sounds like normal life," then it's likely you're intuitively flowing back and forth between adult activity and independent play already. In that case, you can become a little more conscious in making sure that children have times of direct attention and times without your energy. If you have any "must-do" activities that are currently unpleasant (a child who hates getting dressed, or having his nails clipped), then work on elevating them into an *Art*.

On the other hand, if you read the example above and thought, "Well, that might work with other children but she's obviously never met mine," then I offer you long-distance hugs and assure you that habits can change with intention and practice; I've seen it many times.

If your children bicker and fight almost all the time, you may need to do more positive, adult-led activities so they can focus on *you* instead of focusing on one another, and you'll need to help them learn to interact kindly and respectfully with one another. With guidance, over time, they can drop their negative habits and replace them with words, tones and actions that are friendly and gentle.

When you have many children in your care, you will likely spend less time reading the newspaper and more time doing connecting activities, as some children will be energetically "alone" while you're giving direct attention to others. But you can—and should!—still carve out some time for relaxation. One way to do this is to consolidate some times of connection, by gathering everyone together and doing something in a way that everyone enjoys at the same time. Creative activities like circle games and puppet plays are great for this, but even practical activities like a meal can be fun and connecting for everyone. While the meal itself takes more energy to do in this way, it can create a window of time afterward where everyone feels satisfied. Don't waste this window by washing the dishes; use that time to do something you enjoy and love. Once the window closes, you can invite a child who needs connection to clean up the dishes with you. When you have multiple children in your care, making sure that you include at least one child in every must-do task can also ensure that you can take some time throughout the day that's energetically just for you.

When I first started as the teacher in the Toddler Class at a local Waldorf kindergarten in Boulder, Colorado, I made a goal to sit on the couch and crochet for at least five minutes each morning. At the beginning, I could only do two minutes at a time, but after a while, I was able to do two five-minute stretches on the couch, and then three. By the end of the school year, I could sit in my Adirondack chair for twenty minutes at a stretch when we were outdoors, doing handwork and sipping on my iced coffee. Children would come up to show me things or sit on my lap, and eventually it would be time for an activity, a game, or a meal again. Having a solid routine can help children be able to wait for a meal or a game, because they know "in their body" that one is coming up soon.

KEY POINTS

The Big Ideas in *Promoting Independent Play*

Promoting Independent Play

Children benefit from having time when they are not interacting directly with anyone else. Independent play fosters children's abilities to:

- Focus deeply and have longer attention spans.
- Experience the world without the interpretive filter of our commentary.
- Solve problems on their own.
- Process emotions and experiences.

To Give Children Space, without actually leaving:

Be Busy But Available with tasks where your hands are busy but your mind is relatively free.

Set yourself up for success by:

- Being prepared to invite children into your task
- Helping them energetically (with your voice) instead of physically
- Giving them ways to see for themselves when you'll be available
- Letting yourself be drawn back to your task by an invisible rubber band

Recognizing when children are done being alone, for now, and do an adult-led activity.

- Other Ways to Promote Independent Play
- Create welcoming spaces that promote play
- Turn off the screens
- Spend more time outdoors
- Eliminate the phrase "Be careful" from your vocabulary

Create a rhythm to your day where you have adult-led activities alternating with times apart; use the idea of the Living Arts (nurturing, practical, social, and artistic) for times together.

ENDNOTES, CHAPTER 9

1. For example, see: Crockenberg, S., Jackson, S., & Langrock, A. M. (1996). Autonomy and goal attainment: Parenting, gender, and children's social competence. *New Directions for Child and Adolescent Development, 1996*(73), 41-55.
2. White, B. L. (1971). *Human infants: Experience and psychological development.* Oxford, England: Prentice Hall. Cited in Bronson, M. (2000). *Self-regulation in early childhood: Nature and nurture.* Guilford Press.
3. https://en.wikipedia.org/wiki/Flow_(psychology)
4. Kochanska, G. (1997). Mutually responsive orientation between mothers and their young children: Implications for early socialization. *Child Development, 68*(1), 94-112.
5. Tamis-LeMonda, C. S., Bornstein, M. H., & Baumwell, L. (2001). Maternal responsiveness and children's achievement of language milestones. *Child Development, 72*(3), 748-767.
6. Barnett, L. A., & Storm, B. (1981). Play, pleasure, and pain: The reduction of anxiety through play. *Leisure Sciences, 4*(2), 161-175.
7. Cohen, L. J. (2008). *Playful parenting: An exciting new approach to raising children that will help you nurture close connections, solve behavior problems, and encourage confidence.* Ballantine Books, p. 21.
8. Zimmerman, F. J., Christakis, D. A., & Meltzoff, A. N. (2007). Associations between media viewing and language development in children under age 2 years. *The Journal of Pediatrics, 151*(4), 364-368.
9. Fjørtoft, I. (2004). Landscape as playscape: The effects of natural environments on children's play and motor development. *Children Youth and Environments, 14*(2), 21-44.
10. Burdette, H. L., & Whitaker, R. C. (2005). Resurrecting free play in young children: Looking beyond fitness and fatness to attention, affiliation, and affect. *Archives of Pediatrics & Adolescent Medicine, 159*(1), 46-50.
11. Aldinger, C., and O'Connell, M. (2010). *Home away from home: LifeWays care of children and families.* LifeWays North America.

CHAPTER 10

Create a Life That You Love—With Children

This chapter starts with a reminder that both parties in a relationship need to have their needs met. Readers are encouraged to turn the *connection, competence*, and *contributing* lens on their own lives. Suggestions are made for ways to incorporate the things you love into your life with children, making activities short, regular and child-friendly. The chapter ends with a reminder that parenting or caregiving is what we make it, and can truly be a journey of personal growth.

Enjoying *moments* throughout the day is important, but it's not enough to make a *life* feel fulfilling, for our children or for us. We've spent the bulk of this book looking at how to create a life that's fulfilling for children. However, the child is not the only person in this relationship. As we've been exploring, healthy relationships are *mutually responsive*, and both people's needs are important. In our interactions with children, we can also get what we need. Indeed, we must get what we need, if we truly wish to create a life that we love. We must tend to our own passions, not only when our children are being watched by someone else, but in their presence as well.

CONNECTION, COMPETENCE AND CONTRIBUTING—FOR US!

I invite you to take a moment to turn that lens of connection, competence and contribution back on yourself. If you enjoy journaling, do some journaling on this subject. If you like to "think out loud," call a friend and talk about this. Or simply give it some thought.

Connecting. Of course we strive to connect with our children, but who else is in your life with whom you truly connect? Who gives you that feeling of, "Again! Let's do it again!"? Do you have people or activities in your life that generate that sense in you?

Competence. When the need for competence is met, we not only have things that we definitely know we're good at, but we're also actively gaining new knowledge and new skills. We are being challenged in just the right ways to generate aliveness and excitement. What are you doing in your life right now that challenges and supports you this way? Or, does competence elude you completely, or feel like a dream viewed through hazy fatigue?

Contributing. Dedication to family and children is absolutely dedication to "something greater than yourself." If your efforts and energy in this area are meeting your need to make the world a better place, that's wonderful. However, if caring for the family doesn't bring you the appreciation, deeper connection and renewal that you need, that's the way things stand now, and that's okay. It's not a commentary on your love for your children, or your dedication to your family, or anything else. It simply means that, in addition to your time with your family, you also need to make sure you get out and *do something else* that is fulfilling to you.

Other family members, teachers, loving caregivers and friends all play important roles in children's lives, and children thrive from having strong secondary attachments. If you long to work, volunteer, create art to share with others, or something else entirely, then I urge you to create networks of support so you can get the time to do that.

TEND TO YOUR PASSIONS, *WITH* CHILDREN

We sometimes think of ourselves as "putting our lives on hold" while we have young children. Or conversely, we sense that we are trying to lead two lives at once—one with our children, and one when they are being cared for by someone else. How can we integrate ourselves, so we love the life that we live—*with children*? This is not a rhetorical, but a vital, living question.

As a first step, let's start here: If we truly want to create a life that we love *with* children, we would be wise to figure out two things:

1. How can we do what we love, in ways that children can watch and imitate? *and*
2. How can we love the things that we *must* do, because children will watch and imitate whether we love it or not?

Much of this book has been about this second point, albeit somewhat implicitly. Since you've started to implement many of the suggestions from the previous chapters, you have probably found that some of the tasks that felt like drudgery before, have actually become parts of your day that you love. I know that happened for me. As an assistant for a class of one- and two-year-olds, I was changing a *lot* of diapers the year I did my LifeWays Early Childhood Training. When I discovered how to transform each diaper change into a little bit of private time when each child and I could truly connect, that discovery literally transformed my day. Of course, not all aspects of the day were transformed; in six years, I could never quite figure out how to truly enjoy the process of getting ten children ready to play in the snow. But, the results of getting those children outside was always worth it (*sigh*). I "solved" that problem by sharing the work with my co-teachers and assistants.

How about you? What must-do parts of the day still feel like drudgery? Can you outsource them? Trade them? Transform them? "Fake it till you make it"? Or perhaps they're not actually as vital as you've been telling yourself they are. What would happen if you dropped them?

Perhaps getting your child dressed in the morning is a constant struggle. *But I have to get my child dressed!"* you tell yourself. Really? Well maybe, but does your child really need to be dressed before breakfast? What if you ate breakfast in jammies, then took a bath in the morning? Getting your child dressed might be much easier if he's fed and soothed by warm water first. This change might also provide the additional benefit of freeing precious evening time.

If a bath in the morning is not possible because you need to get your little one to childcare or preschool, what about getting him dressed in his clothes the night before and letting him sleep in them? Does this sound radical? You wouldn't have to do this every day, forever, but just until new, positive grooves can be put in place for the morning routine. We have so many "shoulds" in our minds as parents—what if we gave a few of them up in order to enjoy our lives and each other a little more?

How to Do What We Love, in Ways That Children Can Watch and Imitate

Creating a life that we love (with children), is not only about making the must-do parts of our life bearable. We must also incorporate other aspects of what we love into our lives. I encourage you to think about ways to keep those passions alive while you are *with* your children as well.

Children light up when they see us alight with passion. Children get excited to learn about the world when they see us getting excited about the world. How can you do what you love, and what makes you feel most alive, in ways that children can watch and imitate?

When you work to meld the activities you love with activities that are child-friendly, they often have to be transformed in some way. That's okay. The act of transforming your passions into child-friendly activities may spark creativity and send you off in directions you might never have gone otherwise.

Remember: children thrive when we do less, with more awareness and connection. We adults and parents thrive when everything gets done that needs to get done.

Children thrive on regularity and knowing how things go. We adults thrive when we keep our passions alive.

These sets of needs are not mutually exclusive. It is possible to meld them: getting our must-do things done, keeping our passions alive, and doing it all in slow, spacious, connecting ways. We can do it all by making our must-do items connecting, and making our passions child-friendly and regular. It is our responsibility to create a life in which *everyone's* needs get met (not just our children's), and it can be done through thoughtfulness, intention, and practice, practice, practice. I am not saying these things to give you *one more thing* to feel guilty that you're not managing to get done. I am suggesting them as an inspiration to tend to your own passions, to make your own needs a priority, without having to send your children away in order to do so. I'm nudging you toward a life that feels enjoyable in the here and now, that feels enjoyable for your children at the same time. Read these suggestions, but don't take on the challenge of changing anything immediately, unless you are excited to do so. Perhaps you will simply start mulling over how you can do more things that you love, even with young children in the mix.

Let's consider a few examples for making the activities you love child-friendly.

Having Visitors and Making Visits

I am an extrovert and I love social interaction. When I took over being in charge of my toddler class, I made "having visitors" an integral part of my program with the children. We would prepare for our visitors long in advance, making banana muffins or zucchini bread, and talking about how lovely it would be to serve them to our guests.

The next day, my previously invited guest would knock on the door. The children would joyfully rush over and stand back eagerly while I warmly greeted our guest or guests. We'd thank them for coming, take their jackets and bags, and offer them some tea. Then, the adults would sit and chat while the children played. Sometimes our guest might stay for snack or lunch. When the visit was done, we would give them their coats, walk them to the door, thank them for coming, and wave out the window as they walked to their car. The whole visit might be only thirty or forty-five minutes long.

In addition to simply enjoying the company of friends and family, these visits served to increase my enjoyment of my life with children. With a visitor in my classroom, I could see the beautiful space and the pleasant, well-behaved children with fresh eyes. It lifted me out of the mundane and reminded me how sweet and special these little beings really were. The children loved the experience too, and would often play "visitor" with one another, taking each others' imaginary coats and asking if they'd like more tea. I was living a life I loved, in ways that were also nurturing and nourishing to children. While these visits were quite different from what I would have arranged if I had been living without children in my life, they still felt enlivening and renewing for me.

Yoga / Exercise

A friend of mine who loved yoga started her own home-based play program. She did yoga with the children, telling simple stories and acting them out together with yoga movements. During outdoor playtime, she would bring her yoga mat outside and do her own practice while the children played. She always had some extra mats, and children were welcome to come and "do yoga with her." During holiday breaks, she could go to official yoga classes, workshops and retreats, and she said that she approached these "normal" adult classes with new eyes, thinking about how she might share each thing she learned with the children.

Wild Places

Another friend loved spending time in wild places, and she would bundle the children up and head out into the woods in all types of weather. They ate their snacks picnic style, had outdoor stories and puppet shows, created elaborate "fairy houses," and marveled at each change the seasons brought.

Before she lived with children, this friend had done (and led) mountain climbing trips all over the world. Now she is looking in the creek each day to see what's new since the day before. While the way she expresses her passion for wild places has changed with the presence of children, it is still alive and well. It brings her joy and inspires the children. I won't be surprised if, in fifteen years, I hear that her care has inspired some of her former charges to climb to their own heights.

Art Ideas

If you're an artist, why not have a piece that you work on while the children play (pastels or acrylics work better than oils because they don't require set-up time and tolerate your being interrupted). You can also set up small easels with chalk and chalkboards so the children can come and be artists too.

Animals

If you love horses, perhaps you can find a nearby stable that you and the children could visit once a week, or perhaps every other week if that's more feasible. You bring apples and carrots to share with your animal friends, and perhaps even get to help brush them. You draw pictures and thank-you cards for the stable owner. Even if you're not able to ride while children are present, you are sharing your passion with them, and keeping the passion alive in yourself.

Writing

If you're a writer, perhaps you could spend some time writing longhand in a journal, or create children's books together with the children, or join a book club. I joined a book club when my daughter was three weeks old and we still attend regularly. I get to connect with other adults while she plays nearby or sits on my lap. She sees my love of books in many different ways.

Computer Work?

If the activity you love involves work on the computer, you may have to be a little bit more creative while the children are young, as many children cannot abide adults working on the computer. They need to see us actively engaged in activities they can observe and imitate, and sitting and staring at a screen doesn't inspire creative play; it is more likely to pull them out of it. While you save the computer work itself for a time when children are not present, how can you share the underlying passion in ways that children can watch and imitate?

SELF-CARE AND BEING YOUR BEST SELF

Since we parents and caregivers spend so much time taking care of others, it is vital that we prioritize caring for ourselves as well. If we fail to do this, we are not the only ones to suffer: those who depend on us do, too. If we don't care for ourselves, we will surely burn out. This may happen spectacularly, through sudden, stress-related illnesses that force us to stop what we're doing. Or it may happen gradually, over time, showing up moment after moment, as we experience anxiety when we could have had calm, overwhelm when we could have had enjoyment, anger when we could have had patience, or annoyance when we could have been laughing.

- What do you need in order to be your best self?
- How much sleep is optimal for you, and how can you make sure that you get it (or close to it)?
- How much time alone do you need?
- What activities renew you?

- How well are you taking care of your body?
- Do you ask for help when you need it?

Children are resilient, and they don't need us to be perfect, but the better we can be, the better they can be, too. We are modeling for them what it means to be an adult. We are also modeling the various roles we fill: spouse, parent, man, woman, sending messages about each of these.

If you grew up with parenting models you'd prefer not to imitate with your own children, please be extra patient with yourself. Whether you judge that you've been doing a fine job, or not, in your modeling, I want you to know that wherever you are today, you *are enough*. You have what it takes to be a good parent for your children: a firm and loving guide, a positive role model, a provider. The ideal of the "perfect parent" is a trap. But still, our children will benefit when they see us striving to improve ourselves, when they see us learning, when they see us making the effort to be our *best selves* as often as we can. When we make caring for ourselves a priority, devoting the time and effort that self-care demands and deserves, then we are setting ourselves up for success—as well as setting a good example for our children.

MOVING FORWARD WITH THE LESSONS FROM THIS BOOK

When I first did my LifeWays early childhood training, we had a training session every three months. At the end of each session I would return to my classroom, filled with inspiration and ideas of new things to do, or new ways to do old activities. I would make two or three small changes, and life would go on. Three months later I would return to my training and the same ideas would flood in again. I had forgotten them all! I would return to my classroom determined to make all of the changes. I'd make one or two small changes…you get the picture. What I discovered, however, were two things:

1. very small changes can make a very large difference, over time;
2. the more small changes I was able to make, the easier it became to think of new things (and actually do them).

I have been on this path for many years now, and I still fall into negative rituals and power struggles with my own preschooler from time to time. I still have challenges in the classroom. I still have to be kind to myself, and remind myself that a life with children is a path, not a destination.

I mentored a wonderful woman through her LifeWays training, as she worked at a small preschool, and then opened her own home-based childcare program. Years later she shared her experience of working with young children:

> *It's a running joke between myself and my friends and family that I do childcare because it's "cheaper than therapy."*
>
> *Sure, I can go into a therapy session and speak at length with another adult about my issues, how to be mindful, not blow up when I'm angry, be compassionate with myself, etc. But no matter how many therapy sessions I complete, no matter how many mindfulness books I read, nothing will ever be more challenging or rewarding than this sacred task with which I have been entrusted: "Here are some very young children. Make sure they are safe and healthy. Make sure they feel loved and respected. Provide a container in which they can play, experiment, and be who they are. Most of all, don't be a jerk." A simple task, but not always an easy one.*
>
> *When you can't resort to fear-based tactics to get people to do what you want, when you can't simply punish or threaten them into submission, when you*

follow the golden rule to its logical end, then you have to become a better person than you were. It forces you to change. Children have a knack for that, forcing change. Just look at how much they grow from birth to six. It took me a full ten years (as an adult!) to learn how to put myself to bed on time so that I would not be cranky in the morning. Children learn how to walk and talk (and many more skills) typically in just three. Now that's what I call personal growth!

Yes, they are hard to keep up with, and yes it is hard to see them go when they (too quickly) do. But I wouldn't have it any other way. It is to them I am indebted. Thank you.

The children in our lives provide us with amazing challenges, and each challenge is an opportunity to grow. We all miss these opportunities, many times. But the wonderful thing about living with children is that we will have the opportunity to try again. And again. And again. Our children love us beyond measure, and our love for them can serve as a catalyst for our own transformations as well.

KEY POINTS

The Big Ideas in *Creating a Life That You Love—With Children*

In addition to creating a life that's fulfilling for our children, it's important to create a life that's fulfilling for us.

Look at your life through the lens of *connecting*, *competence,* and *contributing*. Do you feel that your current life is meeting all three of those needs? Why or why not?

Tend to Your Passions, *With* Children

Take activities that you love, and figure out how to do them in child-friendly ways

- Involve your children
- Do them regularly

Doing activities with children not only helps to keep your passions alive, helps you continue to find the time to do them without children as well, but can spark creativity and take you in directions you'd never have imagined.

Self-Care and Being Your Best Self

How much sleep do you need to be your best self? How much time alone? What activities renew you? Are you taking care of your body? Do you ask for help when you need it?

Moving Forward with Lessons from this Book

What are your goals as you finish this book? Is your relationship with each of your children mutually responsive? Parenting or caring for young children is an unparalleled opportunity for growth.

APPENDIX: THE BIG IDEAS

Joyful Toddlers & Preschoolers: Create a Life That You and Your Child Both Love

Here are the ideas and suggestions from each chapter, boiled down to their essence. Use this list [*each of these 10 main ideas is elaborated in the section that follows*] as a reference to refresh your relationship(s) when you get stuck in negative rituals. Highlight the ideas that will make the biggest difference for you. Copy the list and post it on your fridge as a visual reminder. Share these ideas with your friends, childcare providers, and in-laws. Remember that small changes can make a big difference over time.

1. Healthy relationships, including parent–toddler relationships, are *mutually responsive.*
2. Most of the time that young children say "no" to us, what they are really saying is, "I don't feel as connected to you right now as I wish I did."
3. We support children in learning to be responsive to us (the First Great Parenting Task) by cultivating a Habit of *Yes.*
4. When we can't transform *no* into *yes* using connection, then explaining and convincing are not likely to work either. Most of the time we should help our children do what we've asked, as kindly as possible.
5. Regular tantrums and meltdowns are often a child trying to tell us that our relationship with them is out of balance.
6. If your anger gets in the way of responding kindly and consistently, it's time to develop some new tools.

7. Help your child learn to be more enjoyable by learning the skill of self-regulation.
8. Transforming housework into enrichment activities allows children to help in meaningful ways, while also creating more time for self-renewal since your housework will be done.
9. We can provide space for children to enter a state of *flow* by being Busy But Available with tasks where our hands are busy but our minds are free.
10. In addition to creating a life that's fulfilling for our children, it's important to create a life that's fulfilling for us.

BIG IDEAS ELABORATED

1. **Healthy relationships, including parent–toddler relationships, are *mutually responsive*.**
   - Being responsive means responding quickly and positively, even when you can't (or won't) do what the other person asks.
   - The Two Great Parenting Tasks of the Toddler Years:
     i. In the toddler years, it is vital that we support our children in learning to control their impulses and practice being responsive to us.
     ii. In the toddler years, it is vital that we adjust our parenting to be responsive to children's needs, rather than reacting to their whims.
   - We focus on the universal needs of *Connection, Competence*, and *Contributing* to set an internal compass to guide our responses to children. Childhood is not just a time of preparation for adulthood, but is as valid as any other time, and children long to live a life that's fulfilling, just like we do.

2. **Most of the time that young children say "no" to us, what they are really saying is, "I don't feel as connected to you right now as I wish I did."**
   - Young children feel connected through different activities than adults do. You can tell if connection is happening when a person's reaction is: "Yes! Let's do it again!"
   - If you want to connect with your child, don't forget to S*M*I*L*E: use Singing, Movement, Imagination, Love, and Exaggeration.
   - If your child is engaging in "attention-seeking" behavior, teach them ways to ask that are more enjoyable to you. In order for this to work, you must respond *just as consistently* as you do to annoying behavior.

3. **We support children in learning to be responsive to us (the First Great Parenting Task) by cultivating a Habit of *Yes*.**
   - Using positive language is a powerful tool because our brains think in pictures and "don't" means very little to that part of the brain.
   - Choosing to assume that children want to be enjoyable and helpful can make a big difference
   - Ask a child once, then say, "Can you do it on your own, or should I help you?" then come and give physical help. Make your help connecting, not punitive.

4. **When we can't transform *no* into *yes* using connection, then explaining and convincing are not likely to work either. Most of the time we should help our children do what we've asked, as kindly as possible.**
   - Dropping requests when we can't convince our children teaches them that they should only have to do the things they feel like doing. Conversely, when we insist upon right

action when they are small, they will grow into people who will do the right thing when they are adults. And they will have the willpower to achieve their dreams.

- When you ask a child to do something, what's a typical response?
    - She tries to explain why she shouldn't have to:

        You're explaining and convincing too much.
    - She throws a tantrum or has a fit:

        You're withdrawing your request too frequently and not insisting often enough
    - It feels like you're constantly making her do things and it's exhausting:

        You're forgetting to use positive language and/or make things connecting. Re-read Chapters 1 and 2.
    - You say, "It looks like you need some help" and your child jumps to do what you've asked:

        Things are in balance. Good job!

5. **Regular tantrums and meltdowns are often a child trying to tell us that our relationship with them is out of balance.**
    - Do a Pouring In the Love Campaign for one week, and see what happens:
        - **The negative behavior melts away**: your child was sending a *Call for Affection*. Continue the campaign and gradually ramp down to a "new normal."
        - **The negative behavior gets worse**: your child is sending a *Call for Boundaries*. Work on developing "high demandingness" while maintaining high levels of warmth. Help them learn to put their desires on hold, and to recover from disappointment.

- **Things Improve Briefly, then Go Back to How they Were:** Your child is likely sending either a *Call for Consistency* or a *Call to Slow Down*. Work on setting up a life for your child that's slower, more spacious, and more regular.

6. **If your anger gets in the way of responding kindly and consistently, it's time to develop some new tools.**
   - Don't wait until your patience is gone to set boundaries. Don't let your child's emotions control yours. Offer olive branches. Repair broken connections. Practice different ways through play.
   - Recognize that negative emotions are often brought on by baggage from the past and fears of the future. However, you can side-step these:

     Ask, "What am I afraid of when s/he does that?"

     Thank yourself, and set that answer aside.

     "What's another possible explanation?"

     "What could *I* do differently that would shift the energy in our interactions?

7. **Help your child learn to be more enjoyable by learning the skill of self-regulation.**
   - As babies grow into children, their regulation gradually goes from being external to being internal. This is not a linear process. The more consistently we can support them, the more easily they can learn.
   - Help children learn to wait: start small, give them ways to see when the waiting will be done, teach them to find things to do while they wait.
   - Help them learn to recover from disappointment by lowering their level of arousal, then choosing something else to focus on.

- Let them practice dealing with frustration: watch, then encourage, then make suggestions, then encourage them to ask for help, then give as little help as needed.
- Staying on task: "What can we do to make this more fun?"

If your child is too intense in some way, think of what "balancing virtue" would transform that into a strength. Commonly helpful virtues include kindness, helpfulness, respectfulness, empathy.

8. **Transforming housework into enrichment activities allows children to help in meaningful ways, while also creating more time for self-renewal since your housework will be done.**
   - Cultivate a *sense of spaciousness* where you have enough attention for your task and your children.
   - Gather everything you'll need so that children can be in motion from beginning till end.
   - Lead with actions rather than words: do the task invitingly, with elements of SMILE.
   - Use imagery and song to shape children's behavior. Keep it small while they're learning. Harness the power of routines.
   - Let children come in and out of your task, and keep doing it spaciously. Don't worry if they don't seem interested.

9. **We can provide space for children to enter a state of flow by being Busy But Available with tasks where our hands are busy but our minds are free.**
   - Inviting play spaces, time outdoors, and limiting screen time also promote independent play.
   - Children will increase their ability and desire to play independently over time. They will check in periodically to make sure we're still available. Eventually they will be ready for more direct adult interaction.

- Healthy daily rhythms are created when we have times of adult-led activities alternating with time where we are energetically apart. Use the idea of the Living Arts (Nuturing, Practical, Social and Artistic) to drive your adult-led activities.

10. **In addition to creating a life that's fulfilling for our children, it's important to create a life that's fulfilling for us.**
    - Figure out how to enjoy, transform, trade, or stop doing the things we MUST do.
    - Tend to your passion by taking activities that you love, and figuring out how to do them in child-friendly ways
    - Parenting can be a path of growth and transformation, if we let it.

When we are aware of what young children need to live a life that's fulfilling, when we support them to learn to become responsive to us while remaining responsive to their deep needs, and when we attend to our own passions in child-friendly ways, we can truly create a life that we and our children *all* love.

FURTHER READING AND RESOURCES

There are many resources out there for parents and early childhood educators, but these are my personal favorites and the ones that have had the greatest effect on my own work and life with children:

GENERAL PARENTING BOOKS:

- *You Are Your Child's First Teacher: Encouraging Your Child's Natural Development from Birth to Age Six,* by Rahima Baldwin Dancy. Ten Speed Press (3rd ed.), 2014.
- *Simplicity Parenting: Using the Power of Less to Raise Calmer, Happier, and More Secure Kids*, by Kim John Payne with Lisa M. Ross. Ballantine Books, 2010.
- *Parenting Without Power Struggles: Raising Joyful, Resilient Kids While Staying Cool, Calm and Collected*, by Susan Stiffelman. Simon & Schuster, 2012.
- *Raising Happiness: 10 Simple Steps for More Joyful Kids and Happier Parents*, by Christine Carter. Ballantine Books, 2010.
- *Playful Parenting: An Exciting New Approach to Raising Children That Will Help You Nurture Close Connections, Solve Behavior Problems, and Encourage Confidence,* by Lawrence Cohen. Ballantine Books, 2002.
- *Free-Range Kids, How to Raise Safe, Self-Reliant Children (Without Going Nuts with Worry)*, by Lenore Skenazy. Jossey-Boss, 2010.

TODDLER-SPECIFIC PARENTING BOOKS:

- *No Bad Kids: Toddler Discipline Without Shame*, by Janet Lansbury. CreateSpace Independent Publishing Platform, 2014.

- *Twelve Alternatives to Time Out: Connected Discipline for Raising Cooperative Children*, by Ariadne Brill. CreateSpace Independent Publishing Platform, 2014.
- *Positive Discipline: The First Three Years: From Infant to Toddler—Laying the Foundation for Raising a Capable, Confident Child* (rev. & updated ed.), by Jane Nelson. Harmony, 2015.
- *Positive Discipline for Preschoolers: For Their Early Years, Raising Children Who are Responsible, Respectful, and Resourceful (Positive Discipline Library)*, by Jane Nelson. Harmony, 2007.

RESOURCES FOR SONGS, ACTIVITIES, ETC.:

- *This Is the Way We Wash A Day (Singing with Children Series Song Book and CD)* (4th ed.), by Mary Thienes Schunemann. Naturally You Can Sing, 2003.
- *Sing A Song with Baby (Singing with Children Series Song Book and CD)*, by Mary Thenes Schunemann. Naturally You Can Sing, 2001.
- *Juniper Tree School of Puppetry Arts* (http://junipertreepuppets.com/). All of her story collections, puppet/story kits, are lovely. Or take one of her classes.
- *Roots, Shoots, Buckets & Boots: Gardening Together with Children*, by Sharon Lovejoy. Workman Publishing Company, 1999.
- *Festivals, Families and Food*, by Diana Carey and Judy Large. Hawthorne Press, 1982.

FAVORITE BLOGS:

- The Parenting Passageway (https://theparentingpassageway.com/)

- Janet Lansbury: Elevating Child Care (http://www.janetlansbury.com/)
- Waldorf in the Home (http://www.waldorfinthehome.org/)

TRAININGS (SOME ARE IN-PERSON; OTHERS CAN BE DONE ONLINE):

- *LifeWays North America* offers Certificate Trainings and online classes: (http://lifewaysnorthamerica.org/)
- *RIE: Resources for Infant Educarers* offers classes, trainings, and conferences (https://www.rie.org/)
- *Mothering Arts* offers online classes and trainings (http://www.motheringarts.com/)
- *Sophia's Hearth* offers a Birth to Seven Certificate, summer courses and weekend workshops (https://www.sophiashearthteachers.org/)
- *Juniper Tree School of Puppetry Arts* offers weekend workshops up to full-year trainings (http://junipertreepuppets.com/)

INDEX

INDEX

INDEX

INDEX

INDEX

INDEX

OTHER TITLES OF INTEREST FROM HOHM PRESS / KALINDI PRESS

FREE RANGE LEARNING

How Homeschooling Changes Everything

by Laura Weldon

Presents eye-opening data about the meaning and importance of natural learning. This data—from neurologists, child development specialists, anthropologists, educators, historians and business innovators—turns many current assumptions about school-based education upside down. The book's factual approach is balanced by quotes and stories from over 100 homeschoolers from the U.S., Canada, Germany, Australia, Ireland, New Zealand, Mexico, India and Singapore. *Free Range Learning* will also encourage and excite those who want their children to have the benefits, but who are timid to approach homeschooling. This is the only book anyone needs to make the choice and start the process of homeschooling children, and is applicable for young people from pre-school through high school.

Paper, 312 pages, 50 b&w photos, $24.95 ISBN: 978-1-935387-09-1

PARENTING, A SACRED TASK

10 Basics of Conscious Childraising

by Karuna Fedorschak

Moving beyond our own self-centered focus and into the realm of generosity and expansive love is the core of spiritual practice. This book can help us to make that move. It highlights 10 basic elements that every parent can use to meet the everyday demands of childraising. Turning that natural duty into a sacred task is what this book is about. Topics include: love, attention, boundaries, food, touch, help and humor.

> "There is no more rigorous path to spiritual development than that of being a parent. Thank you to Karuna Fedorschak for reminding us that parenting is a sacred task." – Peggy O'Mara, Editor and Publisher, *Mothering Magazine.*

Paper, 158 pages, $12.95 ISBN: 978-1-890772-30-7

To Order: 800-381-2700, or visit our websites,
www.hohmpress.com / www.kalindipress.com / www.familyhealthseries.com

OTHER TITLES OF INTEREST FROM HOHM PRESS / KALINDI PRESS

CONSCIOUS PARENTING

Revised Edition with New Material

by Lee Lozowick

Any individual who cares for children needs to attend to the essential message of this book: that the first two years are the most crucial time in a child's education and development, and that children learn to be healthy and "whole" by living with healthy, whole adults.

Offers practical guidance and help for anyone who wishes to bring greater consciousness to every aspect of childraising, including: * conception, pregnancy and birth * emotional development * language usage * role modeling: the mother's role, the father's role * the exposure to various influences * establishing workable boundaries * the choices we make on behalf on our children's education ... and much more.

Paper, $19.95, 336 pages ISBN: 978-1-935387-17-9

CONSCIOUS PARENTING WORKBOOK

A Companion and Study Guide to Conscious Parenting by Lee Lozowick

by Bhadra Mitchell with Karuna Fedorschak, Nancy Lewis, Christine McMaster and Matthew Files

This *Workbook*—companion volume to *Conscious Parenting* by Lee Lozowick—is designed be a useful map for parents, prospective parents and childcare givers, and teachers on this adventure. The *Workbook* follows the original book, covering subjects from enlightened birth practices, breastfeeding, our use of language with children, the limiting of early exposure to technology and negative influences for youngsters, to the creation of environments of safety and sanctuary for our teenagers.

Paper, $19.95, 96 pages ISBN: 978-1-935387-85-5

OTHER TITLES OF INTEREST FROM HOHM PRESS / KALINDI PRESS

IN THE BEST INTEREST OF THE CHILD

A Manual for Divorcing Parents
by Nadir Baksh, Psy.D. and Laurie Murphy, R.N., Ph.D.

This book will help parents save their children unnecessary anguish throughout the divorce process. Written by a licensed clinical psychologist, and a nurse and counselor, the authors have a private practice with families and also work as court-appointed evaluators in child-custody disputes.

Their advice and direction is eminently practical – detailing what adults can expect from a custody battle; what they will encounter in themselves and in their children (emotionally, physically, mentally) during divorce; advising how parents can make sense out of children's questions; offering guidance in making decisions for themselves and their kids; and explaining the ultimate importance of putting the child's needs first.

Paper, 144 pages, $16.95 ISBN: 978-1-890772-73-4

YOU DON'T KNOW ANYTHING . . . !

A Manual for Parenting Your Teenagers
by Nadir Baksh, Psy.D. and Laurie Murphy, R.N., Ph.D.

This book offers immediate and clear help to parents, family members and teachers who are angry, confused, frustrated, sad, or at their wit's end in dealing with their teenagers. Beyond advice for crisis situations, ***You Don't Know Anything . . .!*** informs parents of the new stresses their kids today must cope with, and suggests ways to minimize these pressures for both adults and teens. Patience, caring, vigilance, "street smarts," knowledge of the teenage brain – these are among the many skills that parents today need. The book points the way to those skills, and encourages parents and other adults to resume their legitimate roles on teens' lives.

Paper, 188 pages, $12.95 ISBN: 978-1-890772-82-6

OTHER TITLES OF INTEREST FROM HOHM PRESS / KALINDI PRESS

8 STRATEGIES FOR SUCCESSFUL STEP-PARENTING

by Nadir Baksh, Psy. D. and Laurie Elizabeth Murphy, R.N., Ph.D.

No matter who you are, and how much experience you've had with kids, becoming a step-parent, and "blending of families," is difficult work. The book presents 8 strategies, in the form of action steps, to maximize anyone's chances of success in this endeavor. Written in a non-apologetic voice, the book offers strong and specific direction to address current problems. Vignettes of 30 real-life family situations support the strategies suggested. Issues and examples are applicable cross-culturally, and address needs of both men and women.

Paper, 188 pages, $14.95 ISBN: 978-1-935387-08-4

THE ACTIVE CREATIVE CHILD

Parenting in Perpetual Motion

by Stephanie Vlahov

Active/creative children are often misunderstood by the medical community, by schools, and by their own parents. Their energy is astounding; their inquisitiveness is boundless. Channeling that energy is not only helpful, but necessary. Supporting that inquisitiveness is essential! This book provides specific hints for coping, for establishing realistic boundaries, and for avoiding labels and easy judgments where any child is concerned. Written in a simple, journalistic style, the author draws from her experience with her two active/creative sons, and those of others, to present a handbook of encouragement and genuine help.

Paper, 105 pages, $9.95 ISBN: 978-1-890772-47-5

OTHER TITLES OF INTEREST FROM HOHM PRESS / KALINDI PRESS

TO TOUCH IS TO LIVE

The Need for Genuine Affection in an Impersonal World

by Mariana Caplan
Foreword by Ashley Montagu

The vastly impersonal nature of contemporary culture, supported by massive child abuse and neglect, and reinforced by growing techno-fascination are robbing us of our humanity. The author takes issue with the trends of the day that are mostly overlooked as being "progressive" or harmless, showing how these trends are actually undermining genuine affection and love. This uncompromising and inspiring work offers positive solutions for countering the effects of the growing depersonalization of our times.

> "An important book that brings to the forefront the fundamentals of a healthy world. We must all touch more."—Patch Adams, M.D.

Paper, 272 pages, $19.95 ISBN: 978-1-890772-24-6

YOUNG ENOUGH TO CHANGE THE WORLD

Stories of Kids and Teens Who Turned Their Dreams into Action

by Michael Connolly and Brie Goolbis

The 15 stories of young people from around the world described in *Young Enough to Change the World* are proof that kids and teens today want to make a difference! Each of these has already made a significant contribution to the lives of others. And, most of their projects are still going strong. Their commitments and results will inspire readers everywhere, and encourage us all in knowing that the future of humanity is in busy, dedicated hands.

Paper, 144 pages, $17.95 ISBN: 978-1-935826-38-5

OTHER TITLES OF INTEREST FROM HOHM PRESS / KALINDI PRESS

HEART TO HEART

Connecting With Your Child

by Jeff Goelitz and Elyse April

This is a book about conscious and conscientious childraising. *Heart to Heart* shares inspirational and yet practical information to help parents and caregivers of young children lessen their stress and establish healthier communication in their relationships with children.

Uniquely, designed as a children's book, it encourages adults and children to consider *together* how they can deepen their bonds of love through care, active listening and genuine attention. Picture books as a medium for parenting education are particularly useful. They are fast and easy to read, and generally light-hearted, a fact most appreciated by busy and overstressed parents.

Paper, 32 pages, $9.95 ISBN: 978-1-935387-43-5

STAND UP! *The Courage to Care* / ¡ENFRENTA! *El Valor de Cuidar*

by Elyse April and Regina Sara Ryan

Illustrations by Maria Oglesby

In 12 playful and adventurous scenarios, young or baby animals take a stand that demonstrates courage in the face of a challenge, along with kindness and willingness to help others. Short simple text makes for easy comprehension. The book can serve as a stimulus for lots of adult-child discussion of principles like courage, discernment and caring.

A preventative for the pre-school child, this is a valuable contribution to anti-"bullying" literature that never mentions the word. Instead, it is packed with impressions to encourage creativity, individuality and confidence, skills that can combat the susceptibility to peer pressure so damaging to children.

Paper, 32 pages ISBN: 978-1-942493-17-4 (English) $9.95

Ages (infant-6) ISBN: 978-1-942493-33-4 (Bilingual) $10.95

To Order: 800-381-2700, or visit our websites,
www.hohmpress.com / www.kalindipress.com / www.familyhealthseries.com

OTHER TITLES OF INTEREST FROM HOHM PRESS / KALINDI PRESS

WE LIKE TO EAT WELL / NOS GUSTA COMER BIEN

by Elyse April
Illustrations by Lewis Agrell

What we eat is vitally important for good health … but so is *how* we eat … *where* and *when* we eat … and *how much* we eat … especially in reducing obesity and diabetes II, which have reached epidemic proportions in the U.S.

This book encourages young children and parents to develop the healthy eating habits that can last for a lifetime.

Paper, 32 pages
ISBN: 978-1-890772-69-7 (English) $9.95
ISBN: 978-1-890772-78-9 (Bi-lingual) $10.95

WE LIKE TO HELP COOK / NOS GUSTA AYUDAR A COCINAR

by Marcus Allsop
Illustrations by Diane Iverson

All the young children in these brightly-colored picture books (available in both English and Spanish) are helping adults to prepare healthy and delicious foods—all in accordance with the Healthy Diet Guidelines illustrated by the USDA Food Pyramid. Simple text, plus some rhymes, make the books easy to read, and appealing to both kids and parents. Children help themselves or assist the adults by performing many age-related tasks, like pouring, shaking, washing, mashing and mixing—actions that most young children love to do.

Paper, 32 pages
ISBN: 978-1-890772-70-3 (English) $9.95
ISBN: 978-1-890772-75-8 (Bi-lingual) $10.95

OTHER TITLES OF INTEREST FROM HOHM PRESS / KALINDI PRESS

WE LIKE TO READ / NOS GUSTA LEER
by Elyse April
Illustrations by Angie Thompson

We Like to Read / Nos Gusta Leer provides a new look at how to teach and encourage reading by using play and "attachment parenting"—i.e., lots of physical closeness and learning by example. The upbeat rhyming format provides cues for parents and caregivers on how to provide a foundation for reading while enticing children with game-like activities. The need for this

Paperback, 32 pages

ISBN: 978-1-890772-80-2 (English) $9.95
ISBN: 978-1-890772-81-9 (Bi-Lingual) $10.95

WE LIKE TO LIVE GREEN / NOS GUSTA VIVIR VERDE
by Mary Young
Design by Zachary Parker

This Earth-friendly book provides an introduction to vital environmental themes in ways that will appeal to both young children and adults. We can all recycle and reuse, conserve water or grow a garden! Lively full-color photo montages demonstrate how to make a difference in a world threatened by pollution and ecological imbalance.

Paperback, 32 pages

ISBN: 978-1-935387-00-8 (English) $9.95
ISBN: 978-1-935387-01-5 (Bi-Lingual) $10.95

CONTACT INFORMATION

ABOUT THE AUTHOR

Faith Collins (M.A. in Early Childhood Studies from Roehampton University, London) is a parenting coach, public speaker, and classroom teacher dedicated to supporting relationships with the young children in our lives. Her work is inspired by LifeWays, developed from the pedagogy of Rudolf Steiner and the experience of Waldorf education. She lives in Denver, Colorado with her husband and young daughter, where she runs outdoor parent–child classes in her Play Garden, and is co-director of the Rocky Mountain LifeWays Training.

Contact Information: Her blog and popular online classes are available at (http://joyfultoddlers.com).

ABOUT HOHM PRESS & KALINDI PRESS

Hohm Press is committed to publishing books that provide readers with alternatives to the materialistic values of the current culture, and that promote self-awareness, the recognition of interdependence, and compassion. Our subject areas include parenting, transpersonal psychology, religious studies, women's studies, the arts and poetry.

Kalindi Press, an affiliate of Hohm Press, proudly offers books in natural health and nutrition, as well as the acclaimed Family and World Health Series for children and parents, covering such themes as nutrition, dental health, reading and environmental education.

Contact Information: Hohm Press/Kalindi Press, PO Box 4410, Chino Valley, Arizona, 86323; USA; 800-381-2700, or 928-636-3331; email: hppublisher@cableone.net.

Visit our websites:

www.hohmpress.com   www.kalindipress.com

www.familyhealthseries.com